BUILDING THINKING SKILLS®
Book 3 – Verbal

SERIES TITLES
BUILDING THINKING SKILLS®—PRIMARY
BUILDING THINKING SKILLS®—BOOK 1
BUILDING THINKING SKILLS®—BOOK 2
BUILDING THINKING SKILLS®—BOOK 3 FIGURAL
BUILDING THINKING SKILLS®—BOOK 3 VERBAL

SANDRA PARKS AND HOWARD BLACK

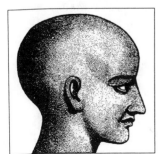

© 1985
CRITICAL THINKING BOOKS & SOFTWARE
www.criticalthinking.com
P.O. Box 448 • Pacific Grove • CA 93950-0448
Phone 800-458-4849 • FAX 831-393-3277
ISBN 0-89455-300-3
Printed in the United States of America

TABLE OF CONTENTS

A VERY IMPORTANT COMMENT ON THE IMPORTANCE OF CLASS DISCUSSION

The following activities were created with the hope that students would use *discussion,* not paper and pencil alone, to stimulate their perception and to develop their analysis skills. Although students may do activities individually in pencil-and-paper form, it is important to follow up each activity with class discussion to foster vocabulary development and to promote better transfer of thinking skills to content learning.

We encourage the use of manipulatives in introducing the exercises, for they provide students with a concrete basis for their discussions and a richer perception of the analysis tasks. For more detailed help, refer to the corresponding *Teacher's Manual and Lesson Plans* for this student book.

ACKNOWLEDGEMENTS

The authors wish to acknowledge Leslie Simon, editor; Bonnie Baker, educational consultant; Penny Van Gundy, layout artist; Janet Holsberg, typographer; and Rigel Chidester for their invaluable contributions to this book.

ANTONYMS—SELECT

Each line contains four words. Read the first word and think about what it means. One of the next three words will mean the **opposite** of the first word. Underline the word that is the **antonym** —or opposite—of the first word.

SIMILARITIES

A-1	preserve	**a.** construct	**b.** destroy	**c.** protect
A-2	deposit	**a.** account	**b.** spend	**c.** withdraw
A-3	ideal	**a.** desirable	**b.** imperfect	**c.** worthy
A-4	idle	**a.** busy	**b.** complex	**c.** simple
A-5	certainty	**a.** belief	**b.** doubt	**c.** proof
A-6	scorn	**a.** disregard	**b.** honor	**c.** reject
A-7	treachery	**a.** loyalty	**b.** plot	**c.** theft
A-8	omit	**a.** avoid	**b.** exclude	**c.** include
A-9	peculiar	**a.** odd	**b.** ordinary	**c.** strange
A-10	conceited	**a.** capable	**b.** loud	**c.** modest
A-11	resist	**a.** oppose	**b.** protest	**c.** submit
A-12	evident	**a.** concealed	**b.** obvious	**c.** questionable

ANTONYMS—SELECT

Each line contains four words. Read the first word and think about what it means. One of the next three words will mean the **opposite** of the first word. Underline the word that is the **antonym** —or opposite—of the first word.

A-13 domestic   **a.** exported   **b.** foreign   **c.** manufactured

A-14 definite   **a.** complete   **b.** neutral   **c.** vague

A-15 decent   **a.** insufficient   **b.** proper   **c.** vulgar

A-16 discharge   **a.** dispel   **b.** fire   **c.** load

A-17 trivial   **a.** partial   **b.** significant   **c.** simple

A-18 thrill   **a.** bore   **b.** rally   **c.** stir

A-19 retain   **a.** lose   **b.** invest   **c.** realize

A-20 sudden   **a.** abrupt   **b.** prolonged   **c.** unexpected

A-21 delay   **a.** arrest   **b.** hasten   **c.** suspend

A-22 weary   **a.** experienced   **b.** refreshed   **c.** worn

A-23 resident   **a.** citizen   **b.** official   **c.** visitor

A-24 mingle   **a.** combine   **b.** prepare   **c.** separate

ANTONYMS—SUPPLY

Each line contains a word. Read the word and think about what it means, then think of a word or words that mean the **opposite** of that word. Write down as many **antonyms**—or opposites—as you can think of for each word.

A-25 mend

A-26 reckless

A-27 combine

A-28 complex

A-29 compliment

A-30 initial

A-31 fixed

A-32 import

A-33 minor

A-34 bald

A-35 innocence

A-36 necessity

ANTONYMS—SUPPLY

Each line contains a word. Read the word and think about what it means, then think of a word or words that mean the **opposite** of that word. Write down as many **antonyms**—or opposites—as you can think of for each word.

A-37   freeze

A-38   remember

A-39   conceal

A-40   construct

A-41   profit

A-42   public

A-43   interior

A-44   farther

A-45   victor

A-46   reward

A-47   offense

A-48   temporary

SYNONYMS—SELECT

Each line contains four words. Read the first word and think about what it means. One of the next three words will mean almost the same thing. Underline the **synonym**—the word that is **most** like the first word.

SIMILARITIES

A-49 average   **a.** excellent   **b.** normal   **c.** unusual

A-50 error   **a.** answer   **b.** mistake   **c.** test

A-51 vast   **a.** empty   **b.** immense   **c.** open

A-52 assemble   **a.** build   **b.** replace   **c.** start

A-53 snarl   **a.** curve   **b.** fiber   **c.** tangle

A-54 grudge   **a.** grievance   **b.** opinion   **c.** remark

A-55 spare   **a.** extra   **b.** lone   **c.** lost

A-56 eliminate   **a.** finish   **b.** project   **c.** remove

A-57 penalty   **a.** decision   **b.** fine   **c.** reward

A-58 linger   **a.** arrive   **b.** depart   **c.** remain

A-59 occupation   **a.** hobby   **b.** profession   **c.** responsibility

A-60 proclaim   **a.** declare   **b.** decline   **c.** devise

A-61 glitter   **a.** gloom   **b.** sparkle   **c.** surface

5

SYNONYMS—SELECT

Each line contains four words. Read the first word and think about what it means. One of the next three words will mean almost the same thing. Underline the **synonym**—the word that is **most** like the first word.

A-62 comment   **a.** meaning   **b.** remark   **c.** thought

A-63 convert   **a.** change   **b.** introduce   **c.** retreat

A-64 persuade   **a.** convince   **b.** doubt   **c.** relate

A-65 misery   **a.** acceptance   **b.** satisfaction   **c.** suffering

A-66 rival   **a.** contest   **b.** opponent   **c.** player

A-67 readily   **a.** rarely   **b.** scarcely   **c.** willingly

A-68 amuse   **a.** calm   **b.** entertain   **c.** instruct

A-69 despise   **a.** reject   **b.** reply   **c.** respect

A-70 attain   **a.** accomplish   **b.** attempt   **c.** fail

A-71 cure   **a.** disease   **b.** infection   **c.** remedy

A-72 endeavor   **a.** effect   **b.** effort   **c.** result

A-73 invent   **a.** conceive   **b.** conclude   **c.** conform

SYNONYMS—SELECT

Each line contains four words. Read the first word and think about what it means. One of the next three words will mean almost the same thing. Underline the **synonym**—the word that is **most** like the first word.

A-74 peer   **a.** chief   **b.** equal   **c.** superior

A-75 peer   **a.** gaze   **b.** listen   **c.** seek

A-76 project   **a.** proceed   **b.** continue   **c.** plan

A-77 project   **a.** enterprise   **b.** ideal   **c.** judgment

A-78 project   **a.** conclude   **b.** receive   **c.** shoot

A-79 project   **a.** forecast   **b.** prove   **c.** solve

A-80 conclusion   **a.** agreement   **b.** argument   **c.** negotiation

A-81 conclusion   **a.** finish   **b.** outset   **c.** route

A-82 conclusion   **a.** fact   **b.** judgment   **c.** reason

A-83 gather   **a.** announce   **b.** assemble   **c.** scatter

A-84 gather   **a.** confuse   **b.** misrepresent   **c.** understand

A-85 gather   **a.** collect   **b.** discover   **c.** disperse

SYNONYMS—SELECT

Each line contains four words. Read the first word and think about what it means. One of the next three words will mean almost the same thing. Underline the **synonym**—the word that is **most** like the first word.

A-86　class　　　　**a.** group　　　　**b.** member　　　　**c.** pupil

A-87　class　　　　**a.** characteristic　**b.** member　　　　**c.** type

A-88　class　　　　**a.** calculate　　**b.** count　　　　**c.** sort

A-89　class　　　　**a.** item　　　　**b.** quality　　　**c.** volume

A-90　share　　　　**a.** collection　　**b.** portion　　　**c.** weight

A-91　share　　　　**a.** divide　　　**b.** prevent　　　**c.** retain

A-92　common　　　**a.** individual　　**b.** private　　　**c.** public

A-93　common　　　**a.** general　　　**b.** restricted　　**c.** specific

A-94　common　　　**a.** exceptional　**b.** ordinary　　　**c.** remarkable

A-95　common　　　**a.** cheap　　　**b.** valuable　　　**c.** worthy

A-96　tear　　　　**a.** creep　　　**b.** remain　　　**c.** rush

A-97　tear　　　　**a.** repair　　　**b.** split　　　　**c.** sustain

SYNONYMS—SUPPLY

Each line contains a word. Read the word and think about what it means, then think of a word or words that mean **almost** the same thing. Write down as many **synonyms**—or similar words— as you can think of.

A-98 quantity

A-99 plunge

A-100 melt

A-101 plead

A-102 oath

A-103 crease

A-104 horror

A-105 flaw

A-106 verse

A-107 lengthen

A-108 competition

A-109 assist

SIMILARITIES

SYNONYMS—SUPPLY

Each line contains a word. Read the word and think about what it means, then think of a word or words that mean **almost** the same thing. Write down as many **synonyms**—or similar words—as you can think of.

A-110 retain

A-111 imagine

A-112 pursue

A-113 corridor

A-114 savage

A-115 profession

A-116 rescue

A-117 quarrel

A-118 sketch

A-119 sole

A-120 uncommonly

A-121 contribute

© 1985 MIDWEST PUBLICATIONS 93950-0448

SYNONYMS AND ANTONYMS—SELECT

Read the first word in each line and think about what it means. One of the next four words means the **opposite** of the first. Circle the opposite word and mark it **A** for **antonym**.

One of the words is **similar** in meaning to the first word. Circle the similar word and mark it **S** for **synonym**.

EXAMPLE:

	S			**A**
stoop	**a.** bend	**b.** crawl	**c.** relax	**d.** stretch

A-122 aged	**a.** ambitious	**b.** elderly	**c.** healthy	**d.** youthful
A-123 wreck	**a.** attempt	**b.** construct	**c.** destroy	**d.** direct
A-124 glance	**a.** gaze	**b.** glimpse	**c.** gloss	**d.** glow
A-125 contrary	**a.** changeable	**b.** exact	**c.** opposite	**d.** similar
A-126 boring	**a.** dull	**b.** lengthy	**c.** stimulating	**d.** tragic
A-127 clasp	**a.** agree	**b.** grasp	**c.** release	**d.** select
A-128 awkward	**a.** clumsy	**b.** graceful	**c.** steady	**d.** straight
A-129 essential	**a.** basic	**b.** distinct	**c.** terminal	**d.** unnecessary
A-130 omit	**a.** direct	**b.** edit	**c.** include	**d.** overlook
A-131 liberal	**a.** financial	**b.** generous	**c.** possessed	**d.** stingy
A-132 keen	**a.** dull	**b.** even	**c.** extra	**d.** sharp
A-133 retreat	**a.** advance	**b.** establish	**c.** prepare	**d.** withdraw
A-134 rival	**a.** associate	**b.** guest	**c.** opponent	**d.** subject

SYNONYMS AND ANTONYMS—SELECT

Read the first word in each line and think about what it means. One of the next four words means the **opposite** of the first. Circle the opposite word and mark it **A** for **antonym**.

One of the words is **similar** in meaning to the first word. Circle the similar word and mark it **S** for **synonym**.

A-135 attentive   **a.** attractive   **b.** considerate   **c.** deceptive   **d.** neglectful

A-136 altogether   **a.** barely   **b.** considerably   **c.** practically   **d.** totally

A-137 effort   **a.** ease   **b.** exertion   **c.** goal   **d.** outcome

A-138 dread   **a.** alertness   **b.** caution   **c.** fearlessness   **d.** fright

A-139 former   **a.** future   **b.** never   **c.** often   **d.** preceding

A-140 forbid   **a.** discourage   **b.** judge   **c.** permit   **d.** prohibit

A-141 destroy   **a.** damage   **b.** destruct   **c.** preserve   **d.** treat

A-142 repel   **a.** attract   **b.** challenge   **c.** repulse   **d.** sustain

A-143 reliable   **a.** conceivable   **b.** dependable   **c.** doubtful   **d.** occasional

A-144 obvious   **a.** acceptable   **b.** evident   **c.** possible   **d.** obscure

A-145 permanently   **a.** currently   **b.** lastingly   **c.** sometimes   **d.** temporarily

A-146 official   **a.** approved   **b.** favorable   **c.** leading   **d.** unauthorized

A-147 prior   **a.** instant   **b.** preceding   **c.** present   **d.** subsequent

A-148 simple   **a.** complete   **b.** complex   **c.** observable   **d.** uncomplicated

SYNONYMS AND ANTONYMS—SUPPLY

Read each word and think about what it means. Think of a word or words that mean **almost** the same thing. In the synonyms column, write as many similar words as you can recall.

Think of a word or words that mean the **opposite** of each word. In the antonyms column, write as many opposite words as you can recall.

	SYNONYMS	ANTONYMS
A-149 bold		
A-150 shout		
A-151 choose		
A-152 seldom		
A-153 defend		
A-154 tilted		
A-155 liberty		
A-156 profit		

SYNONYMS AND ANTONYMS—SUPPLY

List as many synonyms and antonyms as you can think of for the words below.

	SYNONYMS	**ANTONYMS**
A-157 accept		
A-158 proper		
A-159 dispute		
A-160 scarcely		
A-161 risk		
A-162 consequence		
A-163 remember		
A-164 lessen		

HOW ALIKE?—SELECT

Each line contains two words. Think about the ways the two are alike, then underline the sentences that are true of **both**.

A-165 copyright
patent

a. Both apply to novels.
b. Both apply to inventions.
c. Both are recorded by a government agency.
d. Both protect legal rights to new ideas.

A-166 bolt
lock

a. Both are operated by turning.
b. Both can be used to secure doors.
c. Both are always operated by a key.

A-167 fever
temperature

a. Both are used to describe body heat.
b. Both apply to symptoms of illness.
c. Both can be described in measurable degrees.

A-168 journalist
newscaster

a. Both report news.
b. Both must have good language skills.
c. Both write for newspapers.

HOW ALIKE?—SELECT

Each line contains two words. Think about the ways the two are alike, then underline the sentences that are true of **both.**

A-169 deport
exile

a. Both mean leaving a country.
b. Both refer to native citizens.
c. Both are usually government actions.

A-170 compare
contrast

a. Both involve observing similarities.
b. Both involving stressing differences.
c. Both are useful in understanding characteristics.

A-171 language
speech

a. Both involve words.
b. Both can be spoken.
c. Both are only spoken.

A-172 mumble
mutter

a. Both refer to speech.
b. Both sound angry.
c. Both are barely heard.

A-173 childish
childlike

a. Both are complimentary.
b. Both refer to qualities typical of children.
c. Both can be applied correctly to adults as well as children.

HOW ALIKE?—SELECT

Each line contains two words. Think about the ways the two are alike, then underline the sentences that are true of **both.**

A-174 danger
risk

a. Both suggest exposure to injury or loss.
b. Both suggest willingness to take a perilous chance.
c. Both suggest the need for caution.

A-175 blame
criticism

a. Both usually cause discomfort.
b. Both suggest evaluation of fault.
c. Both stress the fixing of responsibility for an error or fault.

A-176 error
lie

a. Both are efforts to deceive.
b. Both are incorrect.
c. Both can have unfortunate consequences.

A-177 salary
wage

a. Both refer to hourly or piecework rates.
b. Both refer to pay.
c. Both are fixed amounts usually paid monthly or twice a month.

HOW ALIKE AND HOW DIFFERENT?

Each line contains two words. Describe how the words are alike and how they are different.

A-178 bush
vine

HOW ALIKE? *Both plants, both migh give fruit, both grow, both have lea*

HOW DIFFERENT? *A bush is shor stubby, they grow in clumps, and the start branching out near the roots. Vines are long and thin, and sta branching farther out.*

A-179 garbage
trash

HOW ALIKE? *Both are taken on We both are really tempting to get by th same basic thing.*

HOW DIFFERENT? *Garbage mainl refers to stuff that goes into the g can. Trash refers to stuff that goes into recycle bin.*

A-180 borrow
steal

HOW ALIKE? *Both refer to taking som*

HOW DIFFERENT? *Borrowing means you have something for awhile and you return it later. Stealing is like robbing.*

A-181 alarm
signal

HOW ALIKE? *Both are warnings, both might make sound.*

HOW DIFFERENT? *Alarm refers to making more sound thay noise. Signal uses more nonverbal ways to get attent*

HOW ALIKE AND HOW DIFFERENT?

Each line contains two words. Describe how the words are alike and how they are different.

A-182　lumber
　　　　　wood

HOW ALIKE? *Both come from trees, both are used to make houses,*

HOW DIFFERENT? *Wood straight from the tree wouldn't be used to build houses. Lumber is used to build houses.*

A-183　author
　　　　　composer

HOW ALIKE? *Both write,*

HOW DIFFERENT? *Author writes books, Composer writes music.*

A-184　explorer
　　　　　pioneer

HOW ALIKE? *Both explore different ~~countries~~, territory and takes risks*

HOW DIFFERENT? *Explorers explore, but a pioneer settler in the land.*

A-185　artery
　　　　　vein

HOW ALIKE? *Both transport blood to organs*

HOW DIFFERENT? *One transports blood without oxygen, and one transports blood with oxygen,*

DENOTATION AND CONNOTATION

Denotation refers to the basic meaning of a word, which is the same from person to person. **Connotation** refers to the positive or negative interpretations that may differ from person to person.

Compare the meaning of "cheap" and "inexpensive." The basic meaning (denotation) of both words is "having a low price." Cheap has the negative connotation of poor quality. Inexpensive has the more positive connotation of acceptable quality.

For each pair of words below, underline the word with the more positive or complimentary meaning (connotation). Write the basic meaning (denotation) that applies to both words on the line provided.

Connotation	**Denotation**
EXAMPLE: cheap, <u>inexpensive</u>	having a low price
A-186 criminal, <u>delinquent</u>	steal stuff
A-187 <u>homemaker</u>, housewife	take care of your house
A-188 guard, <u>security officer</u>	guard things, or people
A-189 job, <u>profession</u>	someones work
A-190 <u>blemishes</u>, pimples	bumps on skins
A-191 lady, <u>female</u>	of the feminen species
A-192 <u>dentures</u>, false teeth	replace real teeth
A-193 <u>pre-owned</u>, used	been owned before

© 1995 MIDWEST PUBLICATIONS 93950-0448

DENOTATION AND CONNOTATION

For each pair of words below, underline the word with the more positive or complimentary meaning (connotation). Write the basic meaning (denotation) that applies to both words on the line provided.

A-194 garbage, <u>refuse</u>　　~~don't want to~~ waste

A-195 kid, <u>youth</u>　　younger

A-196 <u>homely</u>, ugly　　don't look nice

A-197 <u>disagreement</u>, squabble　　not in agreement

A-198 pity, <u>sympathy</u>　　caring for someone

A-199 dead, <u>deceased</u>　　stopped living

A-200 income, <u>revenue</u>　　money

A-201 house, <u>residence</u>　　something someone lives in

A-202 crippled, <u>handicapped</u>　　disabled

A-203 <u>disadvantaged</u>, needy　　don't have much

A-204 male, <u>gentleman</u>　　of the masculine species

A-205 belly, <u>stomach</u>　　organ that digests food

A-206 choose, <u>prefer</u>　　decide on something

DENOTATION AND CONNOTATION

Each group of words below contains a word with a basic denotation, a word with a more positive or formal meaning, and a word that has a more negative or informal meaning.

On the lines provided, mark the basic word **B**, the more positive word **P**, and the more negative word **N**. The positive and negative shades of meaning are connotations.

EXAMPLE:

flower __**P**__, plant __**B**__, weed __**N**__

A-207 aroma __P__, odor __B__, stench __N__

A-208 cozy __P__, cramped __N__, small __B__

A-209 antique __P__, old __B__, worn __N__

A-210 curious __B__, nosy __N__, questioning __P__

A-211 skinny __N__, slender __P__, thin __B__

A-212 behold __P__, observe __B__, spy __N__

A-213 chat __N__, confer __P__, talk __B__

A-214 immature __N__, young __B__, youthful __P__

A-215 little __B__, miniature __P__, puny __N__

WORD BENDERS™—INSTRUCTIONS

A Word Bender is a list of words made by changing letters. Each word in the list has two or more letters that are the same as the word above it. The letters that are to be changed are shown by blank circles.

Here is a Word Bender. Begin with "POST" and end with "LIST." Change only the letters that go in the circles.

P O S T Office
Ⓛ ə ʃ T and found
Not first but I ⓐ ʃ t
Shopping L Ⓘ S T

There is a clue that can help you solve the Word Bender correctly. Notice that there are no circles in either the third or fourth columns. This tells you that the last letters are "S" and "T."

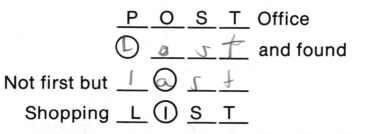

P O S T
Ⓛ o S T
Ɫ ⓐ S T
L Ⓘ S T

Look at the second word; only the first letter should be changed since it is the only one circled. So you have three letters and the phrase clue: ◯ O S T and found.

You have probably figured out that the answer is
Ⓛ O S T.

Now look at the third word; you can bring down the "L" and now have the clue: "Not first but L ◯ S T."

Here is a finished Word Bender:

P O S T Office
Ⓛ O S T and found
Not first but L Ⓐ S T
Shopping L Ⓘ S T

WORD BENDERS™—SYNONYMS

Complete the following exercise using words that have **similar** meaning to the "clue" words at the right.

B-1

D	A	R	K	GLOOM
(p)	a	r	k	PLAYGROUND
p	a	r	(t)	PORTION
(c)	a	r	t	WAGON
c	a	r	(e)	TEND
(p)	a	r	e	PEEL
(f)	a	r	e	PRICE
f	a	r	(m)	TILL
(h)	a	r	m	HURT
(w)	a	r	m	ENTHUSIASTIC
w	(o)	r	m	FISH BAIT
w	o	r	(n)	THREADBARE
(t)	o	r	n	RIPPED
(b)	o	r	n	BIRTH
b	(u)	r	n	SINGE
(t)	u	r	n	SPIN

WORD BENDERS™—SYNONYMS

Complete the following exercises using words that have **similar** meaning to the "clue" words at the right.

SEQUENCES

B-2

S	I	G	N	A	L	WARNING
(D)	(e)	s	i	g	n	PATTERN
d	e	s	i	(r)	(e)	WANT
d	e	s	(e)	r	(t)	ABANDON
d	e	s	e	r	(v)(e)	EARN
(r)	e	s	e	r	v e	EXTRA
(c)(e)(n)	s	e	r	v e		PRESERVE
c o n	(c)	e	r	(n)		INTEREST
(D)(I)(S)	C	E	R	N		RECOGNIZE

B-3

V	I	S	I	T	O	R	GUEST
	v	i	s	i	(o)(r)		SIGHT
(p)(r)(o)	v	i	s	i	(o)	n	CONDITION
p	r	o	v	i	(d)(e)		GIVE
p	r	o	(d)(u)(c)	e			MAKE
p	r	o	d	u	c	(t)	OUTPUT
p	r	o	(j)(e)	c	t		PLAN
P	(E)(R)(F)	E	C	T			FLAWLESS

25

WORD BENDERS™—SYNONYMS

Complete the following exercise using words that have **similar** meaning to the "clue" words at the right.

B-4

M	O	T	I	O	N	MOVEMENT
(n)	o	t	i	o	n	IDEA
(a)	(c)	t	i	o	n	DOING
(f)	(r)	a	c	t	i	o n	PART
f	(u)	(n)	c	t	i	o n	WORK
(J)	U	N	C	T	I	O N	JOINING
(s)	(t)	(a)	t	i	o	n	DEPOT
(n)	a	t	i	o	n	COUNTRY
(r)	a	t	i	o	n	PORTION
R	A	T	I	O		FRACTION

WORD BENDERS™—SYNONYMS

Complete the following exercise using words that have **similar** meaning to the "clue" words at the right.

B-5

P R E V E N T	STOP
i n v e n t	DEVISE
i n t e n d	MEAN
e x t e n d	STRETCH
p r e t e n d	IMAGINE
C O N T E N D	MAINTAIN
c o n t e s t	GAME
c o n s e n t	PERMISSION
p r e s e n t	GIFT
r e s i d e	LIVE
p r e s i d e	DIRECT
p r e s u m e	GUESS
r e s u m e	CONTINUE
c o n s u m e	DEVOUR
C O N F U S E	PUZZLE

SEQUENCES

27

WORD BENDERS™—SYNONYMS

Complete the following exercise using words that have **similar** meaning to the "clue" words at the right.

B-6

R	E	F	R	A	I	N	WITHHOLD
	(s)	(t)	r	a	i	n	STRESS
(r)	(e)	s	t	r	a	i	n	HOLD BACK
r	e	s	t	r	(i)	(c)	(t)	LIMIT
(d)	(i)	s	t	r	i	c	t	SECTION
d	i	s	t	r	(u)	(s)	t	SUSPECT
d	i	s	t	r	(e)	s	(s)	MISERY
d	i	s	t	r	(a)	(c)	(t)	CONFUSE
(R)	(E)	T	R	A	C	T	RECEDE
	(r)	(e)	a	c	t	RESPOND
	r	e	a	c	(h)	ARRIVE
	(p)	r	e	a	c	h	URGE
(A)	(P)	P	R	(O)	A	C	H	COME NEAR

28

WORD BENDERS™—ANTONYMS

Complete the following exercise using words that have the **opposite** meaning to the "clue" words at the right.

B-7

D	E	M	A	N	D	REQUEST
(c)	(o)	(n)	m	a	n	d	FOLLOW
c	o	m	m	(e)	n	d	REBUKE
(r) (e)	c	o	m	m	e	n	d	WARN
c	o	m	m	e	n	( ) ( )	FINISH
c	o	m	m	(o)	n		UNUSUAL
c	o	m	m	o	(t) (i) (o) (n)		QUIET
(p) (r) (o)	m	o	t	i	o	n	DEMOTION
p	r	o	m	o	t	(e)	DISCOURAGE
P	R	O	M	(P)	T		TARDY

SEQUENCES

29

WORD BENDERS™—ANTONYMS

Complete the following exercises using words that have the
opposite meaning of the "clue" words at the right.

B-8

I	N	C	L	U	D	E	ELIMINATE
(○)	(○)	c	l	u	d	e	ADMIT
		c	l	(○)	(○)	(○)	WHISPER
(r)	(e)	c	l				DISPOSE
r	e	c	l	(i)	(n)	(e)	STAND
(d)	e	c	l	i	n	e	ACCEPT
D	E	C	L	(A)	(R)	E	DENY

B-9

R	E	S	T	R	A	I	N	FREE
r	e	s	t	r	(i)	(c)	(t)	ALLOW
(d)	(i)	s	t	r	a	c	t	CONCENTRATE
d	i	s	t	r	(○)	(s)	(○)	COMFORT
d	i	s	t	r	(u)	s	(t)	BELIEVE
d	i	s	t	(○)	(○)	c	t	BLURRED
d	i	s	t	(a)	n	t	(e)	VICINITY
D	I	S	T	A	N	(T)		NEAR

30

FOLLOWING DIRECTIONS—SELECT

Read each set of directions below, then circle the figure that correctly represents the directions.

B-10

DIRECTIONS: Draw a square. Use the top side of the square as the base of a half circle.

FIGURES:

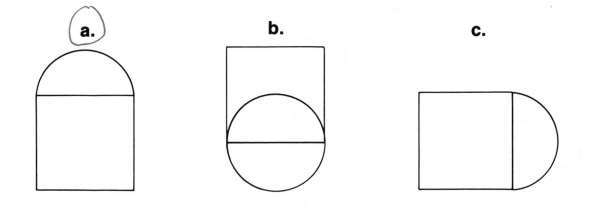

B-11

DIRECTIONS: Draw a vertical line. Use the line as part of a half circle and part of a triangle. The triangle should be to the left of the half circle.

FIGURES:

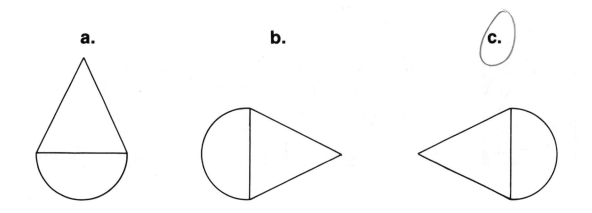

FOLLOWING DIRECTIONS—SELECT

Read each set of directions below, then circle the figure that correctly represents the directions.

B-12

DIRECTIONS: Draw a small square above and touching a larger rectangle.

FIGURES:

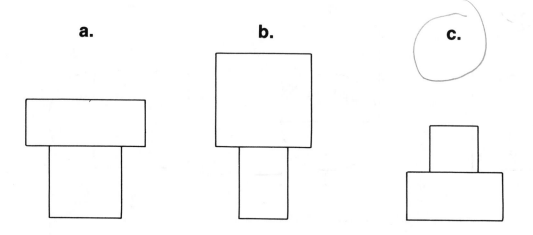

B-13

DIRECTIONS: Draw a large circle. Inside the circle draw a triangle. Inside the triangle draw a rectangle.

FIGURES:

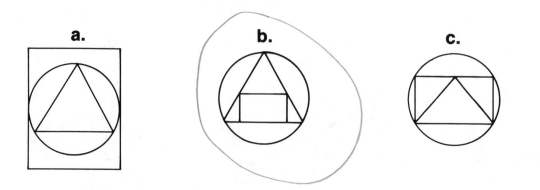

© 1985 MIDWEST PUBLICATIONS 93950-0448

FOLLOWING DIRECTIONS—SELECT

Read each set of directions below, then circle the figure that correctly represents the directions.

B-14

DIRECTIONS: Draw a square and two rectangles. The long side of the rectangles should be the same length as a side of the square. The rectangles should touch opposite sides of the square to form a tall rectangle.

FIGURES:

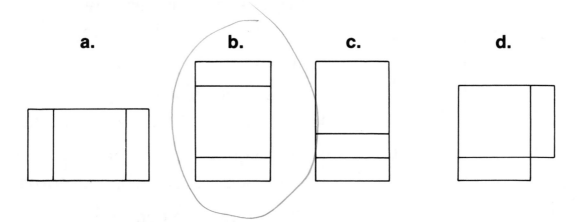

a.   b.   c.   d.

B-15

DIRECTIONS: Draw a rectangle. Divide the rectangle into two equal triangles by drawing a line from the upper right corner to the lower left corner. Draw a square using the left side of the rectangle as the right side of the square.

FIGURES:

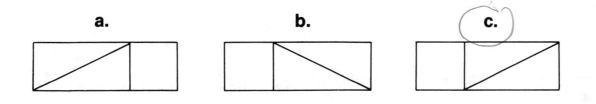

a.   b.   c.

33

FOLLOWING DIRECTIONS—SUPPLY WORDS

Complete the sentences below with the correct words from the Choice Box.

<table>
<tr><td align="center">**CHOICE BOX**

center, left, lower, right, upper</td></tr>
</table>

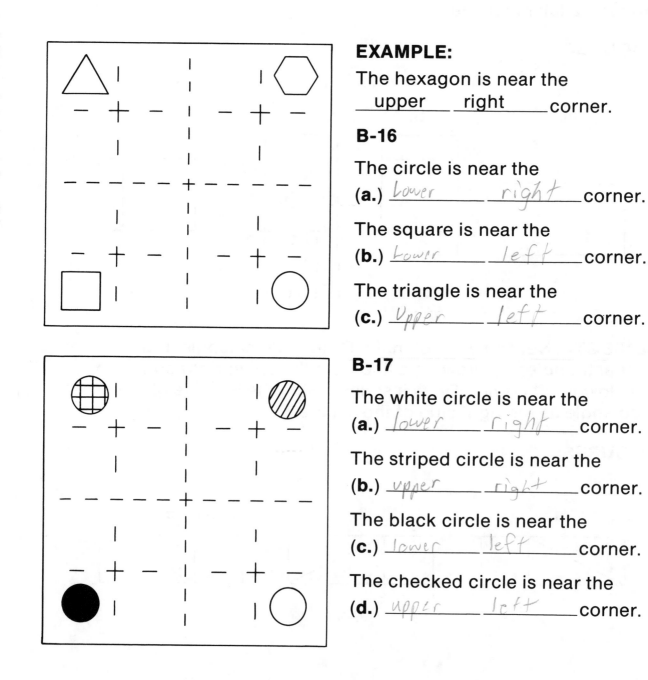

EXAMPLE:

The hexagon is near the
_____upper_____right_____corner.

B-16

The circle is near the
(a.) _lower_____right___corner.

The square is near the
(b.) _lower_____left___corner.

The triangle is near the
(c.) _upper_____left___corner.

B-17

The white circle is near the
(a.) _lower_____right___corner.

The striped circle is near the
(b.) _upper_____right___corner.

The black circle is near the
(c.) _lower_____left___corner.

The checked circle is near the
(d.) _upper_____left___corner.

stop

FOLLOWING DIRECTIONS—SUPPLY WORDS

Complete the sentences below with the correct words from the Choice Box.

CHOICE BOX

above, below, black, center, checked, left,
lower, right, striped, upper

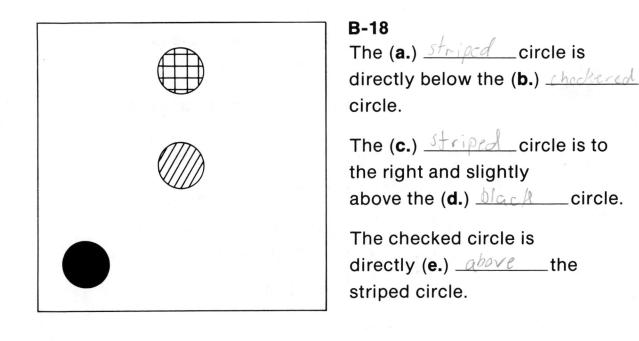

B-18

The (**a.**) _striped_ circle is directly below the (**b.**) _checkered_ circle.

The (**c.**) _striped_ circle is to the right and slightly above the (**d.**) _black_ circle.

The checked circle is directly (**e.**) _above_ the striped circle.

SEQUENCES

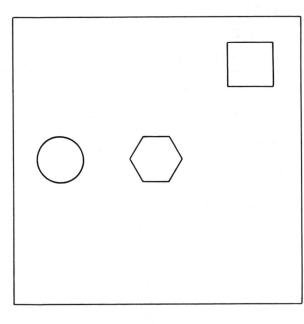

B-19

The hexagon is in the (**a.**) _center_ and also to the (**b.**) _right_ of the circle.

The square is near the (**c.**) _upper_ _right_ corner.

The circle is (**d.**) _left_ of center.

FOLLOWING DIRECTIONS—SUPPLY WORDS

Complete the sentences below with the correct words from the Choice Box.

```
CHOICE BOX
above, below, center, circle, hexagon, large
left, lower, right, small, square, triangle
```

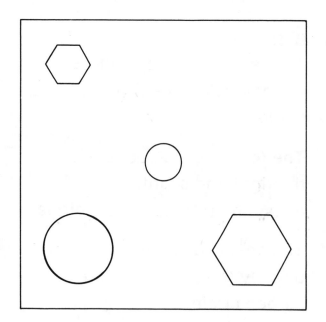

B-20

The small circle is near the (**a.**) _center_ .

The large hexagon is near the (**b.**) _lower right_ corner.

The small hexagon is(**c.**) _above_ the large circle.

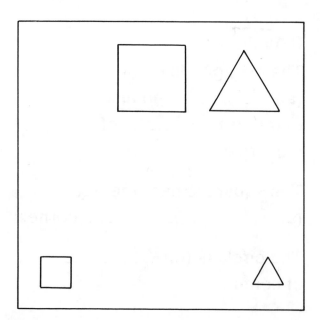

B-21

The large triangle is above the (**a.**) _small triangle_ and to the right of the (**b.**) _large square_ .

The (**c.**) _small triangle_ is near the lower right corner.

FOLLOWING DIRECTIONS—SUPPLY SHAPES

Read the instructions below, then draw the shapes in the square grid as directed.

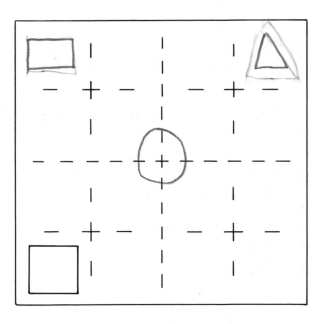

EXAMPLE:

Draw a square near the lower left corner.

B-22

Draw a triangle near the upper right corner.

Draw a circle at the center.

Draw a rectangle near the upper left corner.

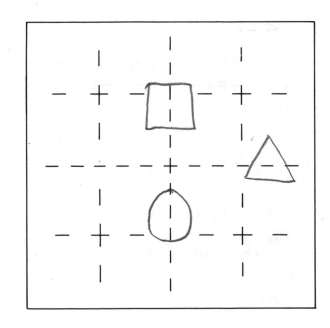

B-23

Draw a triangle to the right of the center.

Draw a circle below the center.

Draw a square above the center.

stop

FOLLOWING DIRECTIONS—SUPPLY SHAPES

Draw the shapes in the square grid as directed by the instructions below. Then complete the sentences to describe the diagrams.

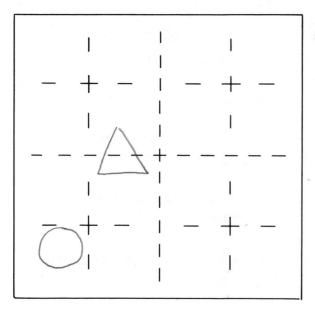

B-24

Draw a triangle to the left of center.

Draw a circle near the lower left corner.

The (**a.**) _circle_ is below the (**b.**) _triangle_ .

The triangle is (**c.**) _above_ the circle.

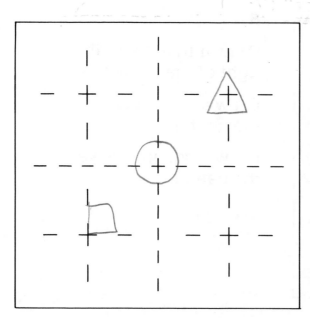

B-25

Draw a triangle above and to the right of a circle located at the center.

Draw a square in a diagonal line with the triangle and circle.

The triangle is near the (**a.**) _upper_ _right_ corner, and the square is near the (**b.**) _lower_ _left_ corner.

FOLLOWING DIRECTIONS—SUPPLY DESIGNS

Read the directions for each problem, then draw the designs step by step, exactly as directed, on the dot grid provided.

B-26 DIRECTIONS: Draw a large rectangle. Draw a small square at the center of the rectangle. Draw a circle near the lower left corner and a triangle near the upper right corner.

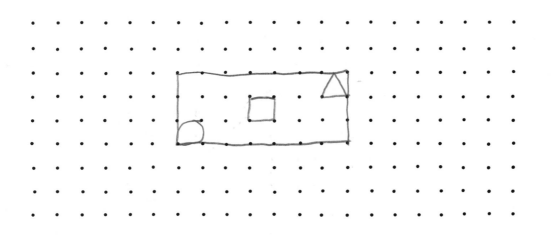

B-27 DIRECTIONS: Draw a small circle to the left of center. At the center draw a square larger than the circle. To the right of center draw a triangle taller than the square.

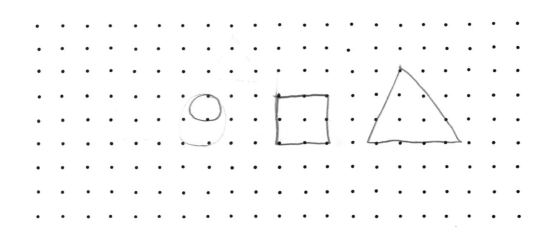

SEQUENCES

FOLLOWING DIRECTIONS—SUPPLY DESIGNS

Read the directions, then draw the designs step by step, exactly as directed, on the dot grid provided.

B-28   DIRECTIONS: Draw a large triangle. Inside the triangle draw the largest square that will fit. Inside the square draw a circle touching the square at four points. Inside the circle draw a rectangle touching the circle at four points.

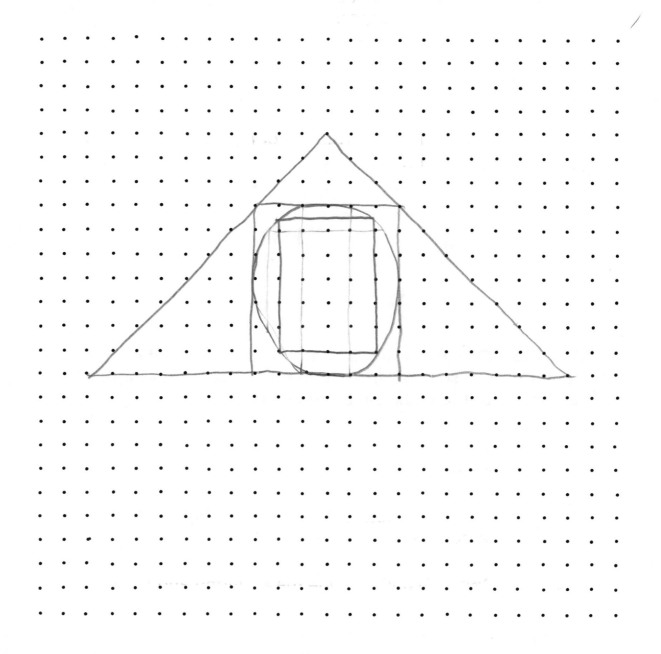

FOLLOWING DIRECTIONS—SUPPLY DESIGNS

Use a whole sheet of paper for each problem. Draw the designs step by step, exactly as directed.

B-29　**a.**　　Draw a small circle in the center of the page.

　　　　b.　　Draw a small square at the midpoint of the bottom edge of the paper.

　　　　c.　　Draw a line from the upper left corner of the page to the circle.

　　　　d.　　Draw a line from the upper right corner of the page to the circle.

　　　　e.　　Draw a line from the circle to the square.

B-30　**a.**　　Mark an "X" at the midpoint of each edge of the paper.

　　　　b.　　Draw lines from midpoint to midpoint to form a tall diamond shape.

　　　　c.　　Mark a "Y" at the midpoint of each side of the diamond.

　　　　d.　　Draw lines connecting the "Y" midpoints to form a rectangle.

　　　　e.　　Write "THINK" inside the diamond and above the rectangle.

SEQUENCES

FOLLOWING DIRECTIONS—SUPPLY DESIGNS

Use a whole sheet of paper for each problem. Draw the designs step by step, exactly as directed.

B-31 **a.** On the left and right edges mark points that are one-fourth of the way down the page.

b. Draw a horizontal line connecting those points.

c. Divide the line into four equal parts.

d. Divide the bottom edge into four equal parts.

e. Connect each point on the horizontal line with the point directly below it.

B-32 **a.** Draw a line from top to bottom that is one-fourth of the page width from the left edge.

b. Divide this vertical line into four equal parts.

c. Divide the right edge into four equal parts.

d. Connect the points one-fourth of the way from the top.

e. Connect the points one-fourth of the way from the bottom.

f. Write "I" in the top right rectangle.

g. Write "DIRECTIONS" in the lower right rectangle.

h. Write "FOLLOWED" in the square.

© 1985 MIDWEST PUBLICATIONS 93950-0448

WRITING DIRECTIONS

In these exercises, you must examine the figure in the box very carefully. Use the lines provided to write a set of directions for drawing each figure. Write the directions carefully so that a classmate could draw the figure from your directions without seeing the figure.

B-33

_____

_____

_____

_____

_____

_____

B-34

_____

_____

_____

_____

_____

_____

SEQUENCES

WRITING DIRECTIONS

In these exercises, you must examine the figure in the box very carefully. Use the lines provided to write a set of directions for drawing each figure. Write the directions carefully so that a classmate could draw the figure from your directions without seeing the figure.

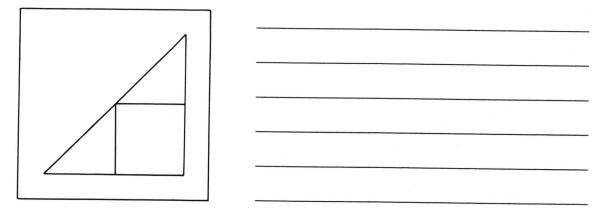
_____
_____
_____
_____
_____
_____

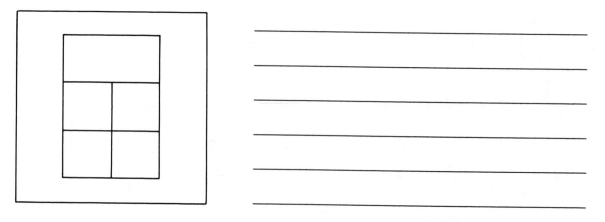
_____
_____
_____
_____
_____
_____

© 1985 MIDWEST PUBLICATIONS 93950-0448

WRITING DIRECTIONS

In these exercises, you must examine the figure in the box very carefully. Use the lines provided to write a set of directions for drawing each figure. Write the directions carefully so that a classmate could draw the figure from your directions without seeing the figure.

B-37

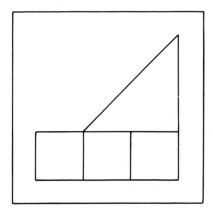

B-38

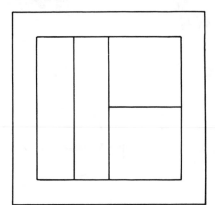

SEQUENCES

STACKING SHAPES—SELECT

Here are four shapes. At the bottom of the page are eight different combinations of shapes, formed by placing one shape on another. Select the stack that fits each description.

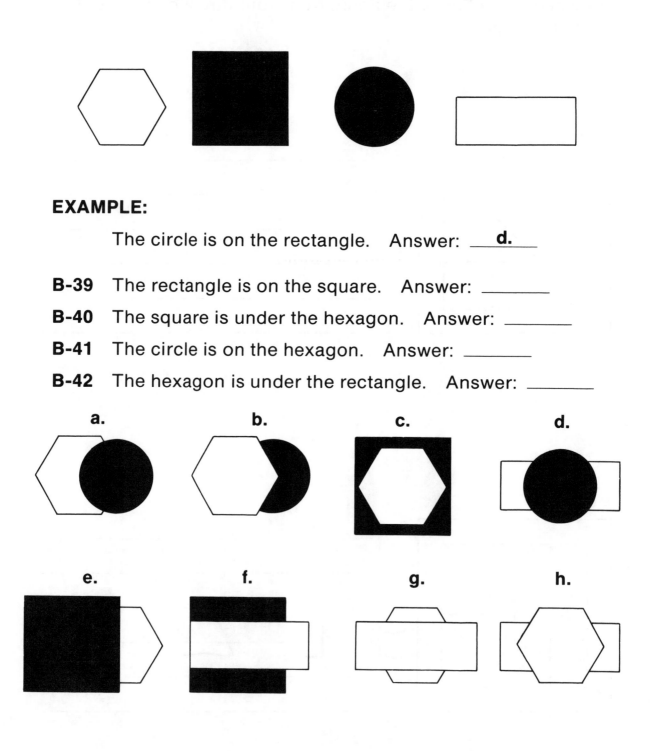

EXAMPLE:

   The circle is on the rectangle.   Answer: _____**d.**_____

B-39   The rectangle is on the square.   Answer: _____

B-40   The square is under the hexagon.   Answer: _____

B-41   The circle is on the hexagon.   Answer: _____

B-42   The hexagon is under the rectangle.   Answer: _____

STACKING SHAPES—SELECT

Here are four shapes. At the bottom of the page are eight different combinations of shapes, formed by placing one shape on another. Select the stack that fits each description.

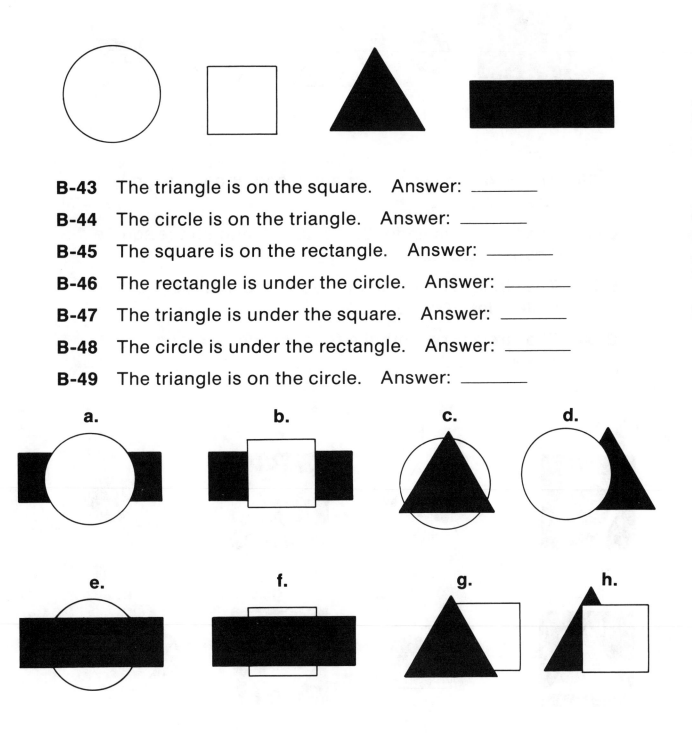

B-43 The triangle is on the square.　Answer: _____

B-44 The circle is on the triangle.　Answer: _____

B-45 The square is on the rectangle.　Answer: _____

B-46 The rectangle is under the circle.　Answer: _____

B-47 The triangle is under the square.　Answer: _____

B-48 The circle is under the rectangle.　Answer: _____

B-49 The triangle is on the circle.　Answer: _____

SEQUENCES

STACKING SHAPES—SELECT

Here are five shapes. At the bottom of the page are eight different combinations of shapes, formed by placing one shape on another. Select the stack that fits each description.

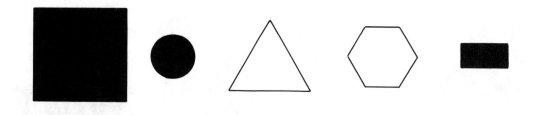

B-50   The hexagon is on the triangle and under the circle.
Answer: _____

B-51   The triangle is under the rectangle and on the square.
Answer: _____

B-52   The circle is on the triangle, and the triangle is on the rectangle.   Answer: _____

B-53   The circle is on both the triangle and hexagon.
Answer: _____

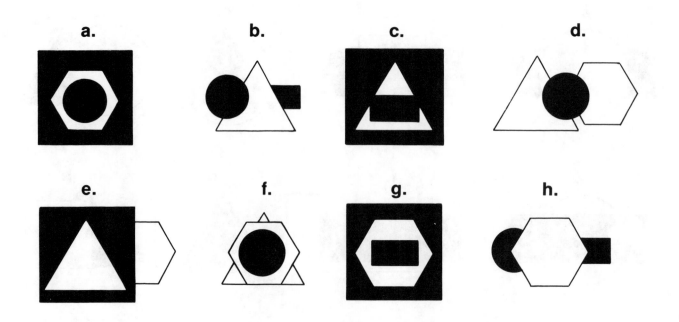

STACKING SHAPES—SUPPLY

Here are three pairs of shapes. Shade them as they will look after they are stacked according to the directions.

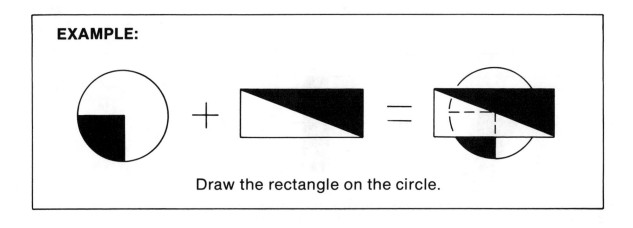

EXAMPLE:

Draw the rectangle on the circle.

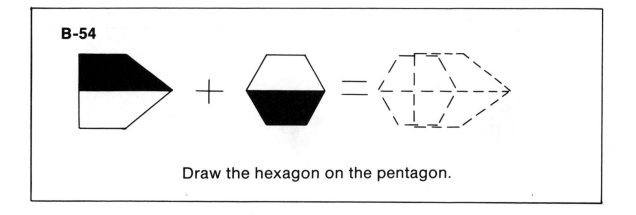

B-54

Draw the hexagon on the pentagon.

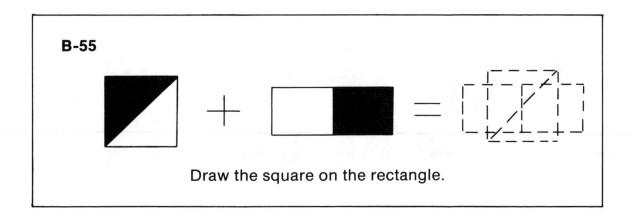

B-55

Draw the square on the rectangle.

SEQUENCES

STACKING SHAPES—SUPPLY

Here are three pairs of shapes. Shade them as they will look after they are stacked according to the directions.

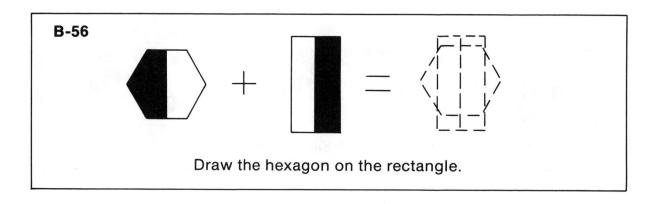

B-56

Draw the hexagon on the rectangle.

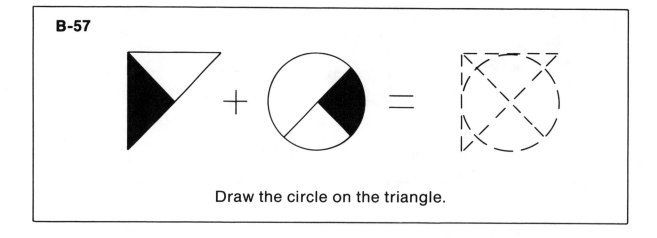

B-57

Draw the circle on the triangle.

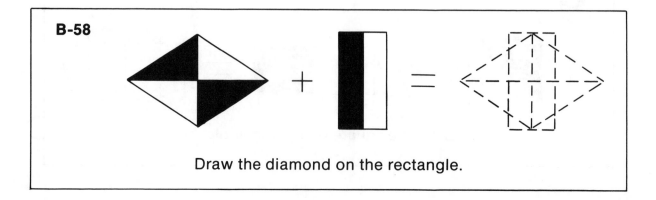

B-58

Draw the diamond on the rectangle.

STACKING SHAPES—SUPPLY

Here are three stacks of shapes. Mark each of them according to the directions given.

B-59

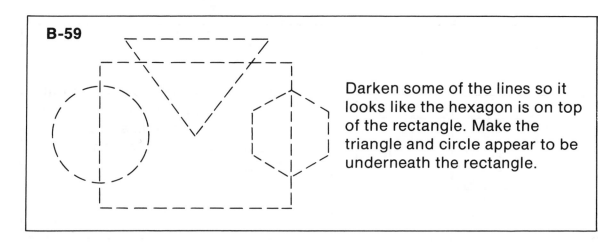

Darken some of the lines so it looks like the hexagon is on top of the rectangle. Make the triangle and circle appear to be underneath the rectangle.

B-60

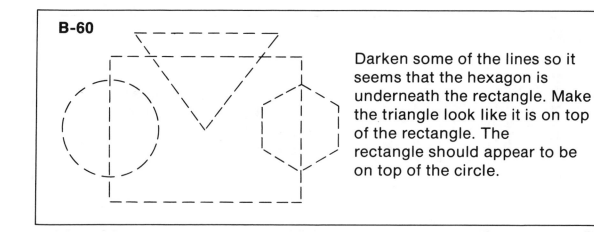

Darken some of the lines so it seems that the hexagon is underneath the rectangle. Make the triangle look like it is on top of the rectangle. The rectangle should appear to be on top of the circle.

B-61

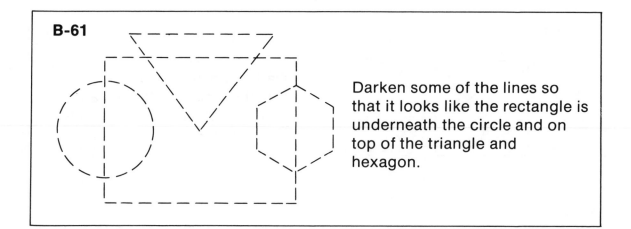

Darken some of the lines so that it looks like the rectangle is underneath the circle and on top of the triangle and hexagon.

SEQUENCES

STACKING SHAPES—SUPPLY

Here are three stacks of shapes. Mark each of them according to the directions given.

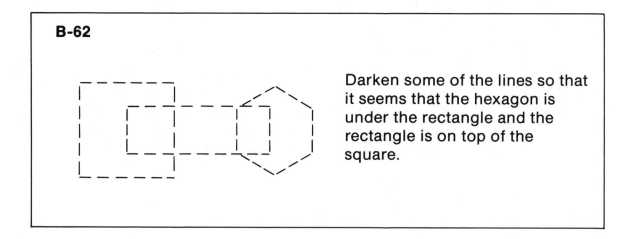

B-62

Darken some of the lines so that it seems that the hexagon is under the rectangle and the rectangle is on top of the square.

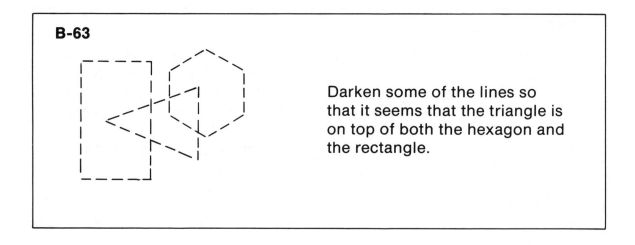

B-63

Darken some of the lines so that it seems that the triangle is on top of both the hexagon and the rectangle.

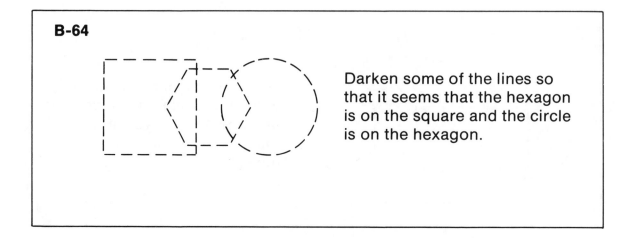

B-64

Darken some of the lines so that it seems that the hexagon is on the square and the circle is on the hexagon.

STACKING SHAPES—SUPPLY

Here are three stacks of shapes. Mark each of them according to the directions given.

B-65

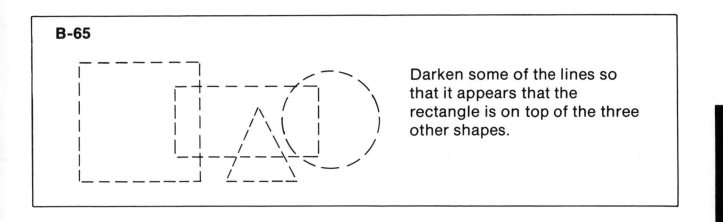

Darken some of the lines so that it appears that the rectangle is on top of the three other shapes.

B-66

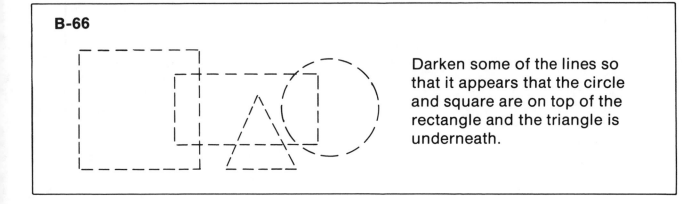

Darken some of the lines so that it appears that the circle and square are on top of the rectangle and the triangle is underneath.

B-67

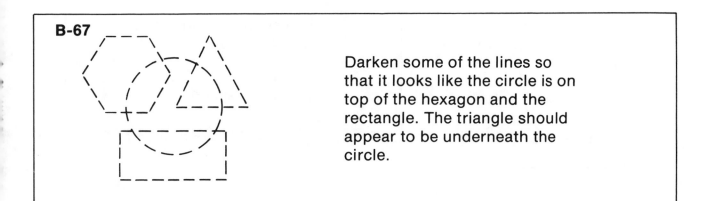

Darken some of the lines so that it looks like the circle is on top of the hexagon and the rectangle. The triangle should appear to be underneath the circle.

SEQUENCES

STACKING SHAPES—EXPLAIN

Supply the words needed to describe the stacks of shapes.

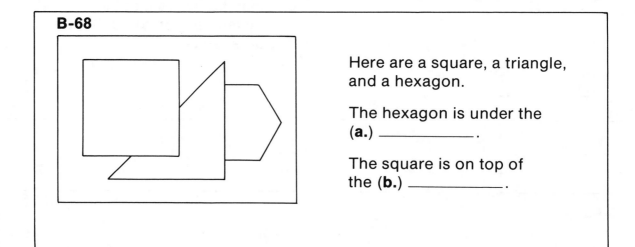

B-68

Here are a square, a triangle, and a hexagon.

The hexagon is under the (**a.**) _____.

The square is on top of the (**b.**) _____.

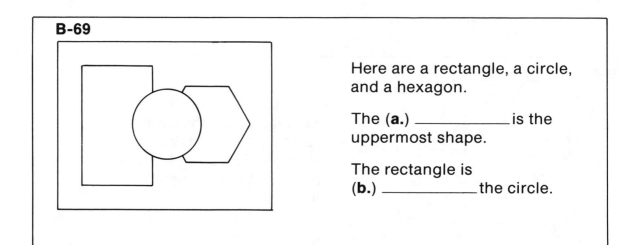

B-69

Here are a rectangle, a circle, and a hexagon.

The (**a.**) _____ is the uppermost shape.

The rectangle is (**b.**) _____ the circle.

STACKING SHAPES—EXPLAIN

Supply the words needed to describe the stacks of shapes.

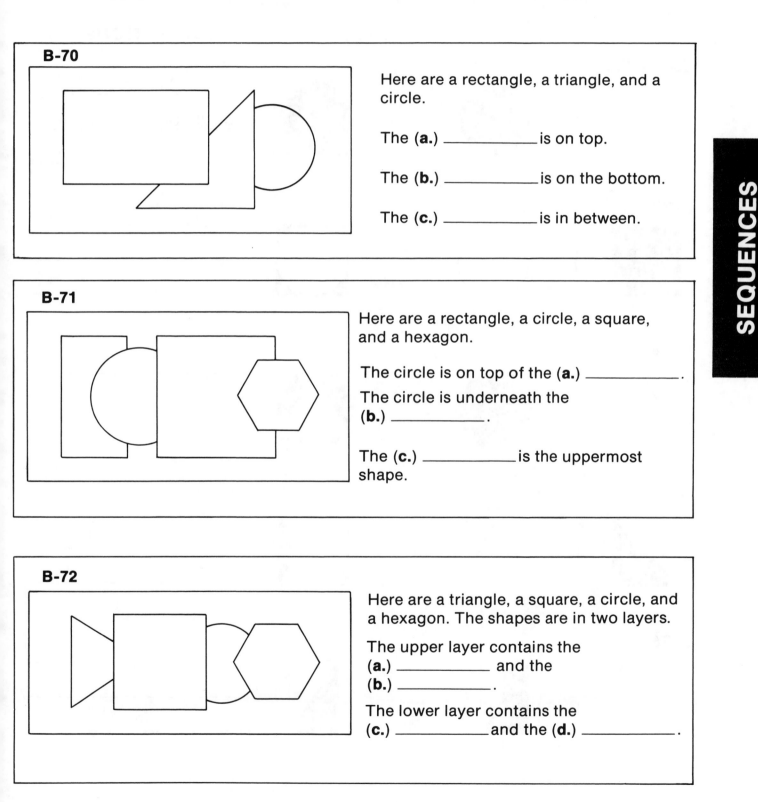

B-70

Here are a rectangle, a triangle, and a circle.

The (**a.**) _____ is on top.

The (**b.**) _____ is on the bottom.

The (**c.**) _____ is in between.

B-71

Here are a rectangle, a circle, a square, and a hexagon.

The circle is on top of the (**a.**) _____.

The circle is underneath the (**b.**) _____.

The (**c.**) _____ is the uppermost shape.

B-72

Here are a triangle, a square, a circle, and a hexagon. The shapes are in two layers.

The upper layer contains the (**a.**) _____ and the (**b.**) _____.

The lower layer contains the (**c.**) _____ and the (**d.**) _____.

SEQUENCES

STACKING SHAPES—EXPLAIN

Write the directions for stacking the shapes to make the figure on the right.

DIRECTIONS

EXAMPLE:

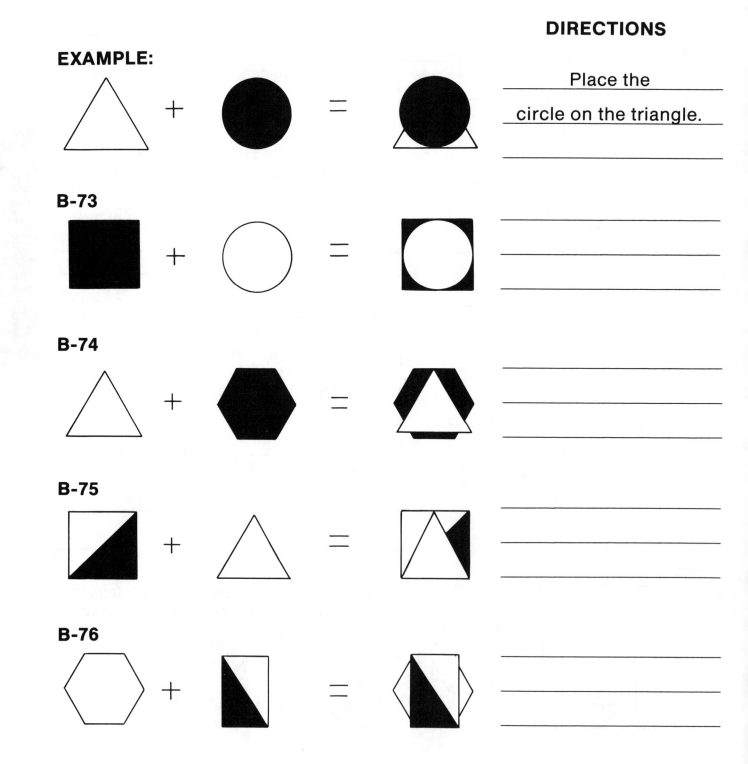

Place the
circle on the triangle.

B-73

B-74

B-75

B-76

STACKING SHAPES—EXPLAIN

Write the directions for stacking the shapes to make the figure on the right.

DIRECTIONS

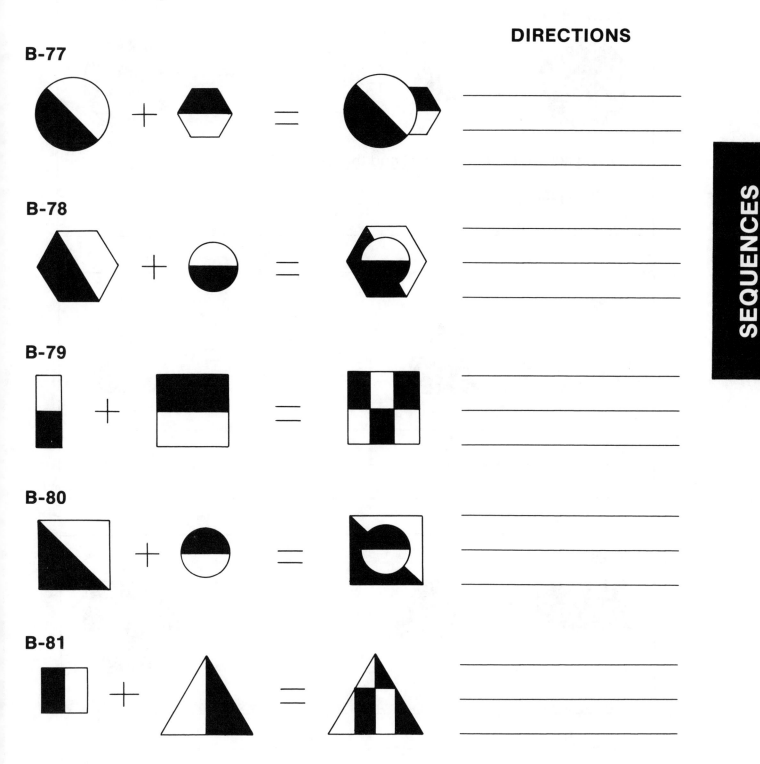

B-77

B-78

B-79

B-80

B-81

STACKING SHAPES—EXPLAIN

Write a verbal description of the sequence illustrated in each problem.

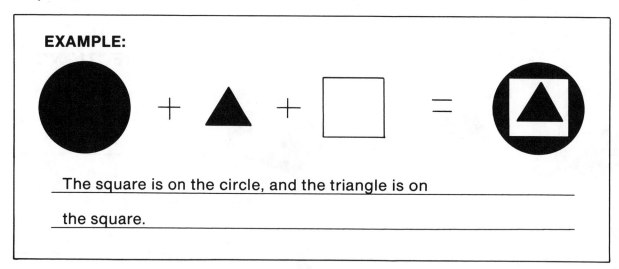

EXAMPLE:

The square is on the circle, and the triangle is on

the square.

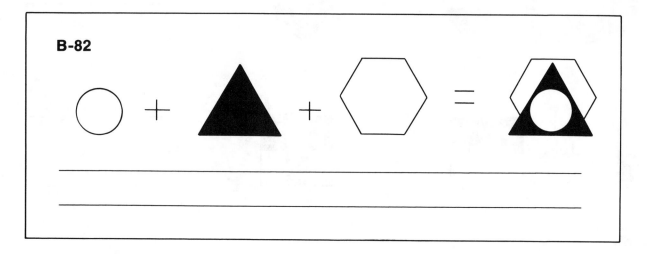

B-82

_____

_____

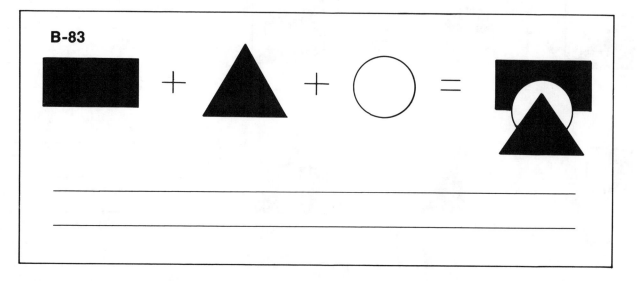

B-83

_____

_____

STACKING SHAPES—EXPLAIN

Write a verbal description of the sequence illustrated in each problem.

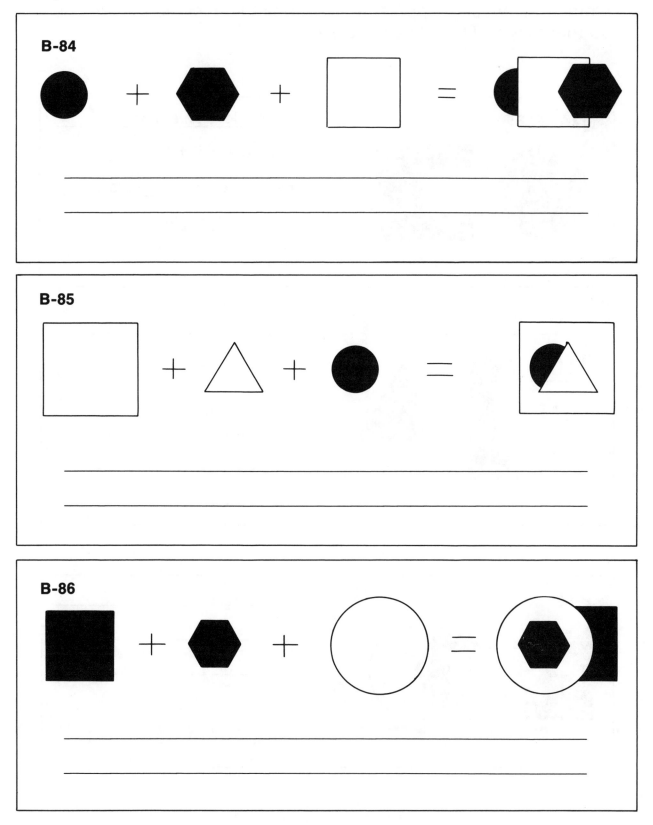

STACKING SHAPES—EXPLAIN

Here are stacks of overlapping shapes. Each shape is either all white or all black. Supply the directions for stacking the shapes so that they will look like the drawing.

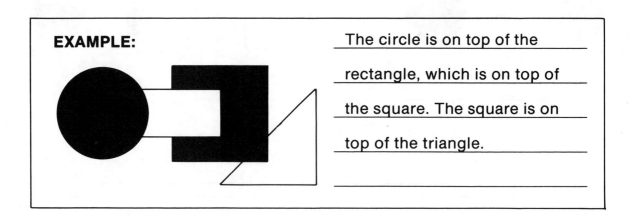

EXAMPLE:

The circle is on top of the rectangle, which is on top of the square. The square is on top of the triangle.

B-87

_____
_____
_____
_____
_____

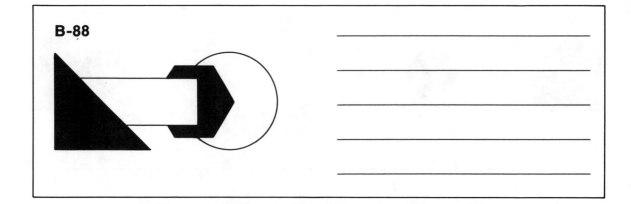

B-88

_____
_____
_____
_____
_____

STACKING SHAPES—EXPLAIN

Here are stacks of overlapping shapes. Each shape is either all white or all black. Supply the directions for stacking the shapes so that they look like the drawing.

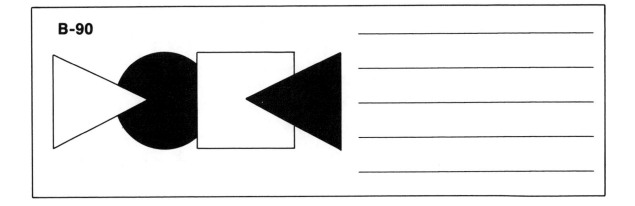

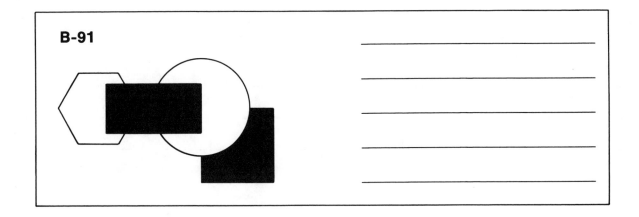

PRODUCE A PATTERN AND WRITE DESCRIPTIONS

Shade parts of each pattern to form any stacking arrangement you choose, then write a description of the stacking arrangement so that another person could reproduce it.

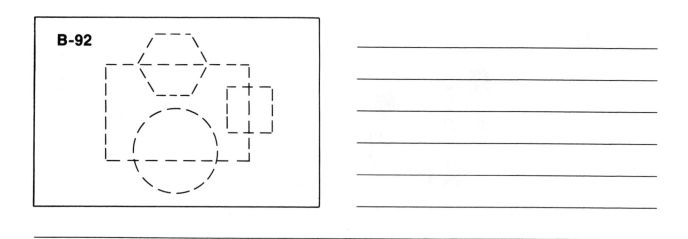

_____
_____
_____
_____
_____
_____

_____
_____

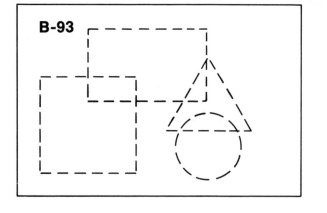

_____
_____
_____
_____
_____
_____

_____
_____

PRODUCE A PATTERN AND WRITE DESCRIPTIONS

Shade parts of each pattern to form any stacking arrangement
you choose, then write a description of the stacking arrangement
so that another person could reproduce it.

B-94

_____
_____
_____
_____
_____
_____

_____
_____

B-95

_____
_____
_____
_____
_____
_____

_____
_____

SEQUENCES

RECOGNIZING DIRECTION

For the problems below, imagine that you are standing on the circle in the middle of this diagram. Then consider the position of the shapes given and determine the direction you are facing and the position of the missing shape.

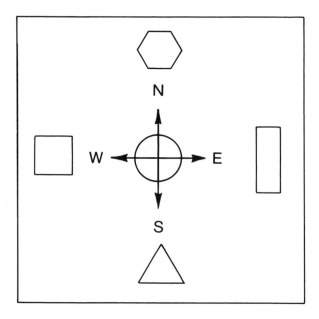

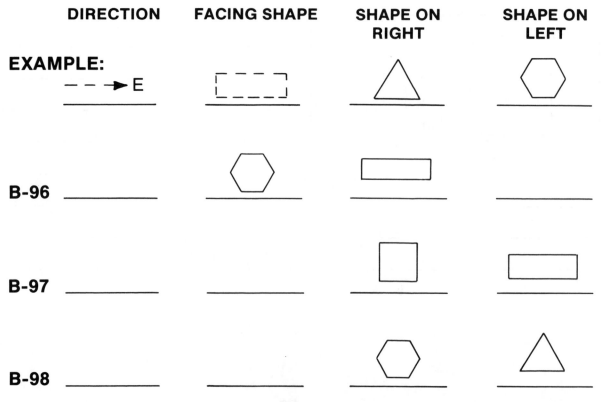

	DIRECTION	FACING SHAPE	SHAPE ON RIGHT	SHAPE ON LEFT
EXAMPLE:	- - ➔ E			
B-96				
B-97				
B-98				

RECOGNIZING DIRECTION

Imagine that you are standing at the center of the large circle and are facing either northeast (NE), northwest (NW), southwest (SW), or southeast (SE). Consider the positions of the shapes given, then determine the direction you are facing and the position of the missing shape.

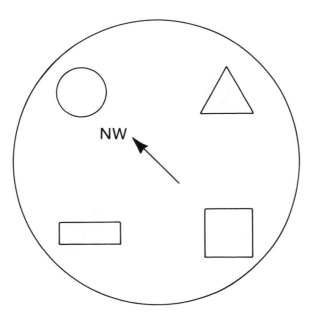

EXAMPLE: If the triangle is on your right and the rectangle is on your left, then you are facing the circle. (Draw the circle in the blank.) If you are facing the circle, you are facing northwest. (Draw in the arrow as shown and mark it NW.)

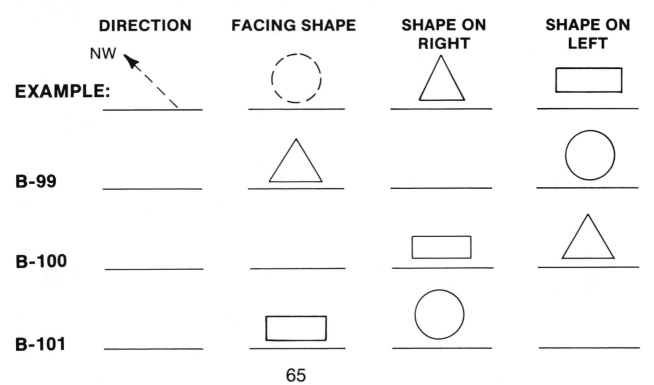

	DIRECTION	FACING SHAPE	SHAPE ON RIGHT	SHAPE ON LEFT
EXAMPLE:	NW	◯	△	▭
B-99		△		◯
B-100			▭	△
B-101	▭	◯		

RECOGNIZING DIRECTION

Imagine that you are standing at the center of the large circle and are facing either northeast (NE), northwest (NW), southeast (SE), or southwest (SW). The direction you are facing is given so that you can draw in the missing shapes.

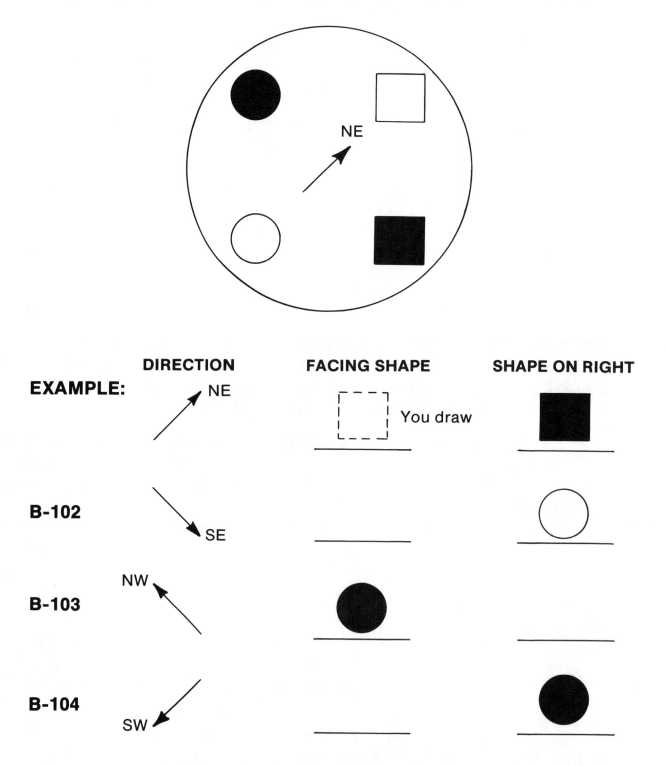

	DIRECTION	FACING SHAPE	SHAPE ON RIGHT
EXAMPLE:	NE	⬚ You draw	■
B-102	SE		◯
B-103	NW	●	
B-104	SW		●

© 1985 MIDWEST PUBLICATIONS 93950-0448

DESCRIBING LOCATIONS ON A GRID

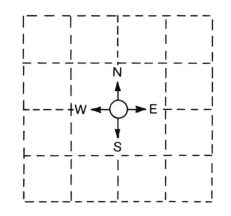

B-105 Put a 1 in the northeast corner of the grid.
Put a 2 in the southwest corner of the grid.
Put a 3 in the southeast corner of the grid.
Put a 4 in the northwest corner of the grid.

For the following exercises, take paths along the dashed lines and make as few turns as needed.

A unit is the length of the side of one of the small squares of the grid.

B-106 How far is it from the northeast corner to the northwest corner?   Answer: _____ units

B-107 How far is it from the northwest corner to the southwest corner? Answer: _____ units

B-108 How far is it from the southwest corner to the northeast corner?   Answer: _____ units

B-109 How far is it from the center of the grid to the northeast corner?   Answer: _____ units

B-110 How far is it from the center of the grid to any corner?   Answer: _____ units

SEQUENCES

DESCRIBING LOCATIONS ON A GRID

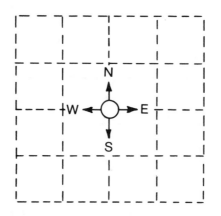

You are standing at the center of the grid facing the northeast corner. You lift your right arm and it points southeast.

B-111 You lift your left arm and it points in which direction?   Answer: _____

B-112 What direction is directly behind you?
Answer: _____

Staying at the center, you now turn so that you are facing southwest.

B-113 What direction is to your left?   Answer: _____

B-114 What direction is behind you?   Answer: _____

Staying at the center, you now turn to face southeast. Northeast is now to your left.

B-115 In relation to you and your position, where is southwest?
Answer: _____

B-116 Where is northwest?   Answer: _____

DESCRIBING LOCATIONS ON A GRID

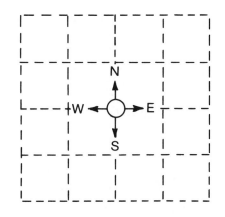

    You are standing at the center of the grid facing north. The direction to the left and north is northwest.

B-117 What direction is to the left and south?
Answer: _____

B-118 What direction is to the right and south?
Answer: _____

B-119 What direction is to the right and north?
Answer: _____

Staying at the center, you now turn and face west.

B-120 What direction is it to your right and behind
you?   Answer: _____

B-121 What direction is to your left and in front of
you?   Answer: _____

Staying at the center, you turn so that northeast is behind you.

B-122 What direction is to your right?   Answer: _____

B-123 What direction is in front of you and to your
left?   Answer: _____

SEQUENCES

DESCRIBING LOCATIONS ON A GRID

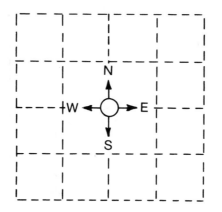

You are standing at the center of the grid.

B-124 Which way are you facing if northwest is behind you?   Answer: _____

You turn so that northwest is on your right.

B-125 Which way are you facing?   Answer: _____

You turn so that east is in front of you and to your right.

B-126 Which way are you facing?   Answer: _____

© 1985 MIDWEST PUBLICATIONS 93950-0448

DESCRIBING LOCATIONS USING MAPS

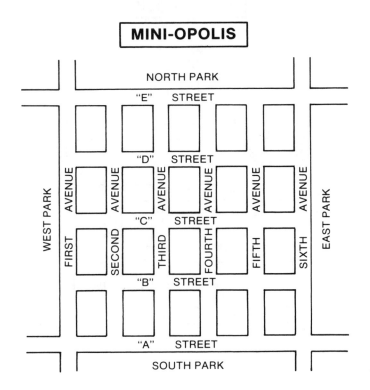

B-127 Print a **P** where Third Avenue and "B" Street cross.
Print a **Q** where Fifth Avenue and "C" Street cross.
Print an **R** at the intersection* of First Avenue and "E" Street.

    a. Which letter (P, Q, or R) is closest to East Park?

        Answer: _____

    b. Which letter is in the northwest corner of the map?

        Answer: _____

*intersection: the place where two or more streets (or lines) cross or meet.

DESCRIBING LOCATIONS USING MAPS

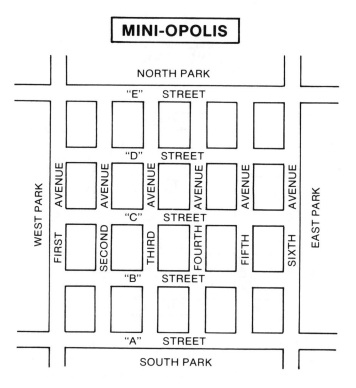

B-128 If you start at First Avenue and "B" Street and travel two blocks north and then three blocks east, where will you be?

Answer: At the intersection of _____ Street and _____ Avenue

B-129 If you start at Fifth Avenue and "D" Street and travel three blocks west and two blocks south, where will you be?

Answer: At the intersection of _____ Street and _____ Avenue

© 1985 MIDWEST PUBLICATIONS 93950-0448

DESCRIBING LOCATIONS USING MAPS

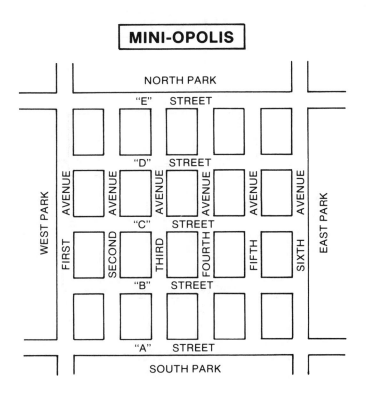

B-130 You are facing North Park. "C" Street is one block behind you; Fifth Avenue is two blocks to your right. What is your location?

Answer: At the intersection of _____ Street and _____ Avenue

B-131 How far are you from East Park?

Answer: _____ blocks

B-132 You have moved and are now facing East Park. Sixth Avenue is two blocks ahead of you; "D" Street is two blocks to your left. What is your location?

Answer: At the intersection of _____ Street and _____ Avenue

B-133 What street or avenue is two blocks behind you?

Answer: _____

DESCRIBING LOCATIONS USING MAPS

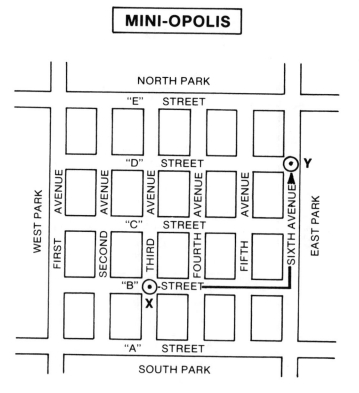

B-134 Describe the path shown by the arrows between points **X** and **Y**.

Answer: _____ blocks _____ on _____ Street
            (number)   (direction)   (name)

and _____ blocks _____ on _____ Avenue
      (number)   (direction)   (name)

B-135 Describe a path from the southwest corner of Mini-opolis to the northeast corner.

Answer: _____ blocks _____ on _____ Avenue
            (number)   (direction)   (name)

and _____ blocks _____ on _____ Street
      (number)   (direction)   (name)

DESCRIBING LOCATIONS ON MAPS

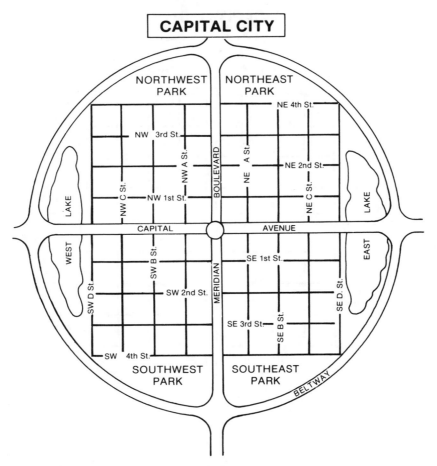

B-136 Put a **P** at the intersection of NE 2nd Street and NE A Street.

Put a **Q** at the intersection of NW 3rd Street and NW B Street.

Put an **R** at the intersection of SE 1st Street and SE C Street.

Put an **S** at the intersection of SW 4th Street and SW C Street.

If the four parts of Capital City are northeast, northwest, southwest, and southeast quarters (quadrants), in what part of Capital City are each of the following located?

Point P? _____   Point Q? _____

Point R? _____   Point S? _____

DESCRIBING DIRECTIONS USING MAPS

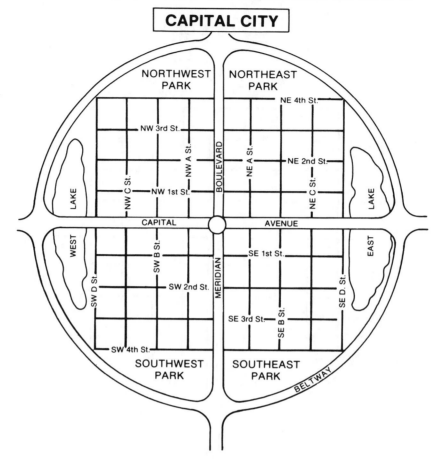

B-137   If you walk along Capital Avenue from West B Street to East A Street, how far do you walk?

Answer: _____ blocks to the _____
        (number)   (direction)

B-138   If you walk along Meridian Boulevard from South 3rd Street to North 2nd Street, how far do you walk?

Answer: _____ blocks to the _____
        (number)   (direction)

B-139   How far is it from the corner of East C Street and Capital to the corner of South 3rd Street and Meridian? (Take a path with only one turn.)

Answer: _____ blocks
        (number)

B-140   Describe the path you imagined.

Answer: _____ blocks _____ and
        (number)   (direction)

_____ blocks _____
(number)   (direction)

© 1985 MIDWEST PUBLICATIONS 93950-0448

DESCRIBING DIRECTIONS USING MAPS

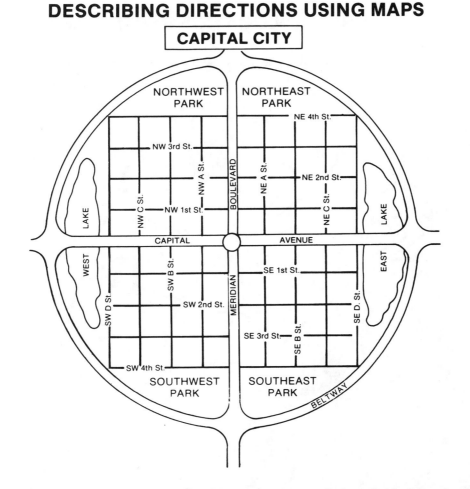

CAPITAL CITY

B-141 The center of the northeast section of Capital City is the intersection of NE 2nd Street and NE B Street. Place an **X** at that point. Place a **Y** at the center of the southeast section of Capital City.

How far is it from X to Y?

Answer: _____ blocks to the _____
         (number)   (direction)

B-142 If you make only one turn in a walk from the center of the northwest quarter to the center of the southeast quarter, how far do you walk?

Answer: _____ blocks
         (number)

B-143 Describe two routes for the preceding walk.

Answer: _____ blocks _____ and _____ blocks _____
         (number)   (direction)   (number)   (direction)

OR _____ blocks _____ and _____ blocks _____
    (number)   (direction)   (number)   (direction)

© 1985 MIDWEST PUBLICATIONS 93950-0448

SEQUENCES

DESCRIBING LOCATIONS WITH MAPS

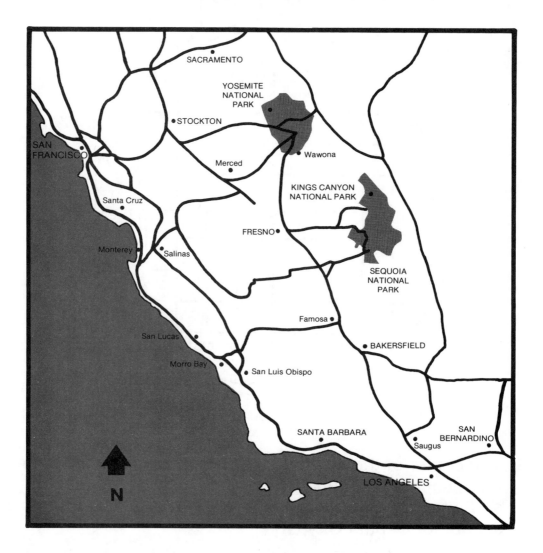

Use the information on this map to answer these questions.

B-144　If you travel south from Wawona in Yosemite National Park, what is the next large city you reach?

Answer: _____

B-145　If you travel southeast from San Luis Obispo, what is the next city you reach?　Answer: _____

B-146　If you travel southwest from Sacramento, what is the next city you reach?　Answer: _____

B-147　If you travel east from Los Angeles, what is the next city marked on the map above?　Answer: _____

DESCRIBING DIRECTIONS WITH MAPS

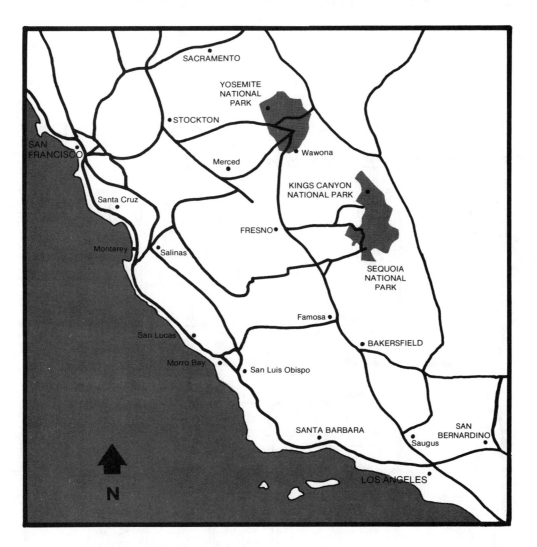

Use the information on this map to answer these questions.

B-148 In what general direction would you travel to go from Los Angeles to Santa Barbara?   Answer: _____

B-149 In what general direction would you travel to go from Santa Cruz to Monterey?   Answer: _____

B-150 In what general direction would you travel to go from San Francisco to Sacramento?   Answer: _____

B-151 In what general direction would you travel to go from Salinas to Yosemite National Park?   Answer: _____

DESCRIBING LOCATIONS AND DIRECTIONS WITH MAPS

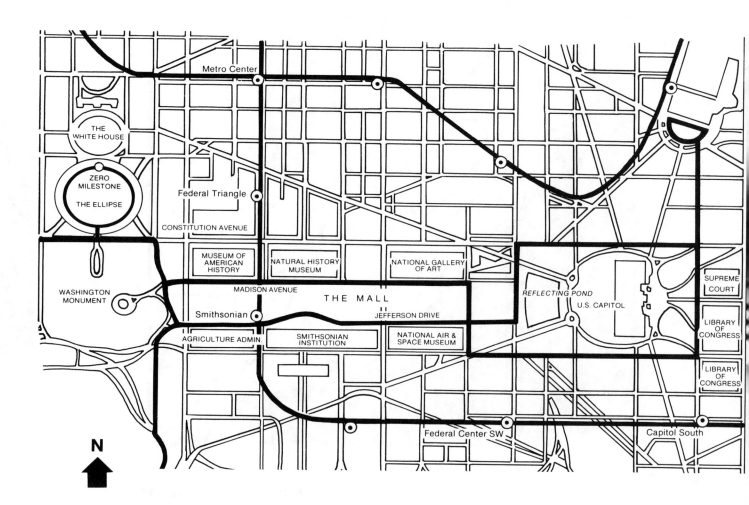

This is a map of the government district of Washington D.C. The symbol ⊙ represents a Metrorail station.

DESCRIBING LOCATIONS AND DIRECTIONS WITH MAPS

Use the map on page 80 to answer these questions.

B-152 If you travel south from the Federal Triangle, what is the next Metrorail stop you reach?   Answer: _____

B-153 If you travel east from the Museum of American History, what is the next building you reach?
Answer: _____

B-154 If you travel north from the Ellipse, what is the next building you reach?   Answer: _____

B-155 If you travel from the south side of the Ellipse to the U.S. Capitol, what would be the most direct route?
Answer: _____ (direction) along
_____ (street or avenue)

B-156 In what direction are you traveling to go from the White House to the National Air and Space Museum?
Answer: _____

B-157 In what direction are you traveling to go from the Library of Congress to the Smithsonian Institution?
Answer: _____

B-158 If you travel on the Metrorail from Metro Center station to Capitol South station, the subway route goes in which directions?
Answer: first _____ and then _____

B-159 If you walk from the U.S. Capitol to the Washington Monument, through what area do you travel?
Answer: _____

DEPICTING DIRECTIONS

B-160 Ms. Rodriguez owns a rectangular piece of land. The northwest corner is shown below as point A. The land extends three miles to the south of point A and five miles to the east of point A.

Draw a sketch of Ms. Rodriguez's land. Each unit on the grid represents one mile.

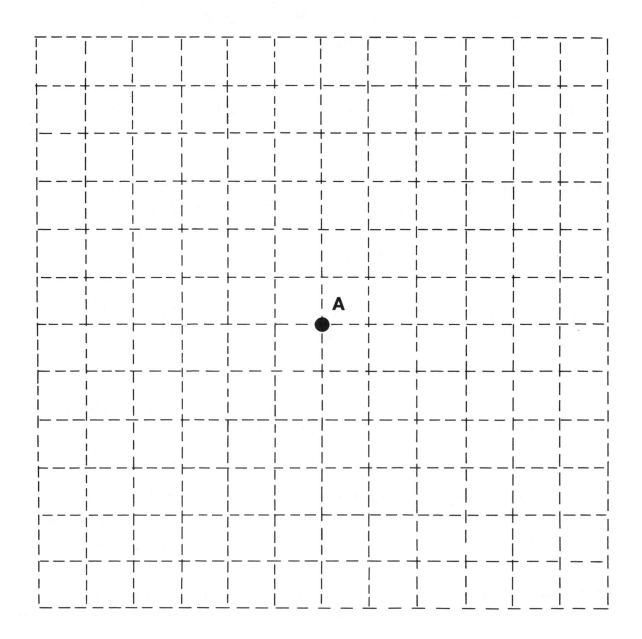

DEPICTING DIMENSIONS

B-161 Mr. Shultz owns some land next to Ms. Rodriguez's land. Mr. Shultz's land is a square—four miles on a side. Point A is the northeast corner of Mr. Shultz's land. Sketch Mr. Shultz's land on the same grid.

B-162 How much of Mr. Shultz's fence is shared by the two neighbors?   Answer: _____ (miles)

B-163 How much fence is required to enclose Ms. Rodriguez's land?   Answer: _____

B-164 How much fence is required to enclose Mr. Shultz's land?   Answer: _____

B-165 Each small square on the grid represents a square mile. How many square miles does Ms. Rodriguez own? Answer: _____

B-166 How many square miles does Mr. Shultz own? Answer: _____

SEQUENCES

DEPICTING DIRECTIONS

B-167 While on vacation, the Itamura family had to detour. They had to go south two miles, east three miles, south one mile, east two miles, and north three miles.

Starting at point **A**, draw the route of their detour. Mark the end of the detour as point **B**.

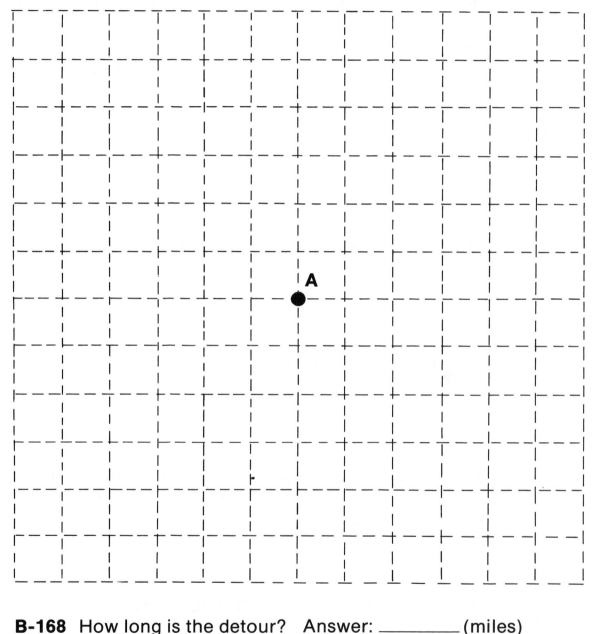

B-168 How long is the detour?   Answer: _____ (miles)

B-169 How far is it (in a straight line) from point A to point B?   Answer: _____

B-170 How much longer than the planned route is the detour? Answer: _____

DEPICTING DIRECTIONS

B-171 Mrs. Perez takes the following route on her errand day. Starting from **H** (home), she travels four miles south to the hairdresser, then five miles east to the lumber yard, two miles north to the post office, three miles west to the supermarket, and two miles north to pick up her children at school. From school she goes directly home.

Sketch Mrs. Perez's route on the grid below.

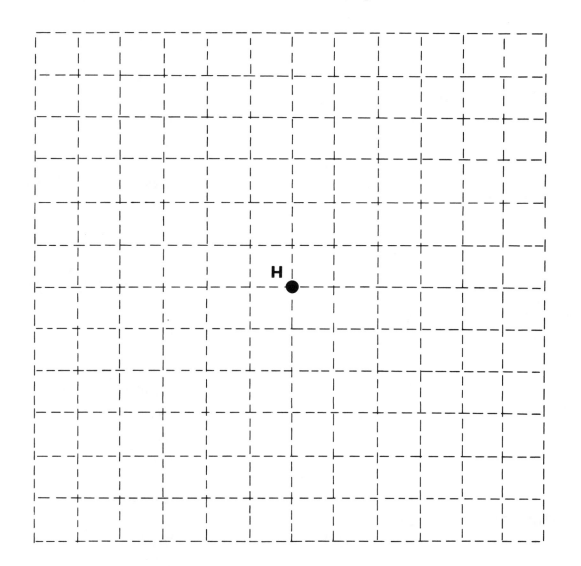

B-172 How far do the Perezes live from the school?
Answer: _____

B-173 In what direction did Mrs. Perez travel to go directly home from school?   Answer: _____

B-174 How long is the total route?   Answer: _____

TIME SEQUENCE—SELECT

The first two words in each group suggest an order of occurrence. In the blank, you should write the word from the CHOICE COLUMN that will continue the time sequence.

B-175 invasion, combat, _____

CHOICE COLUMN
attack
battle
truce

B-176 enroll, attend, _____

CHOICE COLUMN
graduate
register
select

B-177 till, plant, _____

CHOICE COLUMN
harvest
plow
sow

B-178 larva, pupa, _____

CHOICE COLUMN
adult
cocoon
egg

B-179 initial, intermediate, _____

CHOICE COLUMN
original
previous
terminal

B-180 sprout, bloom, _____

CHOICE COLUMN
blossom
bud
wilt

B-181 design, construct, _____

CHOICE COLUMN
build
conceive
occupy

TIME SEQUENCE—SELECT

The first two words in each group suggest an order of occurrence. In the blank, you should write the word from the CHOICE COLUMN that will continue the time sequence.

B-182 attempt, pursue, _____

CHOICE COLUMN
conduct
succeed
undertake

B-183 doubt, inquire, _____

CHOICE COLUMN
determine
investigate
question

B-184 prior, existing, _____

CHOICE COLUMN
following
preceding
previous

B-185 commence, continue, _____

CHOICE COLUMN
begin
conclude
proceed

B-186 income, savings, _____

CHOICE COLUMN
earnings
expenditures
wages

B-187 motive, deed, _____

CHOICE COLUMN
cause
consequence
reason

B-188 conceive, develop, _____

CHOICE COLUMN
conclude
introduce
originate

SEQUENCES

TIME SEQUENCE—RANK

Rewrite each group of words in order of occurrence from earliest to latest.

B-189 memorize, read, recite

_____

B-190 design, distribute, manufacture

_____

B-191 afterward, beforehand, presently

_____

B-192 believe, deliberate, read

_____

B-193 choose, examine, purchase

_____

B-194 action, consequence, plan

_____

B-195 current, obsolete, recent

_____

TIME SEQUENCE—RANK

Rewrite each group of words in order of occurrence from earliest to latest.

B-196 cut, mark, measure

_____

B-197 intermediate, primary, secondary

_____

B-198 outline, research, write

_____

B-199 colonization, discovery, exploration

_____

B-200 contracting, designing, engineering

_____

B-201 crack, crumble, stress

_____

B-202 cook, defrost, serve

_____

SEQUENCES

TIME SEQUENCE—SUPPLY

The first two words in each group suggest an order of occurrence. Think of a word that will continue the time sequence and write it in the blank. Use a dictionary if you need help.

B-203 departure, flight, _____

B-204 lesson, rehearsal, _____

B-205 cause, situation, _____

B-206 early, prompt, _____

B-207 mix, cook, _____

B-208 decide, order, _____

B-209 infection, treatment, _____

B-210 problem, action, _____

B-211 ancient, old, _____

TIME SEQUENCE—SUPPLY

The first two words in each group suggest an order of occurrence. Think of a word that will continue the time sequence and write it in the blank. Use a dictionary if you need help.

B-212 propose, enact, _____

B-213 midday, dusk, _____

B-214 enter, browse, _____

B-215 former, present, _____

B-216 warm, simmer, _____

B-217 question, reason, _____

B-218 jog, stumble, _____

B-219 arrest, trial, _____

B-220 desire, attempt, _____

SEQUENCES

DEGREE OF MEANING—SELECT

The first two words in each group suggest a sequence of rank, degree, size, or order. In the blank you should write the word from the CHOICE COLUMN that will continue the sequence.

B-221 insufficient, adequate, _____

CHOICE COLUMN
abundant
enough
scarce

B-222 admit, ignore, _____

CHOICE COLUMN
acknowledge
confirm
deny

B-223 absurd, possible, _____

CHOICE COLUMN
actual
conceivable
ridiculous

B-224 approval, admiration, _____

CHOICE COLUMN
agreement
credit
devotion

B-225 question, disagree, _____

CHOICE COLUMN
argue
challenge
consider

B-226 urge, push, _____

CHOICE COLUMN
compel
hustle
suggest

DEGREE OF MEANING—SELECT

The first two words in each group suggest a sequence of rank, degree, size, or order. In the blank you should write the word from the CHOICE COLUMN that will continue the sequence.

B-227 advance, maintain, _____

CHOICE COLUMN
attack
charge
retreat

B-228 fretting, worried, _____

CHOICE COLUMN
anxious
concerned
frantic

B-229 ordinary, rare, _____

CHOICE COLUMN
common
unique
unusual

B-230 irrelevant, useful, _____

CHOICE COLUMN
essential
trivial
useless

B-231 fastened, loosened, _____

CHOICE COLUMN
bound
joined
untied

B-232 suggest, request, _____

CHOICE COLUMN
invite
order
prompt

SEQUENCES

DEGREE OF MEANING—RANK

Rewrite each group of words in order from lowest or smallest to highest or largest in degree, rank, size, or order.

EXAMPLE: bellow, cry, whimper

_____ whimper, cry, bellow _____

(arranged by degree of "loudness" from less loud to more loud)

B-233   limit, prohibit, regulate

_____

B-234   dislike, reject, shun

_____

B-235   excited, savage, violent

_____

B-236   acceptance, contempt, criticism

_____

B-237   dull, lustrous, vivid

_____

B-238   vital, significant, urgent

_____

DEGREE OF MEANING—RANK

Rewrite each group of words in order from lowest or smallest to highest or largest in degree, rank, size, or order.

B-239 baboon, chimpanzee, gorilla

_____

B-240 beacon, bulb, candle

_____

B-241 citizen, patriot, traitor

_____

B-242 admirable, ideal, typical

_____

B-243 dissatisfied, grouchy, hostile

_____

B-244 risk, peril, security

_____

B-245 confirm, deny, suggest

_____

B-246 extinct, common, rare

_____

SEQUENCES

DEGREE OF MEANING—SUPPLY

The first two words in each sequence suggest a degree, rank, size, or order. Think of a word that will continue the sequence and write it in the blank. Use a dictionary if you need help.

EXAMPLE: behind, beside, ____ahead____

B-247 solo, duet, _____

B-248 faint, loud, _____

B-249 precede, accompany, _____

B-250 hopeless, conceivable, _____

B-251 seldom, regularly, _____

B-252 more, same, _____

B-253 scent, odor, _____

B-254 possible, probable, _____

B-255 flicker, glow, _____

DEGREE OF MEANING—SUPPLY

On each line, write a word that means **less than** and a word that means **more than** the given word.

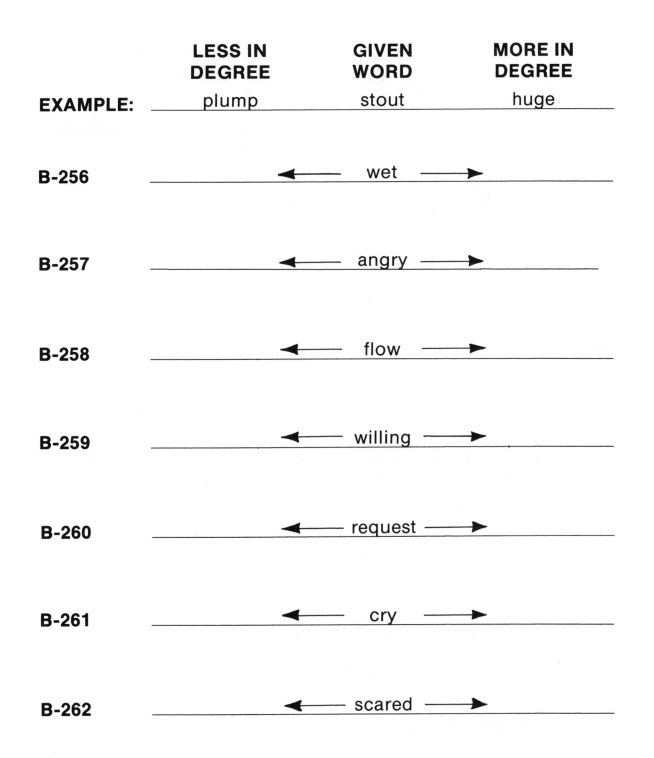

	LESS IN DEGREE	GIVEN WORD	MORE IN DEGREE
EXAMPLE:	plump	stout	huge
B-256		← wet →	
B-257		← angry →	
B-258		← flow →	
B-259		← willing →	
B-260		← request →	
B-261		← cry →	
B-262		← scared →	

TRANSITIVITY—COMPARISON

In these exercises, things are being compared according to some characteristic they have in common. Use the diagram to list the items in the order requested.

B-263 The official air-speed record is more than three times the cruising speed of a Boeing 707 and one-and-one-half times that of the Concord jet.

List these air speeds in order, beginning with the slowest.

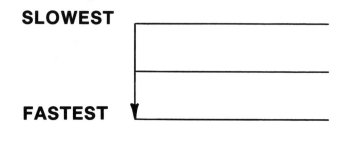

SLOWEST

FASTEST

B-264 The whale shark is one-and-one-half times as long as the great white shark; the blue whale is one-and-one-half times as long as the whale shark. An adult great white shark is about 40 feet long.

Calculate the length of each of these marine animals and list them in order, beginning with the largest.

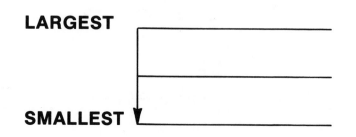

LARGEST

SMALLEST

TRANSITIVITY—COMPARISON

In these exercises, objects are being compared according to size. Use the diagram to list the objects in the order requested.

B-265 The Pentagon has almost twice the volume of the Great Pyramid of Cheops; the Colosseum in Rome has half the volume of the Great Pyramid. St. Peter's Cathedral is larger than the Colosseum, but smaller than the Great Pyramid.

List these buildings in order of size, beginning with the largest.

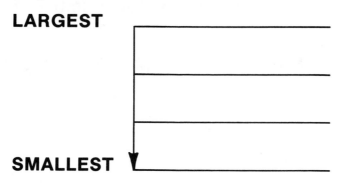

LARGEST

SMALLEST

B-266 A soccer field is larger than an American football field; a regulation skating rink is about one-third the size of a football field. An ice skating rink has about two and one-half times the area of a baseball diamond (infield).

List these playing fields in order of size, beginning with the smallest.

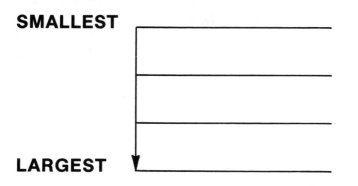

SMALLEST

LARGEST

TRANSITIVITY—COMPARISON

In these exercises, events or places are being compared. Use the diagram to list the items in the order requested.

B-267 Almost 300,000 Americans died in World War II, compared to 53,500 in World War I. Civil War casualties, counting Union and Confederate deaths, amounted to four times the number of Americans who died in World War I. American casualties in Vietnam were about 6,000 less than for World War I.

List these wars in order of the number of American casualties and calculate the approximate number of deaths.

	WAR	NUMBER OF CASUALTIES
MOST	_____	_____
	_____	_____
	_____	_____
LEAST	_____	_____

B-268 In 1975 Tokyo had the greatest population density in the world, 15,500 people per square kilometer. The population density of Tokyo was two and one-half times that of Chicago. The number of people per square kilometer in Mexico City was 2,300 more than the 9,300 per square kilometer in New York City.

List these cities in order of population density and calculate the number of people per square kilometer (sq km).

	CITY	PEOPLE PER SQ KM
MOST	_____	_____
	_____	_____
	_____	_____
LEAST	_____	_____

© 1985 MIDWEST PUBLICATIONS 93950-0448

TRANSITIVITY—TIME ORDER

In these sentences, events are compared according to the time of their occurrence. List the events in order of occurrence from earliest to latest.

B-269 The League of Nations was formed between World War I and World War II. The United Nations was formed after World War II.

List these events in order of occurrence from earliest to latest.

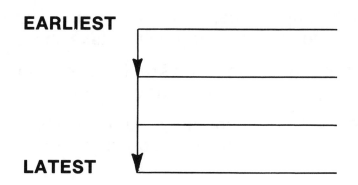

EARLIEST

LATEST

B-270 Franz Schubert died before Peotr Tchaikovsky was born. Richard Wagner was born during Schubert's lifetime and died during Tchaikovsky's lifetime.

List these musicians in the order in which they were born.

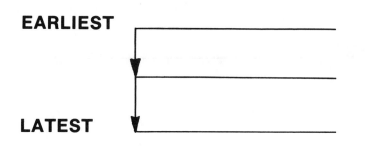

EARLIEST

LATEST

TRANSITIVITY—TIME ORDER

B-271 Number these sequences in order of occurrence from the earliest to the latest. Use the time line below to list the stages of a butterfly's development.

_____ When the butterfly leaves the cocoon it is a fully developed adult.

_____ Upon hatching from the egg, the larva begins its search for food.

_____ During the pupa stage, while the forming butterfly is still in the cocoon, the adult wings take shape.

_____ The egg stage, which is the first in the development of a butterfly, may last for many months.

_____ A day or so before beginning the pupa stage, the larva stops eating and spins a cocoon.

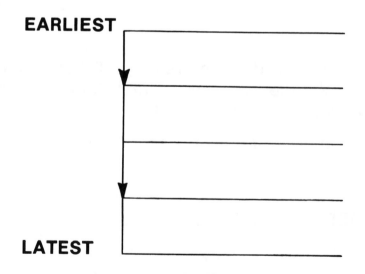

EARLIEST

LATEST

© 1985 MIDWEST PUBLICATIONS 93950-0448

TRANSITIVITY—TIME ORDER

B-272   Number these facts regarding the development of the computer in order of occurrence from the earliest to latest. Then list the forms of calculating machines on the time line below.

_____ The earliest analog computer was developed by Lord Kelvin in 1872.

_____ The oldest form of calculating machine is the abacus.

_____ Charles Babbage, who designed the first digital computer, died in 1872.

_____ In 1959 Robert Noyce developed the silicon microchip circuits that allowed the development of the modern small computer.

_____ In 1942 the first electronic computer was developed in the United States.

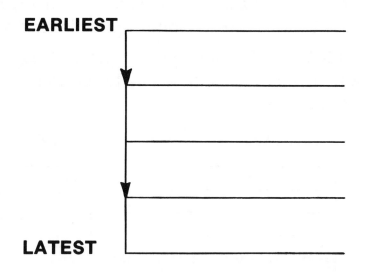

EARLIEST

LATEST

SEQUENCES

TRANSITIVITY—TIME ORDER

B-273 Number these facts regarding the development of space exploration in order of occurrence from earliest to latest. Then list the eight space events and the corresponding presidential administrations in the same order.

_____ The orbital flight of John Glenn occurred during the second year of President Kennedy's term.

_____ During President Johnson's second year in office, the Gemini program launched pairs of American astronauts into space, leading to unmanned lunar landings.

_____ During January 1961, the first month of President Kennedy's term, a chimpanzee named "Ham" became the first subject launched into space by the United States.

_____ The Russians put the space satelite "Sputnik" into orbit during the Eisenhower presidency, about two years before Kennedy was elected.

_____ Following the Surveyor missions, Neil Armstrong became the first man to walk on the moon.

_____ Because of the successful chimpanzee flight, Alan Sheppard became the first American in space during the first year of Kennedy's administration.

_____ Surveyor I made a successful unmanned moon landing during the third year of theJohnson administration.

_____ In July 1969, Neil Armstrong broadcast to the American people from the lunar surface and talked with President Nixon from space.

	SPACE EVENTS		ADMINISTRATIONS
EARLIEST			
LATEST			

TRANSITIVITY—MULTIPLE TIME LINES

B-274 If you know the dates of the presidential terms, you can plot the development of space exploration and presidential administrations on the same time line. Take the information from the preceding exercise to complete this multiple time line.

Label each administration on the left. Place each space event on the right of the time line at the approximate time each occurred.

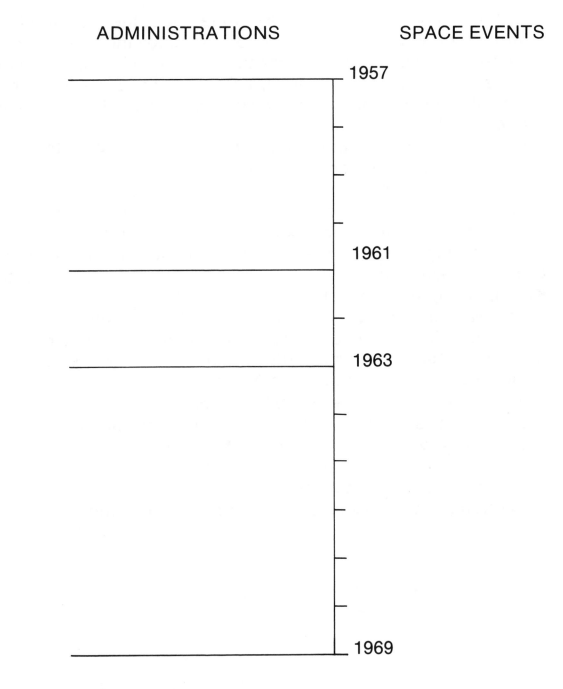

ADMINISTRATIONS   SPACE EVENTS

1957

1961

1963

1969

SEQUENCES

TRANSITIVITY—MULTIPLE TIME LINES

B-275   The use of multiple time lines allows the reader to make interesting, sometimes surprising, connections. Enter the events detailed here on the multiple time line provided on the following page.

In 1945, only months after the detonation of the test atomic bomb, World War II came to an end. The following year the first session of the U.N. General Assembly was held in London. Two years after the end of the war, U.S. Secretary of State George Marshall proposed the European Recovery Plan, also known as the Marshall Plan.

In 1948, only a year after India's independence, Mahatma Gandhi was assassinated. Israel became an independent state during the same year.

In 1949 Vietnam was established as a nation, as Chiang Kai-shek withdrew Nationalist Chinese forces to Formosa, leaving Mao Tse-tung to establish a Communist government in mainland China. In 1950 Communist North Korean troops invaded South Korea, prompting U.N. forces to enter the conflict.

Postwar scientific discoveries advanced health and communication technology. During the same year the atomic bomb was tested at Alamogordo, vitamin A was synthesized. Three years later the antibiotics Aureomycin and Chloromycetin were introduced, followed in 1949 by cortisone and neomycin.

Only a year after the end of the war an electronic brain was built at Pennsylvania University. In 1947 the transistor was invented by Bardeen, Brattain, and Shockley.

The invention of xerography by Chester Carlson in 1946 revolutionized the business and communications industries.

TRANSITIVITY—MULTIPLE TIME LINES

B-275 Enter the political events and the scientific events detailed
on the preceding page on this multiple time line.

POLITICAL EVENTS   SCIENTIFIC EVENTS

— 1945 —

— 1946 —

— 1947 —

— 1948 —

— 1949 —

— 1950 —

© 1985 MIDWEST PUBLICATIONS 93950-0448

SEQUENCES

TRANSITIVITY—MULTIPLE TIME LINES

B-276 Trace the events of the following two passages on the multiple time line provided on the following page.

The Development of Television

The evolution of television can be traced from the 1892 invention by Sir William Crookes, J. J. Thomson, and K. F. Braun of the cathode-ray tube with fluorescent screen. In 1907 the shadow of a metal figure was projected on the screen of a cathode-ray tube by the Russian physicist Boris Rosing. This experiment led to the development of the picture tube.

As with many technological innovations, the first few milestones were spread over a number of years. It was not until 1925 that a recognizable image of a human face was transmitted successfully by the Scottish inventor John Logie Baird. This event spurred the development of television. In 1928 the first scheduled television broadcast was carried out in Schenectady, N.Y. In 1929 Bell Laboratories began experiments that led to color television.

In 1938 the first commercial television transmitting antenna was erected on top of the Empire State Building. The following year, at the New York World's Fair, Franklin Delano Roosevelt became the first president to be televised. His image was broadcast only around the fairgrounds.

Although the first regular television broadcasts began in 1941, the interest in expanding the television industry took a backseat to arms' production in World War II. By 1950, however, there were 1.5 million T.V. sets in the United States. In 1951 color television was introduced in the United States. By 1954 television was an established factor in America, reaching 29 million homes.

The Career of Walt Disney

Walt Disney was born in Chicago in 1901. When he was only 18 he took a job with the Kansas City Ad Film Company, which made crude "animated" slide displays for advertising. Disney made several short animated films of fairy tales. In 1923 he took a sample fairy tale film with him to California and set up his first studio in his uncle's garage in Los Angeles.

In 1928 Disney produced the first sound cartoon, *Steamboat Willy*, introducing Mickey Mouse, whose high voice was supplied by Disney himself for the next 20 years. In 1929 Disney linked animated figures to classical music in his short *Silly Symphonies*, an art form he developed into the full-length feature film *Fantasia*, which appeared 11 years later.

In 1931 Disney introduced color to the cartoon in *Flowers and Trees*. He presented Goofy in 1932 in *Mickey's Review* and Donald Duck in 1934 in *Wise Little Hen.* In 1937 Disney produced the first full-length animated film, *Snow White.*

In 1953 Disney added live-action films to his productions, introducing *The Living Desert.* In 1954 he entered television broadcasting with the series *Disneyland,* followed the next year by the *Mickey Mouse Club.*

© 1985 MIDWEST PUBLICATIONS 93950-0448

108

TRANSITIVITY—MULTIPLE TIME LINES

B-276 Enter the events in the development of television and the career of Walt Disney on this multiple time line.

TELEVISION   DISNEY

— 1890 —

— 1895 —

— 1900 —

— 1905 —

— 1910 —

— 1915 —

— 1920 —

— 1925 —

— 1930 —

— 1935 —

— 1940 —

— 1945 —

— 1950 —

— 1955 —

SEQUENCES

TRANSITIVITY—MULTIPLE TIME LINES

B-277 Use the information in the following passage to complete the multiple time line below.

In 1900 the population of the U.S. was around 76.1 million, nearly 6.5 million more than the 1895 population. In the five years preceding 1900, about 1.3 million people immigrated to the U.S. In the next five years, from 1900 to 1904, about 3 million people immigrated.

Between 1905 and 1909 immigration increased 50 percent more than in the previous five-year period. Immigration between 1910 and 1914 was the same as for the 1905 - 1909 period.

The population increase between 1900 and 1905 was about 7.7 million. The population increase between 1905 and 1910 was about equal to the total number of immigrants admitted from 1905 to 1914. By 1915 the U. S. population had reached 100.5 million.

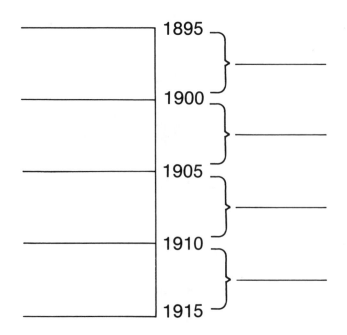

TRANSITIVITY—FAMILY TREES

Family-tree diagrams are used to show relationships between generations in a family. By the use of symbols, the diagram helps you organize relationships between:

> husband and wife
> parents and children
> sister and brother

Here are the symbols, their meaning, and their connections.

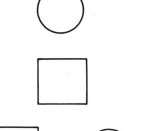

○ = female (woman)

□ = male (man)

□—○ = husband & wife—this relationship is shown by the line connecting the square and circle

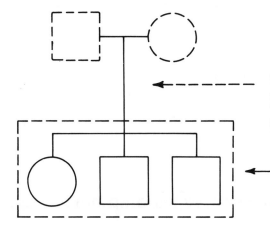

this line means that the husband and wife have children

this group of symbols means the children are two boys and a girl

TRANSITIVITY—FAMILY TREES

B-278   In this family-tree diagram, circles represent females and squares represent males. Use the clues to label the diagram, then answer the questions below the diagram.

CLUES:

1. James and Sarah Levy have a son named Harry.
2. Harry has an aunt named Mary.
3. Mary has a brother named Leon.
4. Leon's father and mother are Walter and Barbara Winston.

DIAGRAM:

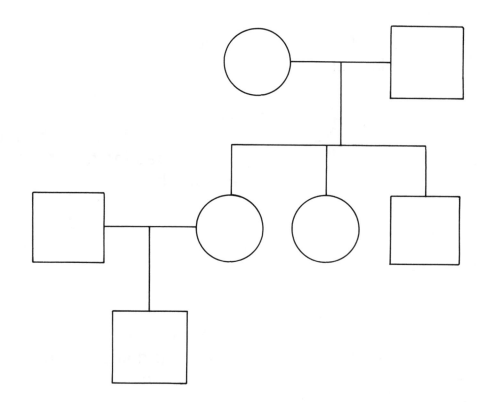

QUESTIONS:

a. What is the name of Harry's grandmother? _____

b. What is Leon's last name? _____

c. What is the name of Harry's uncle? _____

TRANSITIVITY—FAMILY TREES

B-279 In this family-tree diagram, circles represents females and
squares represent males. Use the clues to label the
diagram, then answer the questions below the diagram.

CLUES:

1. Ivan Jones married Betty Green, and they have two
   children named Charles and Helen.
2. Charles Jones was named for his grandfather on his
   dad's side of the family.
3. Helen Jones was named for her mother's sister.
4. Ivan's sister and mother have the same name.
5. Charles has an aunt named Elizabeth.
6. Arthur and Grace Green have three children.
7. Betty Green has a brother named David.

DIAGRAM:

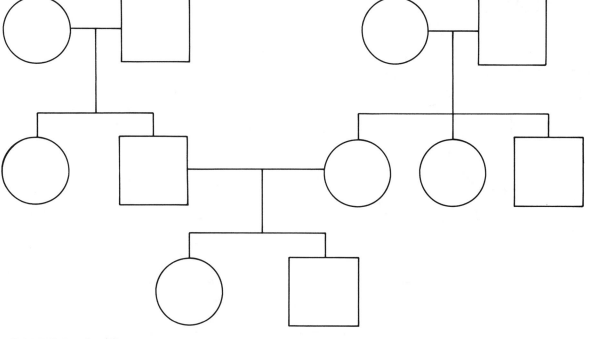

QUESTIONS:

a. Helen Jones has two grandfathers. Name them:

_____ and _____

b. Charles Jones has an uncle. Name him: _____

TRANSITIVITY—FAMILY TREES

B-280   In this family-tree diagram, circles represent females and squares represent males. Use the clues to label the diagram.

CLUES:

1. Fred Williams has three sisters.
2. Grace Thomas has two brothers.
3. Harold Williams, Jr., has two sisters.
4. Fred Williams has a grandfather named John.
5. Fred Williams has a sister, an aunt, and a grandmother named Lillian.
6. Irene Williams has an aunt named Nancy and an uncle named David.
7. Fred Williams was named for an uncle.
8. Pauline Williams was named for her grandmother Pauline Thomas.

DIAGRAM:

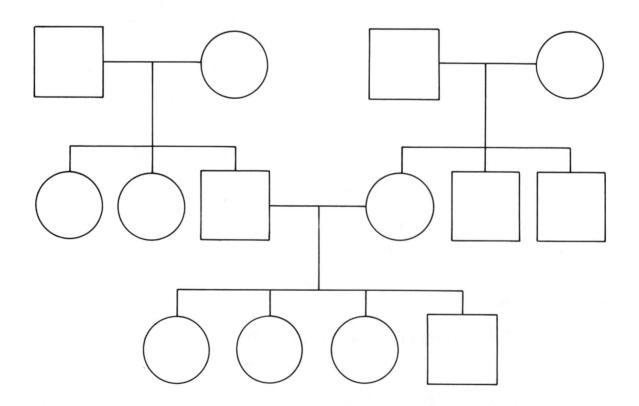

DEDUCTIVE REASONING—INSTRUCTIONS

A MIND BENDER™ is a problem in matching lists. Making a chart helps you work the problem. Here is a Mind Bender involving three people and their pets.

EXAMPLE:

Michael, Sarah, and Tina own a cat, a goldfish, or a parakeet.

From the clues below, match each pet with the proper owner.

a. Tina is allergic to animal fur.

b. Michael's pet does not use kitty litter or live in a cage.

Step 1: From the clue "Tina is allergic to animal fur," you can figure out that Tina does not own the cat. Find the row marked "T" for Tina and write NO in the column marked "C" for cat.

	C	G	P
M			
S			
T	NO		

Step 2: The second clue, "Michael's pet does not use kitty litter or live in a cage," tells you that Michael does not own a cat or a bird. Find the row marked "M" for Michael and write NO in both the "C" (for cat) column and the "P" (for parakeet) column.

	C	G	P
M	NO		NO
S			
T	NO		

DEDUCTIVE REASONING—INSTRUCTIONS

Step 3: You know that each person owns a pet. Since neither Michael nor Tina owns the cat, Sarah must be the cat owner. Write a YES in the "S" row and the "C" column.

	C	G	P
M	NO		
S	YES		
T	NO		

Step 4: Since Sarah owns the cat, Sarah does not own the goldfish or the parakeet. Write NO in the "S" row in both the "G" column and the "P" column.

	C	G	P
M	NO		NO
S	YES	NO	NO
T	NO		

Step 5: By the same kind of reasoning, you see that the only vacancy in the "M" row is in the "G" column. From this, you figure out (**deduce**) that Michael is the goldfish owner. Write a YES in this position.

	C	G	P
M	NO	YES	NO
S	YES	NO	NO
T	NO		

Step 6: Since Michael owns the goldfish, then neither Sarah nor Tina owns the goldfish. You have already figured out (deduced) that Sarah doesn't own the goldfish. Now you know that Tina doesn't either. Mark NO in the "T" row and the "G" column.

	C	G	P
M	NO	YES	NO
S	YES	NO	NO
T	NO	NO	

Step 7: The only vacancy on the chart is in the "T" row and the "P" column. You now know that Tina is the parakeet owner.

DEDUCTIVE REASONING—TRANSITIVE ORDER

B-281

Bob, Joe, Freddy, and Christy are all in grade school (1st, 2nd, 4th, and 6th grades). From the clues below, match each child with his or her grade.

a. No student has been held back or skipped a grade.

b. Joe is about three years younger than Bob.

c. Christy is about four years older than Freddy.

	B	C	F	J
1				
2				
6				

B-282

Four World War II tanks have the following gun sizes: 49mm, 75mm, 88mm, and 100mm. The larger the gun, the more powerful it is. From the clues below, match each tank with its gun.

a. The Tiger tank has a larger gun than either the American or British tank.

b. The Sherman tank is American.

c. The SU-100 has the most powerful gun.

d. The Crusader, a British tank, has the least powerful gun.

	C	Sh	SU	T
49				
75				
88				
100				

SEQUENCES

DEDUCTIVE REASONING—TRANSITIVE ORDER

B-283

Use the following clues to determine the running speeds of a cheetah, deer, elephant, and fox.

a. The largest animal is the slowest.

b. The fastest weighs less than half as much as a deer.

c. A fox can't catch a deer or a cheetah.

	Running Speed km/hr			
	38	64	79	112
Cheetah				
Deer				
Elephant				
Fox				

B-284

Use the following clues to compare the orbit times of Jupiter, Mercury, Pluto, and Venus.

a. Jupiter has the shortest rotation time, but has neither the longest nor the shortest orbit time.

b. Pluto has an orbit time about 22.5 times that of Jupiter.

c. Mercury has a shorter rotation time and a shorter orbit time than Venus.

	Orbit Time in yrs.			
	1/4	2/3	11	248
Jupiter				
Mercury				
Pluto				
Venus				

DEDUCTIVE REASONING USING YES-NO STATEMENTS

B-285

Totino, Warpenburg, Schleinstein, and Kavana live in the U.S.S.R., Czechoslovakia, Chile, and Zambia. From the clues below, match the residents with their countries.

a. Kavana's country has no seacoast.
b. Schleinstein's country isn't in South America.
c. Totino doesn't live in the southern hemisphere, but Kavana does.
d. Totino's country is farther north than Schleinstein's.

	K	S	T	W
Chile				
Czechoslovakia				
U.S.S.R.				
Zambia				

B-286

Mr. Jaworski, Miss Roberts, Mrs. Bradley, and Mr. Forsythe are all dog owners. From the clues below, match the dogs (Collie, German Shepherd, Great Dane, and Dachshund) with their owners.

a. Miss Roberts does not own a dog that has fleas.
b. Neither Mr. Jaworski nor Mrs. Bradley owns the Great Dane.
c. Mr. Forsythe knows the German Shepherd and Dachshund owners.
d. Mr. Jaworski and Mr. Forsythe don't know each other.
e. German Shepherds and Great Danes have fleas.

	B	F	J	R
Collie				
Great Dane				
German Shepherd				
Dachshund				

SEQUENCES

DEDUCTIVE REASONING USING YES-NO STATEMENTS

B-287

Fred, Ken, Ross, and Tim are married. Their wives' names are Betty, Lora, Mary, and Pam. From the clues below, match the men with their wives.

a. Pam and Mary are sisters.

b. Ross's best friend is Fred.

c. Ross is an only child.

d. Pam's sister married Tim's brother.

e. Betty and Ross's best friend are married.

f. Lora is married to Ken's brother.

	F	K	R	T
B				
L				
M				
P				

MULTI-FACTOR DEDUCTIVE REASONING

B-288

Phillippe, Letitia, Cicero, and Beaumont are from Greece, Spain, France, and England; they were born in 1942, 1931, 1946, and 1935. They each visited their home country recently.

Use the following clues to figure out where and when each of them was born.

- **a.** Phillipe is older than Letitia but younger than Cicero.
- **b.** Beaumont is older than Cicero.
- **c.** The oldest is not from Greece or Spain.
- **d.** The youngest is not from England or France.
- **e.** The second oldest visited Athens.
- **f.** The next to youngest is not from England.

OLDEST   1931   _____

                 1935   _____

                 1942   _____

YOUNGEST   1946   _____

	E	F	G	S
B				
C				
L				
P				

SEQUENCES

MULTI-FACTOR DEDUCTIVE REASONING

B-289

George, Jim, and Sam left class for basketball, football, and swimming practice. The guidance office looked for the last names Carey, Roberts, and Wolfe.

Use the following clues to match first and last names. In each clue the two names do not belong to the same person.

a. George and Carey do not go to basketball practice.

b. Sam and Wolfe do not go to football practice.

c. Jim and Roberts do not go to swimming practice.

d. Jim and Carey do not go to football practice.

	FIRST NAMES			SPORT		LAST NAMES	
	G	J	S		C	R	W
				Basketball			
				Football			
				Swimming			

SPORT	FIRST NAME	LAST NAME
Basketball	_____	_____
Football	_____	_____
Swimming	_____	_____

NEGATION—DETERMINING "YES-NO" RULES

RULE BOX
YES—color is the same   NO—color is not the same

Follow the arrows from START TO FINISH. On each arrow write **YES** or **NO** according to the YES-NO rule.

EXAMPLE:

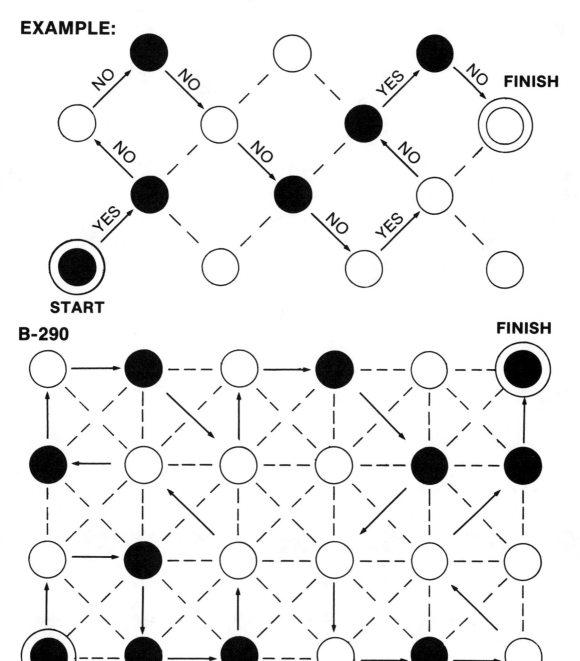

SEQUENCES

B-290

NEGATION—DETERMINING "YES-NO" RULES

RULE BOX
YES—color is the same   NO—color is not the same

Follow the arrows from start to finish. On each arrow write **YES** or **NO** according to the YES-NO rule.

B-291

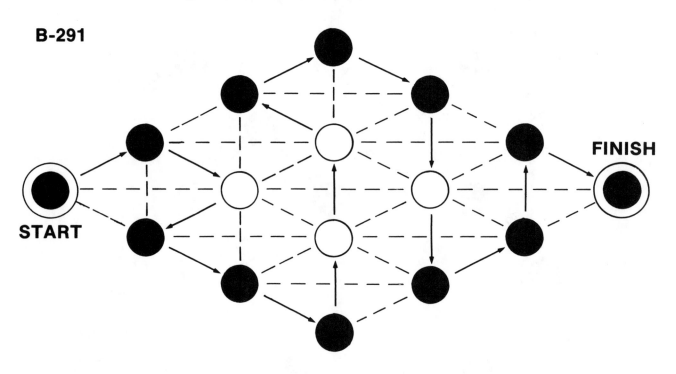

B-292

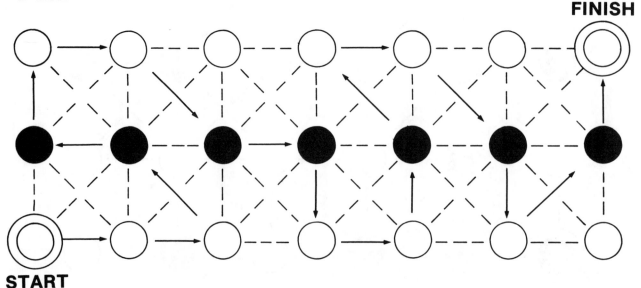

NEGATION—FOLLOWING YES-NO RULES

RULE BOX

YES—color is the same   NO—color is not the same

Darken the correct circles along the path from START to FINISH by following the YES-NO rule.

EXAMPLE:

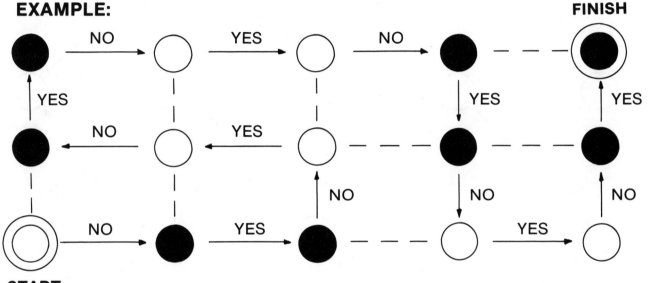

B-293

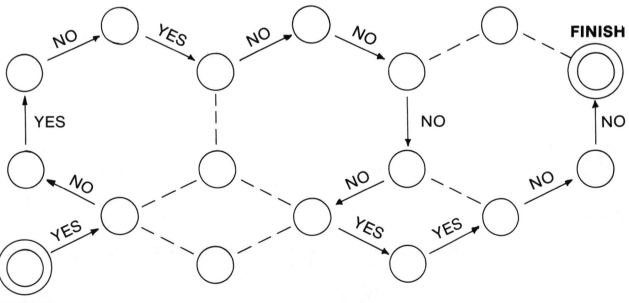

NEGATION—FOLLOWING YES-NO RULES

RULE BOX
YES—color is the same   NO—color is not the same

Darken the correct circles along the path from START to FINISH by following the YES-NO rule.

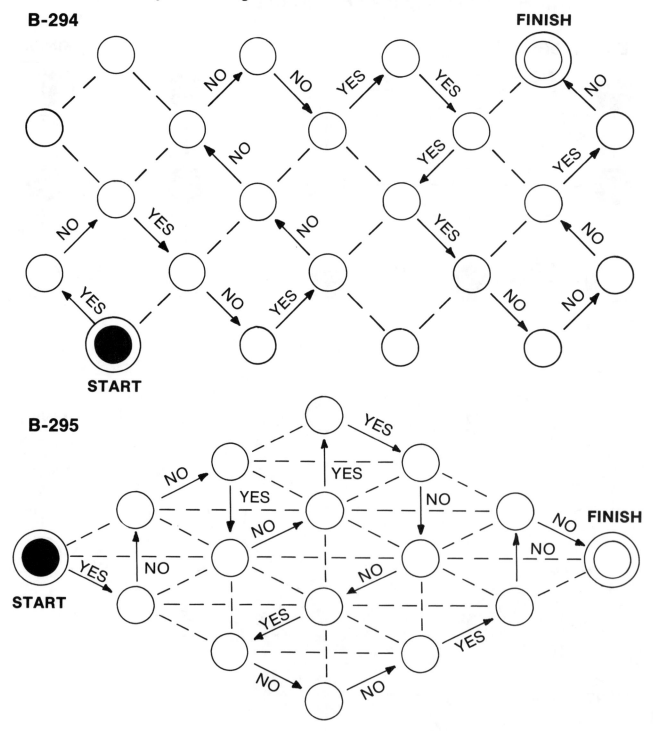

B-294

B-295

NEGATION—SUPPLY THE RULE

RULE BOX

YES—color is the same   NO—color is not the same

In each exercise below, there are three paths from START to FINISH. One path is dotted○ ○ ○, one path is solid_____, and one path is dashed_ _ _ . Supply the rule for each path.

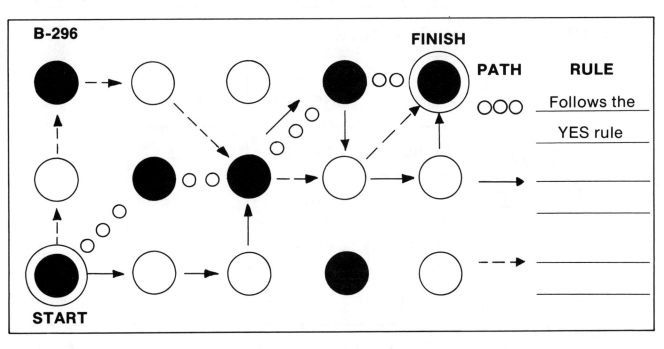

B-296

PATH	RULE
○○○	Follows the ____ YES rule
→	
- - →	

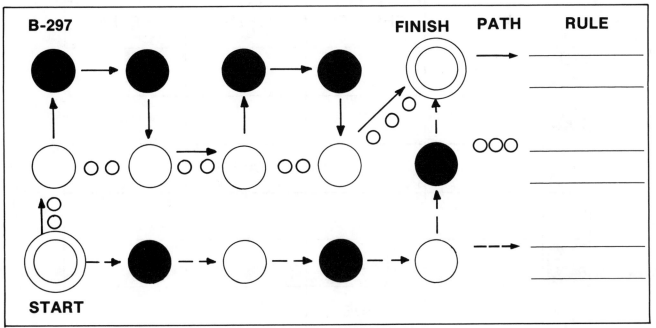

B-297

PATH	RULE
→	
○○○	
- - →	

NEGATION—COMPLETING TRUE-FALSE TABLES

This group of shapes has been used to produce the TRUE-FALSE tables below.

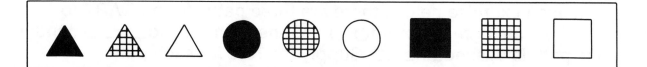

EXAMPLE: Here is a complete TRUE-FALSE table.

	IT IS WHITE	IT IS CHECKED	IT IS NOT CHECKED
▲ (filled triangle)	FALSE	FALSE	TRUE
⊕ (checked circle)	FALSE	TRUE	FALSE
☐ (white square)	TRUE	FALSE	TRUE

B-298   Complete this table.

	IT IS WHITE	IT IS CHECKED	IT IS NOT WHITE	IT IS NOT CHECKED
(checked square)	FALSE			
(filled circle)				TRUE
(white triangle)			FALSE	
(white circle)	TRUE			
(filled square)		FALSE		
(checked triangle)		TRUE		

© 1985 MIDWEST PUBLICATIONS 99050-0448

NEGATION—COMPLETING TRUE-FALSE TABLES

This group of shapes has been used to produce the TRUE-FALSE table below.

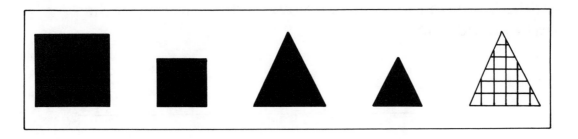

B-299 In each row, draw the shape that is described by the TRUE-FALSE statements.

SHAPE	IT IS NOT LARGE	IT IS NOT SQUARE	IT IS NOT CHECKED
■	FALSE	FALSE	TRUE
▲	TRUE	TRUE	TRUE
	FALSE	TRUE	TRUE
	TRUE	FALSE	TRUE
	FALSE	TRUE	FALSE

SEQUENCES

NEGATION—COMPLETING TRUE-FALSE TABLES

EXAMPLE: Shade the figures below so that they meet the following conditions.

> 1. Large figures are not striped.
> 2. Hexagons are not checked.
> 3. There is only one gray figure.
> 4. No small figure is checked.

In each space on the grid write **True** or **False**, depending on whether the figure can be shaded to fit the conditions given.

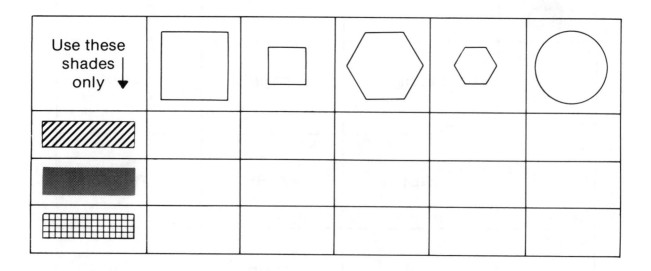

A detailed solution follows on the next page.

© 1985 MIDWEST PUBLICATIONS 93950-0448

NEGATION—COMPLETING TRUE-FALSE TABLES

Clue 1 - "Large figures are not striped." Write **F** (for false) in the "striped" row under all the large figures.

striped	F		F		F
gray					
checked					

Clue 2 - "Hexagons are not checked." Write **F**s in the "checked" row and the "hexagon" columns.

striped	1-F		1-F		1-F
gray			T		
checked			F	F	

If the large hexagon is neither striped nor checked, then it must be gray.

Clue 3 - "There is only one gray figure." Since we have deduced from clues 1 & 2 that the hexagon is gray, no other figure can be gray. In the "gray" row mark all the other figures **F**.

striped	1-F		1-F		1-F
gray	F	F	2-T	F	F
checked	T		2-F	2-F	T

If the large square and circle are neither striped nor gray, then they must be checked.

Clue 4 - "No small figure is checked." Write an **F** in the "checked" row and remaining "small" column.

striped	1-F	T	1-F	T	1-F
gray	3-F	3-F	2-T	3-F	3-F
checked	3-T	F	2-F	2-F	3-T

If the small square and small hexagon are neither gray nor checked, then they are striped.

NEGATION—COMPLETING TRUE-FALSE TABLES

B-300   Shade the figures below so that they meet the following conditions.

1. Squares are not striped.
2. The circle is not checked.
3. No large figure is gray.
4. No small figure is checked.
5. No hexagon is striped.

In each space on the grid write **True** or **False**, depending on whether the figure can be shaded to fit the conditions given.

Use these shades only ↓	□ (large square)	□ (small square)	⬡ (large hexagon)	⬡ (small hexagon)	○ (circle)
(striped)					
(gray)					
(checked)					

NEGATION—COMPLETING TRUE-FALSE TABLES

B-301   Shade the figures below so that they meet the following conditions.

1. Polygons are not gray.
2. Small figures are not striped.
3. There is one gray figure.
4. Large polygons* are not striped.

In each space on the grid write **True** or **False**, depending on whether the figure can be shaded to fit the conditions given.

Use these shades only ↓	□	□	⬡	⬡	◯
▨ (striped)					
▬ (gray)					
▦ (grid)					

* A polygon is a closed figure having sides that are all line segments.

SEQUENCES

NEGATION—COMPLETING TRUE-FALSE TABLES

B-302   Shade the figures below so that they meet the following conditions.

> 1. It is not true that the circle is gray.
> 2. Large figures are not checked.
> 3. Squares are not striped.
> 4. Small figures are not gray.
> 5. Hexagons are not striped.

In each space on the grid write **True** or **False**, depending on whether the figure can be shaded to fit the conditions given.

Use these shades ↓ only ▼	□	◻	⬡	⬡	◯
(striped)					
(gray)					
(checked)					

NEGATION—COMPLETING TRUE-FALSE TABLES

B-303   Shade the figures below so that they meet the following conditions.

> 1. Small figures are not striped.
> 2. No figure is gray.
> 3. Non-polygons* are striped.
> 4. The squares are not shaded alike.
> 5. The non-square polygons are shaded alike.

In each space on the grid write **True** or **False**, depending on whether the figure can be shaded to fit the conditions given.

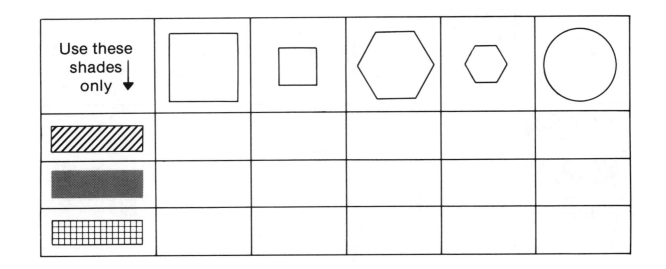

* A polygon is a closed figure having sides that are all line segments.

© 1985 MIDWEST PUBLICATIONS 93950-0448

NEGATION—COMPLETING TRUE-FALSE TABLES

B-304 Shade the figures below so that they meet the following conditions.

> 1. No large polygon is striped.
> 2. Small figures are not shaded the same.
> 3. Large figures are not shaded the same.
> 4. No square is checked.
> 5. No hexagon is gray.
> 6. No small figure is striped.

In each space on the grid write **True** or **False**, depending on whether the figure can be shaded to fit the conditions given.

Use these shades only ↓	☐	▫	⬡	⬡	◯
▨ (striped)					
▬ (gray)					
▦ (checked)					

CONJUNCTION—FOLLOWING "AND" RULES

The use of the term NOT affects the meaning of statements. The term AND also produces special conditions of meaning. In the following exercises, write **Yes** if the statement is true; write **No** if the statement is false.

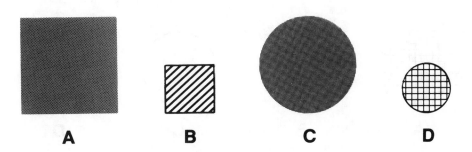

A   B   C   D

EXAMPLE:

Figure A is large and round. __NO__
Figure B is small and square. __YES__

B-305

    a. Figure B is small and gray. _____

    b. Figure C is large and black. _____

    c. Figure C is round and large. _____

    d. Figure D is small and square. _____

    e. Figure D is small and checked. _____

    f. Figure A is large and striped. _____

    g. Figure A is large and square. _____

    h. Figure B is large and striped. _____

    i. Figure B is small and striped. _____

SEQUENCES

CONJUNCTION—FOLLOWING "AND" RULES

In the following exercises, we are combining AND and NOT rules.
Write **Yes** if the statement is true; write **No** if the statement is false.

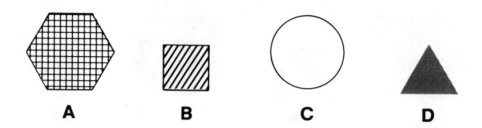

A   B   C   D

EXAMPLE:

Figure A is checked and not square. ___YES___

Figure A is checked and not a hexagon. ___NO___

B-306

a. Figure B is a square and not striped. _____

b. Figure C is a circle and not striped. _____

c. Figure D is a triangle and not large. _____

d. Figure C is not a polygon and is white. _____

e. Figure B is not a triangle and not striped. _____

f. Figure A is not a square and not checked. _____

g. Figure D is not a circle and not striped. _____

h. Figure B is not small and not checked. _____

i. Figure D is not a square and not white. _____

CONJUNCTION—FOLLOWING "AND" RULES

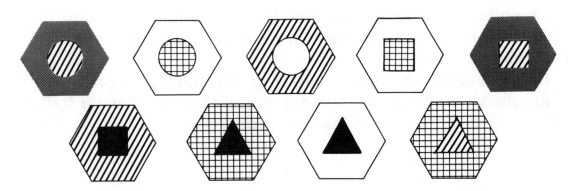

B-307 Draw the hexagons from above that are white and have checked figures in the center.

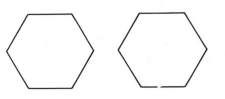

B-308 Draw the hexagons from above that are not white and have striped figures in the center.

B-309 Draw the hexagons from above that are not gray and not striped.

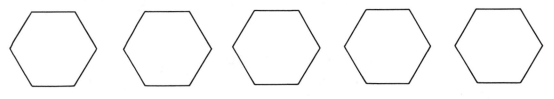

B-310 Draw the hexagons from above that are not white and do not have a circle in the center.

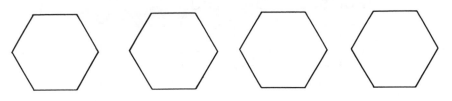

CONJUNCTION—INTERPRETING "AND" RULES

The effect of AND on the meaning of statements can be illustrated by the flow of water through a pipe having more than one control valve.

In these exercises water is flowing into the pipe from the left. The following symbols represent valves that allow water to flow when open and that stop the flow when closed.

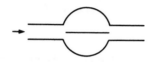
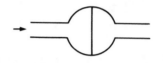

valve open—water flows   valve closed—water does not flow

Given the following combinations of valves in a pipe line, answer **Yes** if water will flow. Answer **No** if water will not flow.

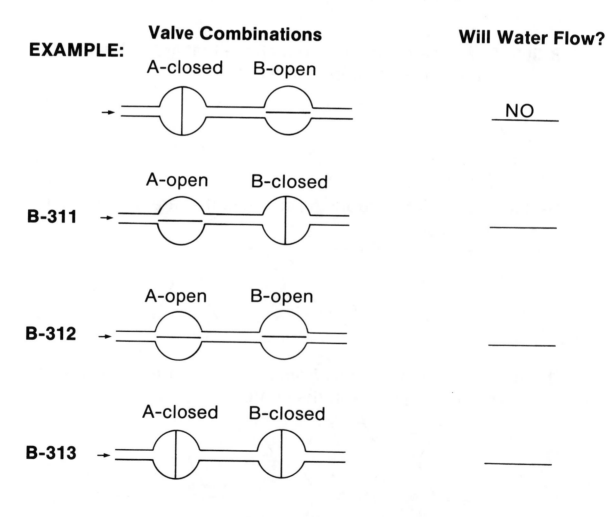

Valve Combinations   **Will Water Flow?**

EXAMPLE:

A-closed   B-open

                                           NO

B-311

A-open   B-closed

                                           _____

B-312

A-open   B-open

                                           _____

B-313

A-closed   B-closed

                                           _____

CONJUNCTION—INTERPRETING "AND" RULES

In the table below, the expression "A and B" represents valve output (water flow).

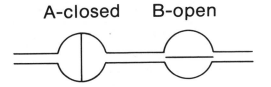

A-closed   B-open

This valve combination is represented in the first row of the table.

B-314 Complete the following table by copying each valve combination and indicating whether it will allow the water to flow.

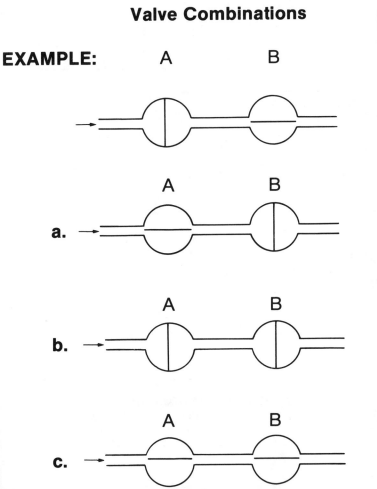

Valve Combinations

A	B	A and B
off	on	NO

CONJUNCTION—INTERPRETING "AND" RULES

Complete the last box in each of the following rows, remembering that "A and B" represents valve output (water flow).

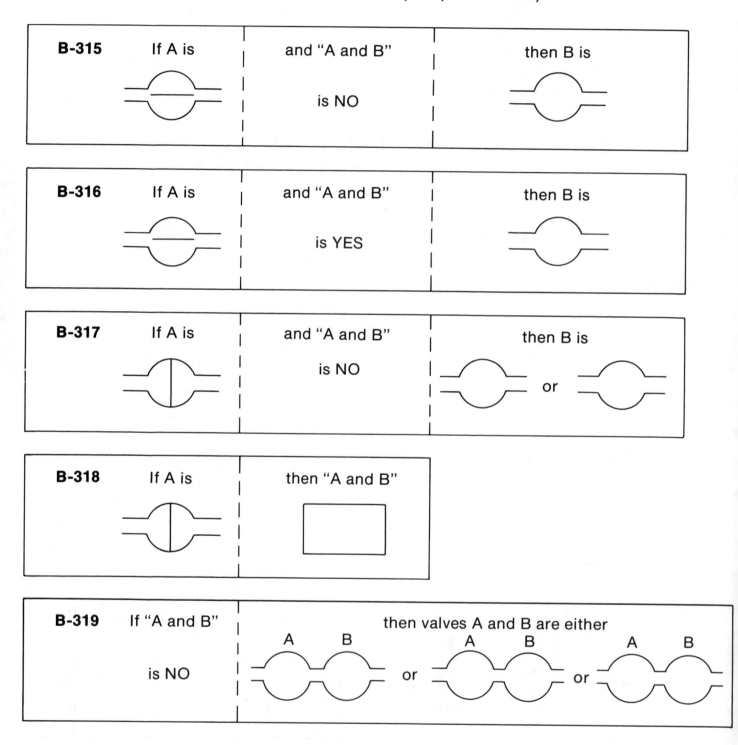

CONJUNCTION—APPLYING "AND" RULES

B-320   Find a path from START to FINISH. Each two neighboring figures on this path must have:

the same size <u>and</u> shape (for example: ▨—☐)

or

the same shape <u>and</u> pattern (for example: ▦—▦)

or

the same pattern <u>and</u> size (for example: ■—▲)

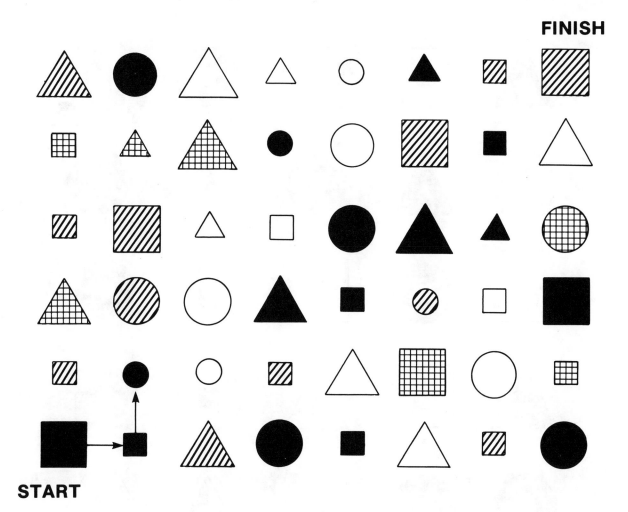

CONJUNCTION—APPLYING "AND" RULES

B-321 Find the path from START to FINISH by following these rules.

1. When moving in horizontal directions (⟷), each two neighboring figures must have the same color (white or black).
2. When moving in vertical directions (↑ ↓), each two neighboring figures must have a different shape, and the figures inside them must be the same shape.

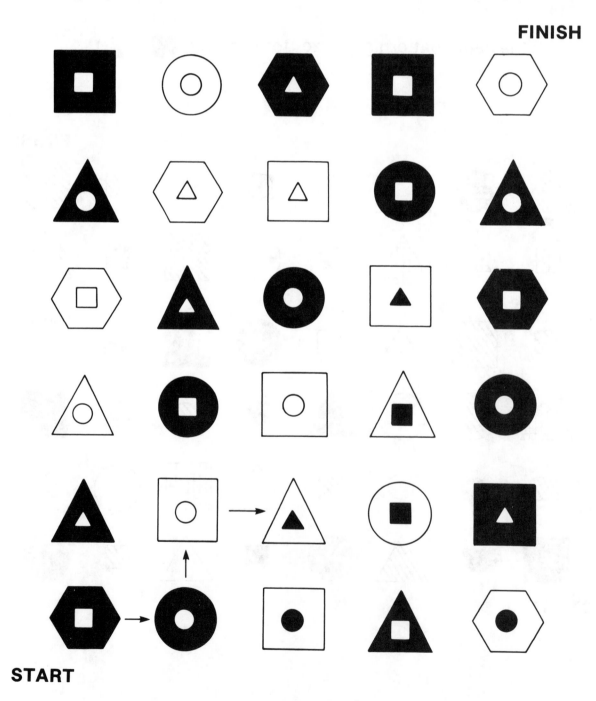

CONJUNCTION—APPLYING "AND" RULES

B-322 Complete the maze by drawing figures at the intersections of the lines. Use these rules.

1. You can move from one intersection to the next only when the figures at the intersections have:
   the same size and shape
   or
   the same shape and same pattern
   or
   the same pattern and the same size

2. You can move only along the dark arrows
3. You can use patterns: white, gray, or striped
                 shapes: circle, square, or triangle
                  sizes: large or small

SEQUENCES

FINISH

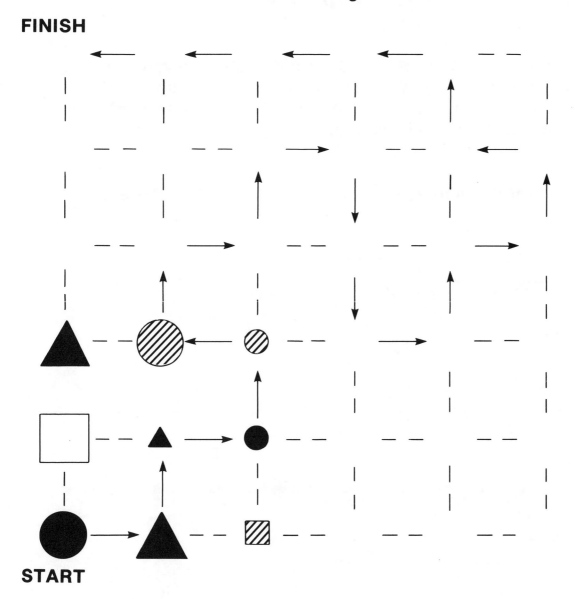

START

DISJUNCTION—INTERPRETING "AND/OR" RULES

The phrase AND/OR is often found in written and spoken language. AND/OR logic is a basis for electrical circuitry and computer languages. These exercises illustrate the effect on meaning when the AND/OR connective is used.

Look at the valve combinations below. On the blank, enter **YES** if water will flow; enter **NO** if water will not flow.

EXAMPLE: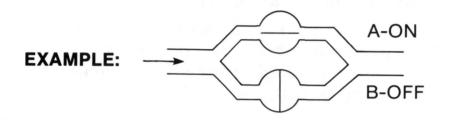

Water enters pipes A and B from the left. The valve in pipe A is open (ON), while the valve in pipe B is shut (OFF).
Will water flow out? YES (because the water has a path through pipe A even if pipe B is closed).

Valve Combinations   **Will Water Flow?**

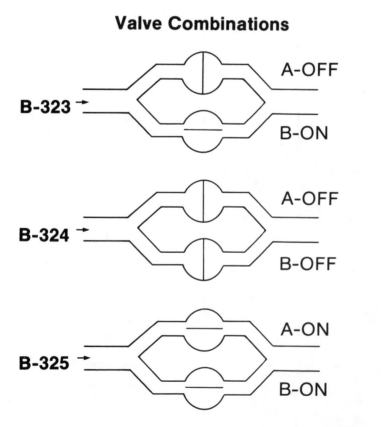

_____

_____

_____

DISJUNCTION—INTERPRETING "AND/OR" RULES

In the table below, the expression "A and/or B" represents valve output (water flow).

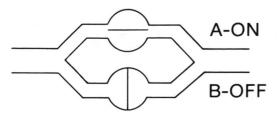

This valve combination is represented in the first row of the table.

B-326 Complete the table by copying each valve combination and indicating whether it will allow the water to flow.

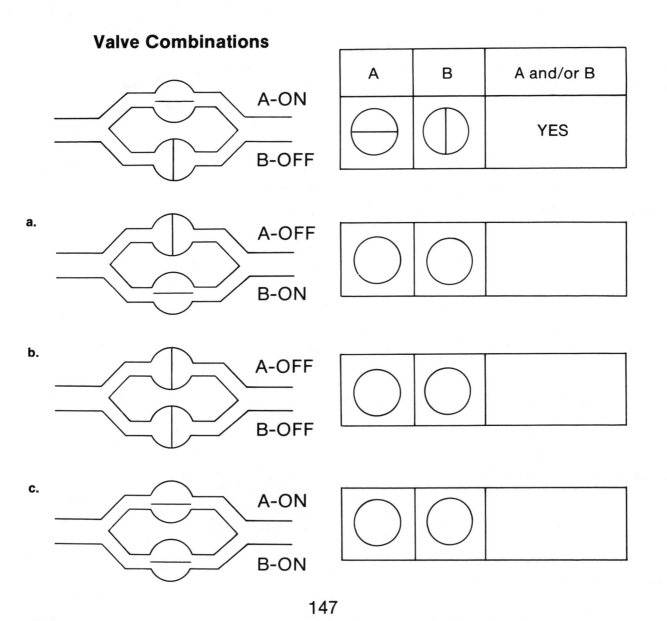

SEQUENCES

DISJUNCTION—INTERPRETING "AND/OR" RULES

Complete the last box in each of the following rows, remembering that "A and/or B" represents valve output (water flow).

B-327	If A is	and "A and/or B" is YES	then B is

B-328	If A is	and "A and/or B" is NO	then B is

B-329	If A is	and "A and/or B" is YES	then B is ___ or ___

B-330	If A is	then "A and/or B" is ☐

B-331	if B is	then "A and/or B" is ☐

B-332	If "A and/or B" is YES	then valves A and B are either ___ or ___ or ___ A B A B A B

148

DISJUNCTION—FOLLOWING AND/OR RULES

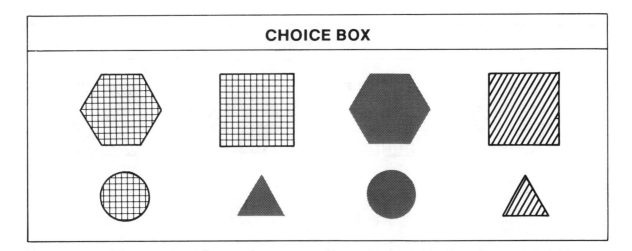

CHOICE BOX

Use the figures above to fill the boxes below according to the characteristics given for each set. Draw the remaining figures in the space outside the box.

EXAMPLE:

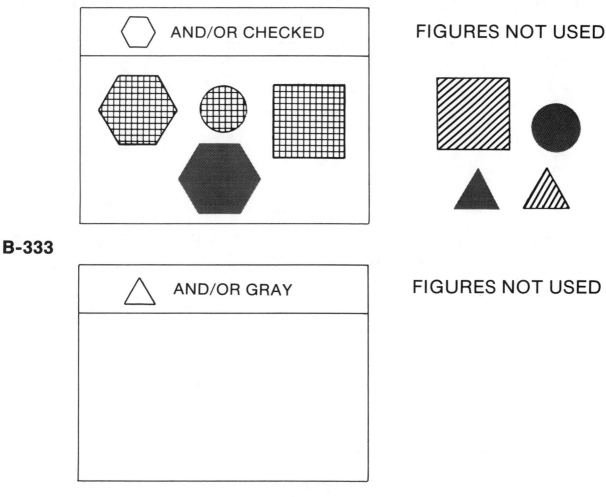

AND/OR CHECKED

FIGURES NOT USED

B-333

AND/OR GRAY

FIGURES NOT USED

DISJUNCTION—FOLLOWING AND/OR RULES

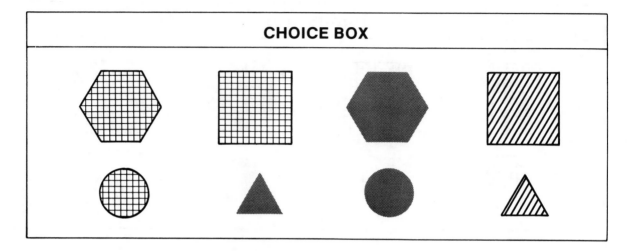

Use the figures above to fill the boxes below according to the characteristics given for each set. Draw the remaining figures in the space outside the box.

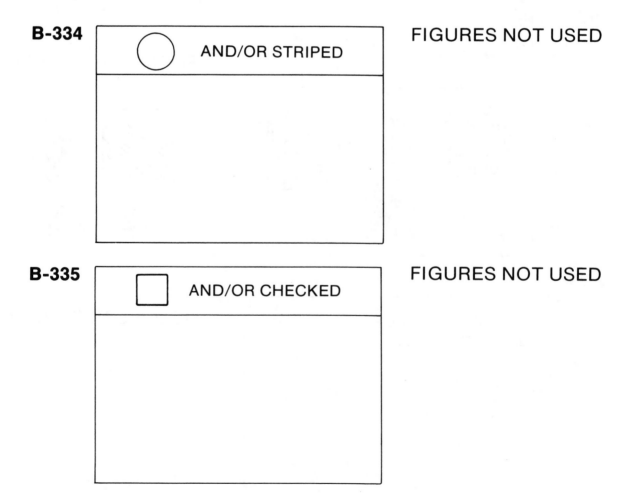

B-334　　　　　　　　AND/OR STRIPED　　　　　FIGURES NOT USED

B-335　　　　　　　　AND/OR CHECKED　　　　　FIGURES NOT USED

DISJUNCTION—FOLLOWING AND/OR RULES

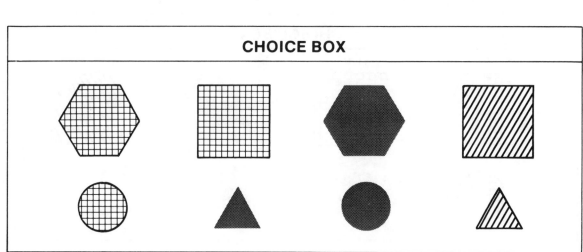

CHOICE BOX

The following sets contain figures from the Choice Box above. Fill in the characteristic missing from the heading of each set, then draw the remaining figures in the space outside the box.

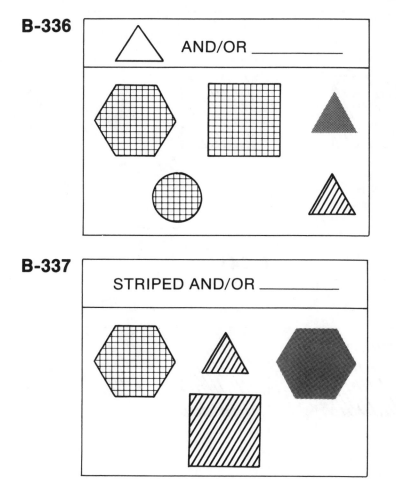

B-336

△ AND/OR _____

B-337

STRIPED AND/OR _____

FIGURES NOT USED

FIGURES NOT USED

SEQUENCES

DISJUNCTION—FOLLOWING AND/OR RULES

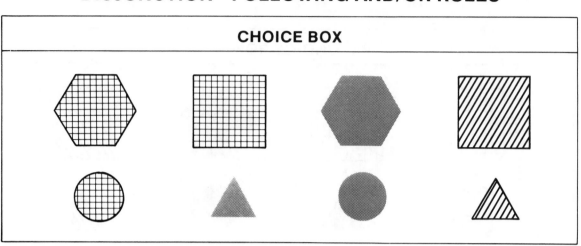

CHOICE BOX

The following sets contain figures from the Choice Box. Fill in the characteristics missing from the headings of each set.

B-338

B-339

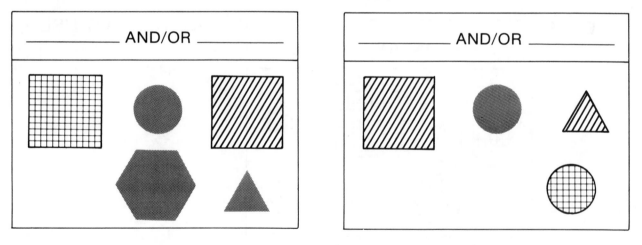

_____ AND/OR _____

_____ AND/OR _____

B-340

B-341

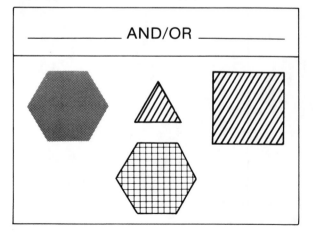

_____ AND/OR _____

_____ AND/OR _____

DISJUNCTION—FOLLOWING AND/OR RULES

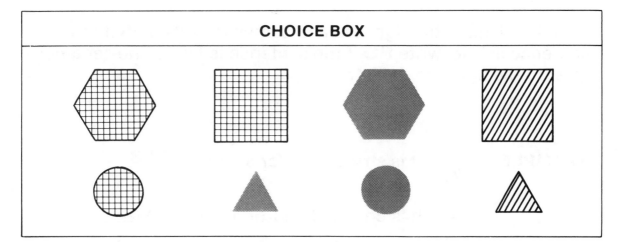

Look at the figures that have not been used in each set. Then draw the figures that belong in each set and fill in the characteristics missing from the headings.

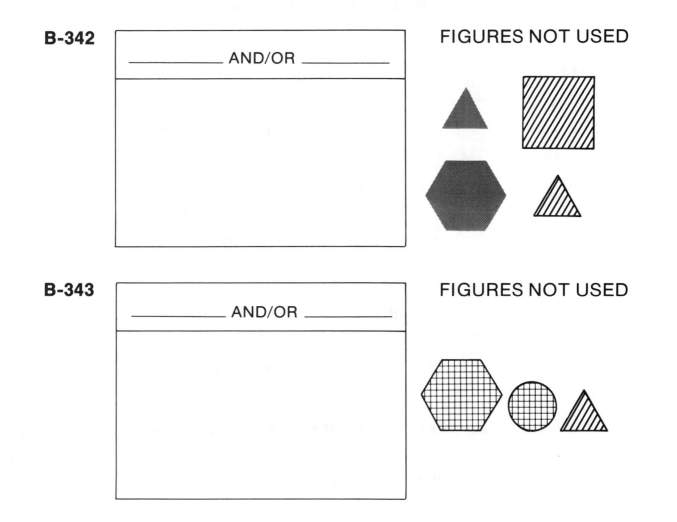

B-342

_____ AND/OR _____

FIGURES NOT USED

B-343

_____ AND/OR _____

FIGURES NOT USED

SEQUENCES

DISJUNCTION—FOLLOWING AND/OR RULES

In the blank to the right of each sentence write **YES** if the sentence is true; write **NO** if the sentence is false. The sentences refer to the figure to the left.

EXAMPLE: It is striped and/or a circle. __YES__

It is checked and/or a circle. __YES__

It is checked and/or a square. __NO__

It is striped and/or a square. __YES__

B-344   It is a triangle and/or gray. _____

It is a triangle and/or striped. _____

It is a square and/or gray. _____

It is a circle and/or striped. _____

B-345   It is checked and/or a square. _____

It is striped and/or a square. _____

It is striped and/or a triangle. _____

It is checked and/or a triangle. _____

DISJUNCTION—FOLLOWING AND/OR RULES

Selecting from the Choice Box, draw the figures for which the first sentence in each exercise is true. The next two sentences help you narrow the field to one figure for which all three sentences are true.

EXAMPLE:

1. It is checked and/or a circle (select all the shapes that follow rule 1).

2. It is checked and/or a square (select from line 1 the shapes that also follow rule 2).

3. It is striped and/or a circle (select from line 2 the shape that also follows rule 3).

Answer: _____

B-346 It is gray and/or a square.

It is checked and/or a circle.

It is checked and/or a triangle.

Answer: _____

B-347 It is striped and/or a triangle.

It is striped and/or a square.

It is gray and/or a triangle.

Answer: _____

IMPLICATION—FOLLOWING IF-THEN RULES

For each group of shapes below, cross out the shapes that do not fit the rule.

EXAMPLE 1:

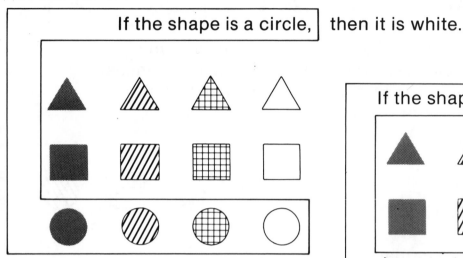

Step 1: Draw a solid line around the figures described by the IF statement. (Notice that the squares and triangles are not being considered.)

Step 2: Draw a dashed line around the figures described by the THEN statement.

Step 3: Look at the figure enclosed by both the solid line and the dashed line (the white circle). Only figures described by both the IF and THEN statements "fit the rule." Cross out the other circles.

B-348   If the shape is checked, then it is a triangle.

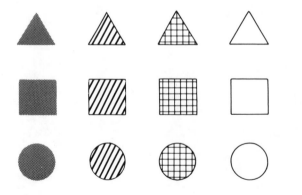

IMPLICATION—FOLLOWING IF-THEN RULES

For each group of shapes below, cross out the shapes that do not fit the rule.

EXAMPLE 2:

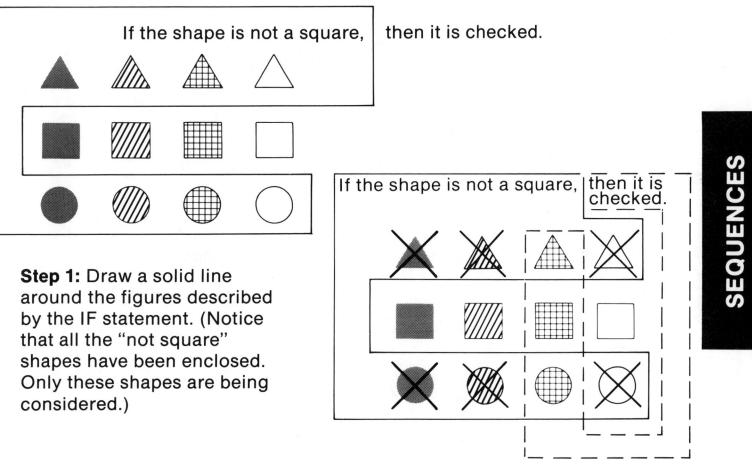

Step 1: Draw a solid line around the figures described by the IF statement. (Notice that all the "not square" shapes have been enclosed. Only these shapes are being considered.)

Step 2: Draw a dashed line around the figures described by the THEN statement.

Step 3: Look at the figures enclosed by both the solid line and the dashed line (the checked triangle and the checked circle). These figures fit the rule. The other triangles and circles outside the dashed line do not fit the rule; they should be crossed out.

Note: The squares also fit the rule, since there are no restrictions on the squares. The phrase "and the squares can have any shading" is implied in the rule.

IMPLICATION—FOLLOWING IF-THEN RULES

For each group of shapes below, cross out the shapes that do not fit the rule.

B-349   If the shape is not a circle, then it is white.

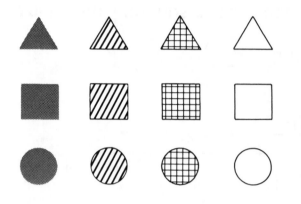

B-350   If the shape is a triangle, then it is not checked.

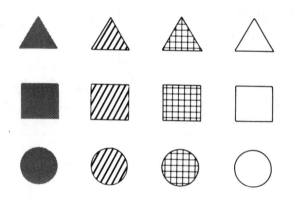

B-351   If the shape is not a square, then it is checked.

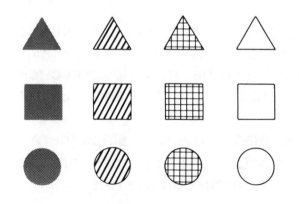

IMPLICATION—FOLLOWING IF-THEN RULES

For each group of shapes below, cross out the shapes that do not fit the rule.

EXAMPLE 3:

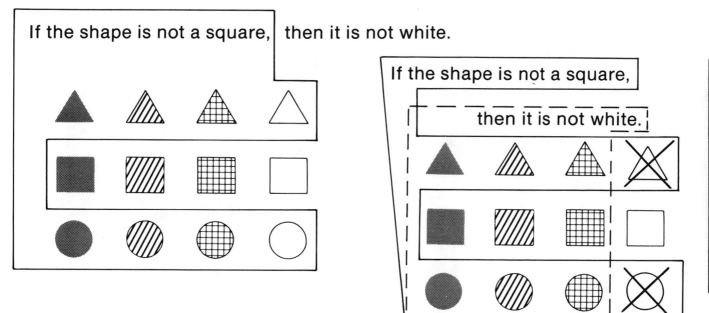

Step 1: Draw a solid line around the figures described by the IF statement.

Step 2: Draw a dashed line around the figures described by the THEN statement.

Step 3: Look at the figures enclosed by both the solid line and the dashed line (the non-white triangles and circles). These figures fit the rule. The white triangle and circle don't fit the rule and are outside the dashed line; they should be crossed out.

Remember: The shapes not described by the IF statements, the squares, also fit the rule.

IMPLICATION—FOLLOWING IF-THEN RULES

For each group of shapes below, cross out the shapes that do not fit the rule.

B-352 If the shape is a circle, then it is not striped.

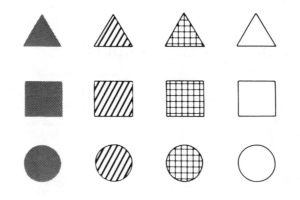

B-353 If the shape is not a triangle, then it is not gray.

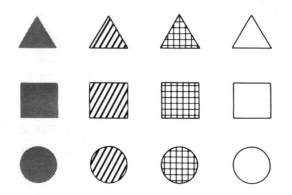

B-354 If the shape is not striped, then it is not a circle.

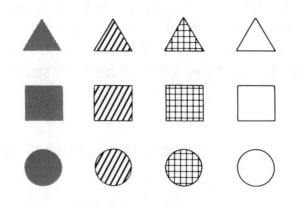

© 1985 MIDWEST PUBLICATIONS 93950-0448

IMPLICATION—FOLLOWING IF-THEN RULES

Decide in which group(s) of shapes (**a.** and/or **b.**) <u>all</u> the shapes fit the rule.

EXAMPLE:

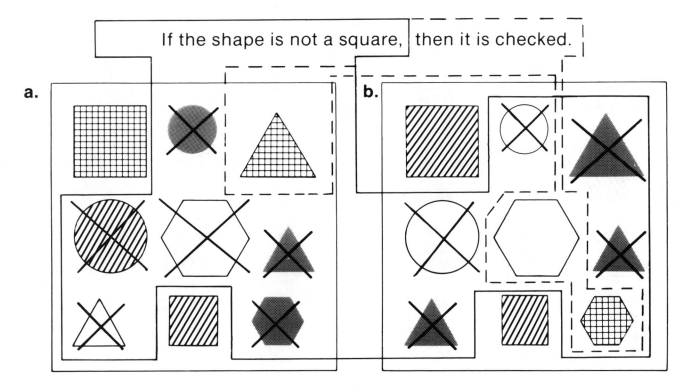

If the shape is not a square, then it is checked.

a.   **b.**

Step 1: Draw a solid line around the figures described by the IF statement.

Step 2: Draw a dashed line around the figures described by the THEN statement.

Step 3: The shapes that "fit the rule" are enclosed by both the solid line (depicting the IF statement) and the dashed line (depicting the THEN statement). Cross out the shapes that do not fit the rule (that is, the shapes within the solid line but outside the dashed line).

Step 4: Decide in which group(s), <u>all</u> the shapes fit the rule.

Answer: Neither a. nor b., since only some of the shapes in each group fit the rule.

IMPLICATION—FOLLOWING IF-THEN RULES

Decide in which group(s) all the shapes fit the rule.

B-355   If the shape is gray, then it is a triangle.

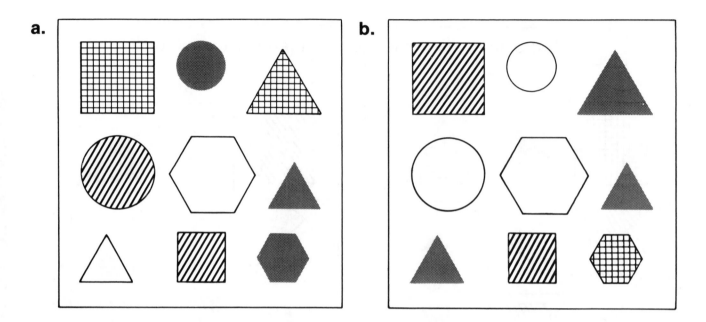

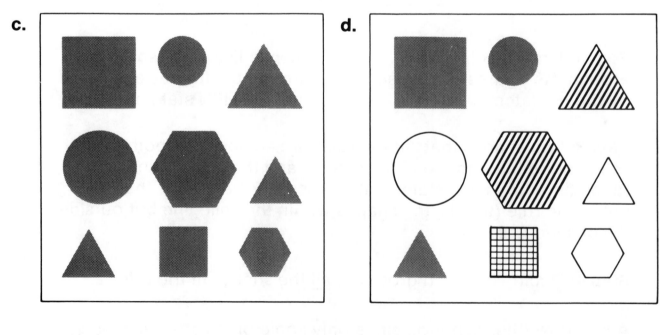

Answer: All shapes in group(s) _____ fit the rule.

IMPLICATION—FOLLOWING IF-THEN RULES

Decide in which group(s) all the shapes fit the rule.

B-356   If the shape is a circle, then it is white.

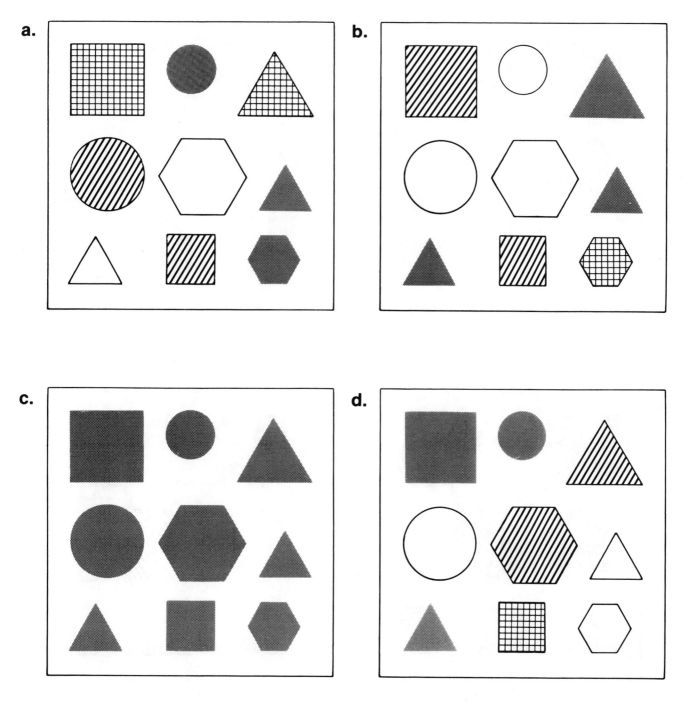

Answer: All shapes in group(s) _____ fit the rule.

IMPLICATION—FOLLOWING IF-THEN RULES

Decide in which group(s) all the shapes fit the rule.

B-357 If the shape is not a circle, then it is gray.

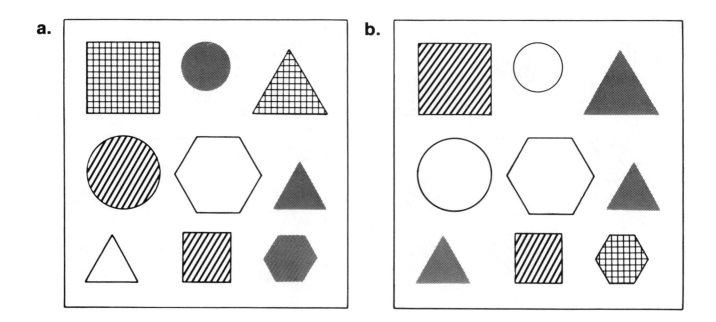

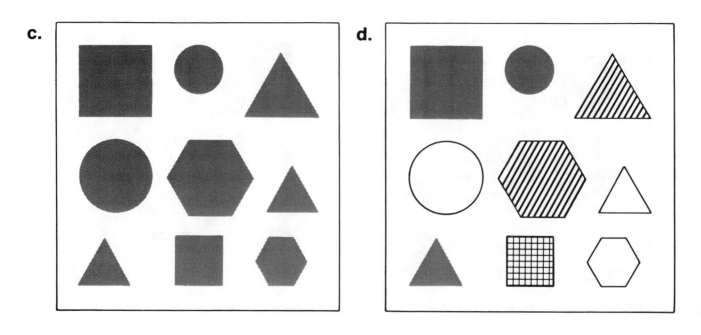

Answer: All shapes in group(s) _____ fit the rule.

IMPLICATION—APPLYING "IF-THEN" RULES

Mark the shapes in the diagram so that they all fit the rule.

EXAMPLE: If the shape is not a triangle,   then it is gray.

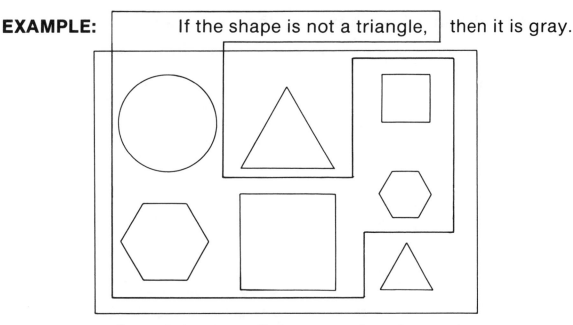

Step 1: Locate all the non-triangles and enclose them within a solid line.

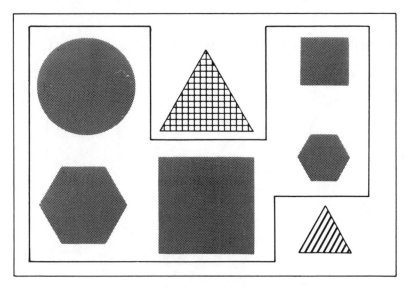

Step 2: Within the solid line that encloses the shapes described by the IF statement, shade **all** the shapes gray.

Remember: The triangles are not restricted by the rule and can be marked **any way**, including gray.

SEQUENCES

IMPLICATION—APPLYING "IF-THEN" RULES

Mark the shapes in each diagam so that they all fit the rule.

B-358   If the shape is a hexagon, then it is gray.

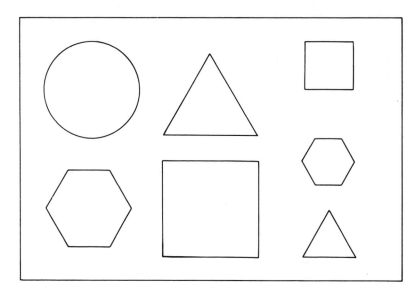

B-359   If the shape is not a circle, then it is striped.

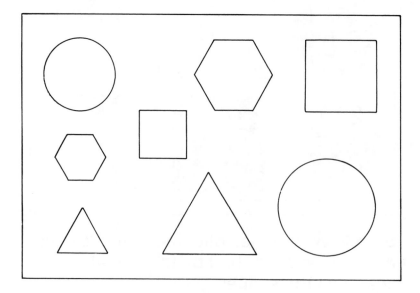

© 1985 MIDWEST PUBLICATIONS 93950-0448

IMPLICATION—APPLYING "IF-THEN" RULES

Mark the shapes in each diagram so that they all fit the rule.

B-360   If the shape is not a hexagon, then it is not checked.

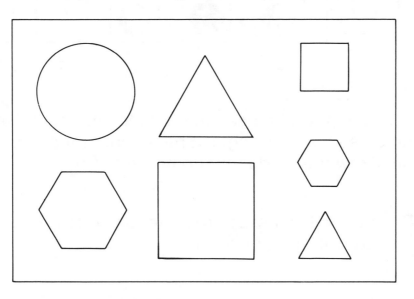

B-361   If the shape is not a polygon,* then it is not white.

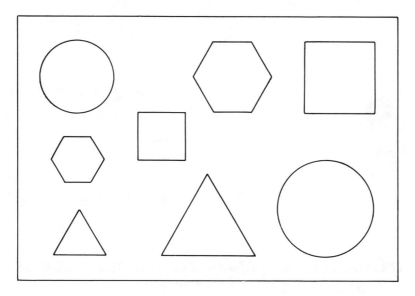

* A closed figure having sides and angles. The sides are all line segments.

IMPLICATION—FOLLOWING IF-THEN RULES

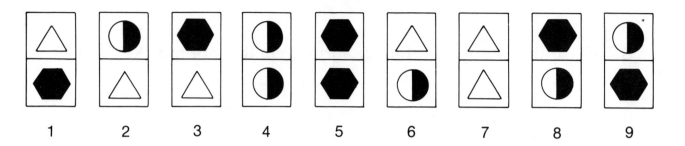

1   2   3   4   5   6   7   8   9

These nine cards will be used in the following exercises. Each card is marked so that a triangle, a hexagon, or a circle appears in each half. Draw the cards that do **not** fit the rule.

EXAMPLE: If there is a hexagon in the lower half, then there is a circle in the upper half.

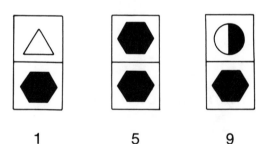

1   5   9

Step 1: The IF statement directs attention to all the cards with a hexagon in the lower half.

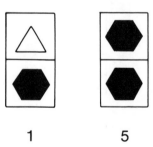

1   5

Step 2: The THEN statement, "there is a circle in the upper half," says that card 9 fits the rule. This leaves cards 1 and 5 as those that do not fit the rule and that are to be drawn.

Remember: Because there are no restrictions on cards 2, 3, 4, 6, 7, and 8, they also fit the rule.

IMPLICATION—FOLLOWING IF-THEN RULES

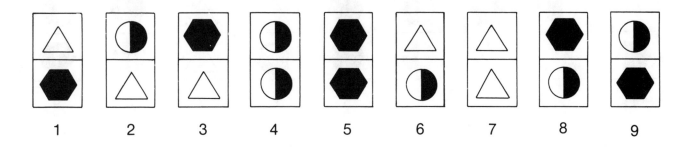

1   2   3   4   5   6   7   8   9

These nine cards will be used in the following exercises. Draw all the cards that do **not** fit the rule.

B-362 If there is a triangle in the lower half, then there is a hexagon in the upper half.

B-363 If there is no triangle in the lower half, then there is a hexagon in the upper half.

B-364 If there is a circle in the upper half, then there is a triangle in the lower half.

IMPLICATION—FOLLOWING IF-THEN RULES

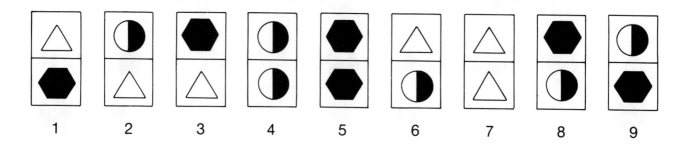

1   2   3   4   5   6   7   8   9

These nine cards will be used in the following exercises. Draw all the cards that do **not** fit the rule.

B-365 If there is a circle in the upper half, then there is no triangle in the lower half.

B-366 If there is no circle in the upper half, then there is a hexagon in the lower half.

B-367 If there is no circle in the upper half, then there is no hexagon in the lower half.

INTERPRETING THREE CONNECTIVES

When the three connective terms AND, AND/OR, and NOT are used in combination, the meaning of statements becomes more complex.

The effect of these three terms on the meaning of statements depends on where in the statement each appears.

Again, water flow through valves will be used to illustrate AND and AND/OR rules. Now the symbol "Λ" will be used for AND; the symbol "V" will be used for AND/OR.

means the valve is OPEN, water will flow through

means the valve is CLOSED, water will not flow through

Complete the following tables. You may want to refer to pages 140-142 and/or pages 146-148 for a reminder.

SEQUENCES

B-368

A and B		A Λ B
A	B	A Λ B
(open)	(open)	YES
a. (open)	(closed)	
b. (closed)	(open)	
c. (closed)	(closed)	

B-369

A and/or B		A V B
A	B	A V B
(open)	(open)	YES
a. (open)	(closed)	
b. (closed)	(open)	
c. (closed)	(closed)	

INTERPRETING THREE CONNECTIVES

Water flow has been used to illustrate how the use of a connective term (AND, AND/OR) will affect the meaning of a statement.

The location and action of the valves determine whether water will flow. The position and combination of AND (Λ) and AND/OR (V) determine the meaning of a statement.

Keeping this in mind, complete the following tables.

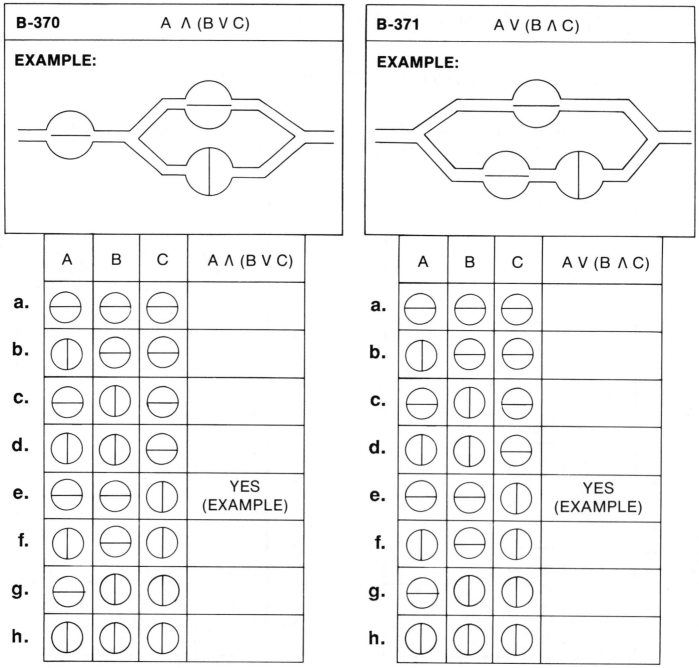

© 1985 MIDWEST PUBLICATIONS 93950-0448

INTERPRETING THREE CONNECTIVES

Each diagram on the left has several valve combinations that will allow water to flow. Illustrate these possibilities by marking the blanks on the right ⊖ (open) or ⊘ (closed).
Remember that "∧" means AND and "V" means AND/OR.

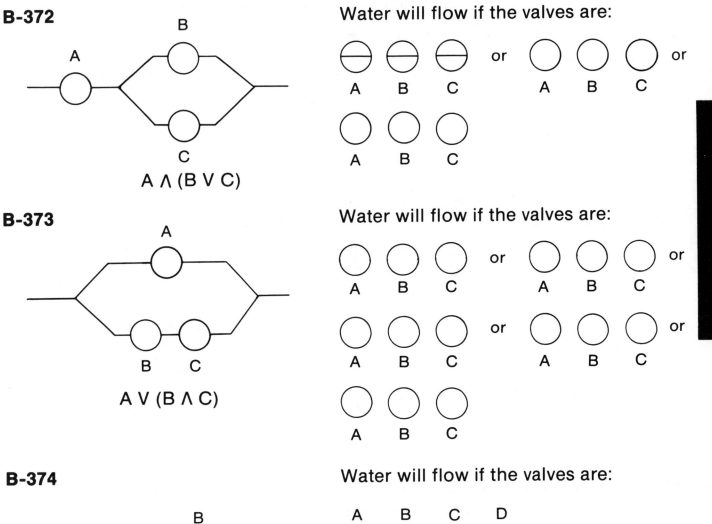

B-372

B

A

A ∧ (B V C)

Water will flow if the valves are:

⊖　⊖　⊖　　or　　○　○　○　　or
A　B　C　　　　　A　B　C

○　○　○
A　B　C

B-373

A

B　C

A V (B ∧ C)

Water will flow if the valves are:

○　○　○　　or　　○　○　○　　or
A　B　C　　　　　A　B　C

○　○　○　　or　　○　○　○　　or
A　B　C　　　　　A　B　C

○　○　○
A　B　C

B-374

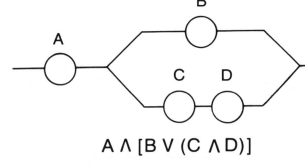

B

A

C　D

A ∧ [B V (C ∧ D)]

Water will flow if the valves are:

A　B　C　D

○　○　○　○　　or

○　○　○　○　　or

○　○　○　○　　or

○　○　○　○　　or

○　○　○　○

SEQUENCES

INTERPRETING THREE CONNECTIVES

Each diagram on the left has several valve combinations that will allow water to flow. Illustrate these possibilities by marking the blanks on the right ⊖ (open) or ⦶ (closed). Remember that "Λ" means AND and "V" means AND/OR.

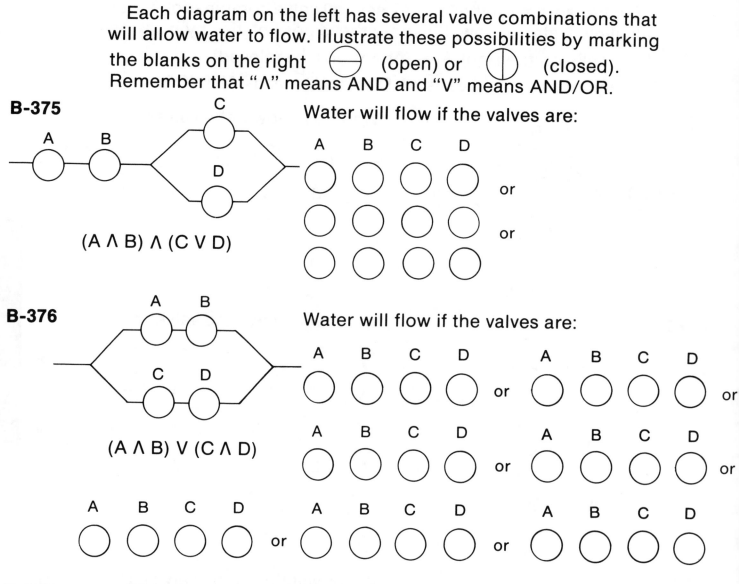

B-375

(A Λ B) Λ (C V D)

Water will flow if the valves are:

B-376

(A Λ B) V (C Λ D)

Water will flow if the valves are:

© 1985 MIDWEST PUBLICATIONS 93950-0448

B-377 This series of valve combinations will help you figure out which of the valves in the diagram below should be marked A, B, and C.

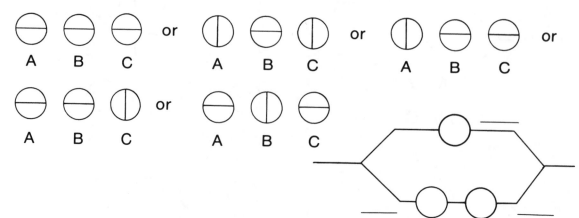

174

USING THREE CONNECTIVES

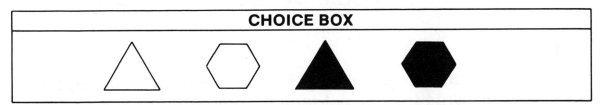

Selecting from the Choice Box, draw the figures for which the first sentence in each exercise is true. The next two sentences help you narrow the field to one figure for which all three sentences are true.

B-378

1. It is black and/or it is a hexagon.

2. It is white and/or it is a triangle.

3. It is black and/or it is a triangle.

Answer: _____

B-379

1. It is black and/or it is a hexagon.

2. It is white and/or it is a triangle.

3. It is white and/or it is a hexagon.

Answer: _____

B-380

1. It is not white and/or not a triangle.

2. It is not black and/or not a triangle.

3. It is not white and/or not a hexagon.

Answer: _____

B-381

1. It is not white and/or not a triangle.

2. It is not black and/or not a triangle.

3. It is not black and/or not a hexagon.

Answer: _____

USING THREE CONNECTIVES—CONJUNCTION

B-382

Each of the sentences below refers to one of the four regions in the diagram. Write the correct region number in the blanks provided.

CIRCLES

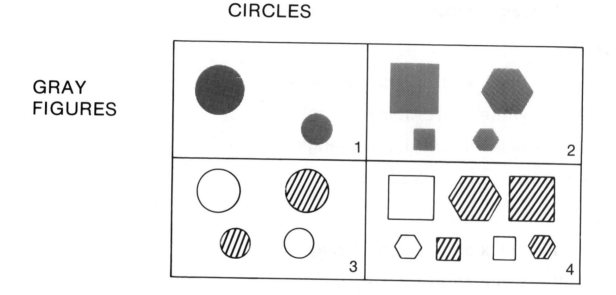

GRAY
FIGURES

EXAMPLE: The figures are gray and they are circles. __Region 1__

a. The figures are not gray and they are not circles. _____

b. The figures are gray and are not circles. _____

c. The figures are not gray and they are circles. _____

d. The figures are gray and/or they are circles. _____

e. The figures are not gray and/or they are not circles. _____

USING THREE CONNECTIVES—CONJUNCTION

These symbols will be used for the following exercises:

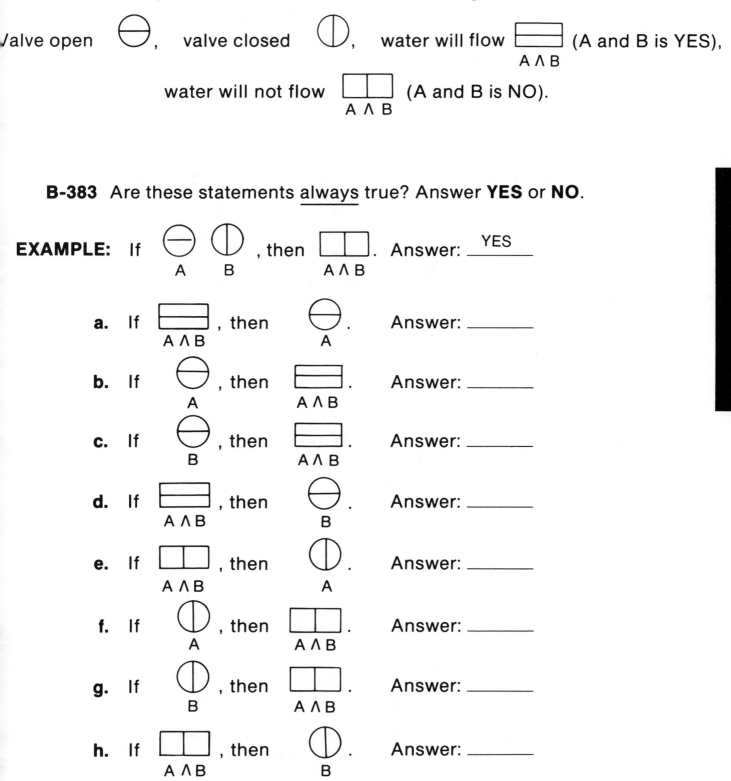

B-383 Are these statements <u>always</u> true? Answer **YES** or **NO**.

USING THREE CONNECTIVES—DISJUNCTION

These symbols will be used for the following exercises:

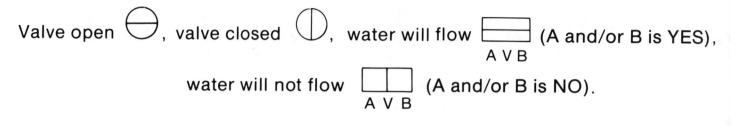

Valve open ⊖, valve closed ⊘, water will flow ▭ (A and/or B is YES),

water will not flow ▯ (A and/or B is NO).

B-384 Are these statements <u>always</u> true? Answer **YES** or **NO**.

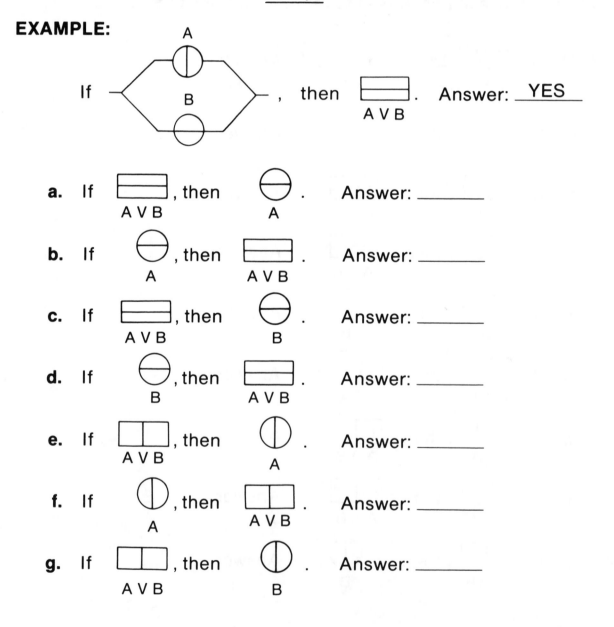

EXAMPLE:

If (A, B) , then ▭. Answer: <u>YES</u>
A V B

a. If ▭ , then ⊖ . Answer: _____
    A V B   A

b. If ⊖ , then ▭ . Answer: _____
    A   A V B

c. If ▭ , then ⊖ . Answer: _____
    A V B   B

d. If ⊖ , then ▭ . Answer: _____
    B   A V B

e. If ▯ , then ⊘ . Answer: _____
    A V B   A

f. If ⊘ , then ▯ . Answer: _____
    A   A V B

g. If ▯ , then ⊘ . Answer: _____
    A V B   B

APPLYING THREE CONNECTIVES

Find your way through the mazes without breaking this rule:
If you are on a white field, then the next field you enter is striped.

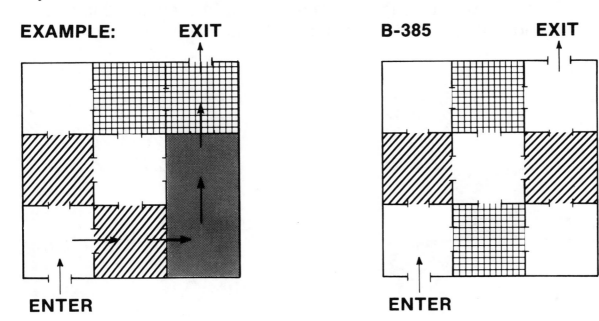

EXAMPLE: **EXIT**   **B-385**   **EXIT**

ENTER   ENTER

Find your way through the mazes without breaking this rule:
If you are on a white field, then the next field you enter is not striped.

B-386   **EXIT**

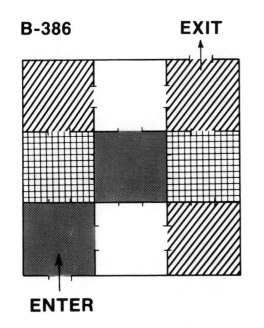

ENTER

B-387   **EXIT**

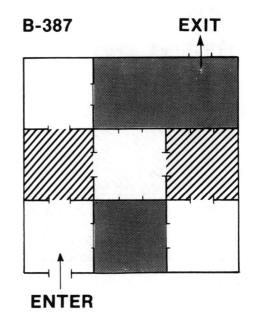

ENTER

APPLYING THREE CONNECTIVES

Find your way through the mazes without breaking this rule:
If the field you are on is not white, then the field you enter is striped.

B-388   **EXIT**   **B-389**   **EXIT**

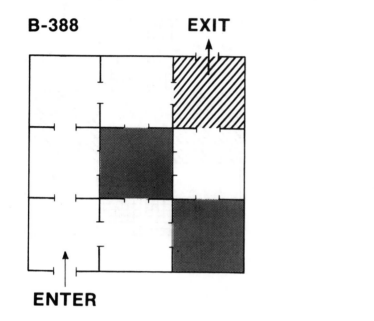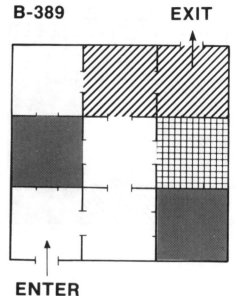

Find your way through the mazes without breaking this rule:
If the field you are on is not white, then the field you enter is not striped.

B-390   **EXIT**   **B-391**   **EXIT**

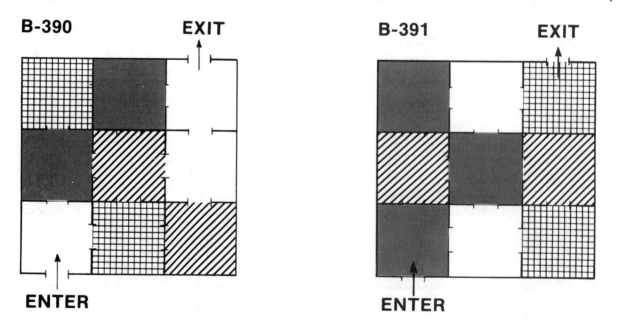

CAUSE-EFFECT WORDS—SELECT

The following pairs of words are commonly used together. In some instances the relationship is cause-to-effect or reason-to-result.

On the line by each pair of words, write **C-E** if the first word commonly <u>causes</u> or results in the second; write **NO** if the first word <u>does</u> <u>not</u> commonly result in the second.

EXAMPLE:

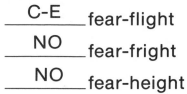

__C-E__ fear-flight
__NO__ fear-fright
__NO__ fear-height

Since fear may result in flight, mark that line "C-E." Fear and fright are synonyms, not a cause-effect relationship; mark the second pair "NO." One may be afraid of heights, but fear does not commonly cause height; mark that line "NO."

B-392

a. _____ achievement-recognition

b. _____ taste-honey

c. _____ vibrations-sound

d. _____ intent-purpose

e. _____ colleague-associate

f. _____ flood-damage

g. _____ quart-liquid

h. _____ running-stamina

i. _____ violation-fine

j. _____ salt-thirst

SEQUENCES

CAUSE-EFFECT WORDS—SELECT

Write **C-E** on the line provided if the first word commonly causes or results in the second. Write **NO** if the first word <u>does not</u> commonly result in the second.

B-393

a. _____ gravity-falling

b. _____ mystery-suspense

c. _____ sound-music

d. _____ ability-talent

e. _____ famine-hunger

f. _____ advocate-supporter

g. _____ whispering-hoarseness

h. _____ misconduct-punishment

i. _____ cold-numbness

j. _____ release-discharge

k. _____ blow-bruise

l. _____ virus-illness

m. _____ sum-parts

n. _____ suffering-distress

o. _____ astonishment-wonder

CAUSE-EFFECT WORDS—SUPPLY

Give one or more effects or results for the following causes or reasons.

	CAUSES/REASONS	EFFECTS/RESULTS
EXAMPLE:	worry	tension, frown
B-394	fire	_____
B-395	quality	_____
B-396	imbalance	_____
B-397	practice	_____
B-398	hurricane	_____
B-399	reading	_____
B-400	supply	_____
B-401	stretch	_____
B-402	noise	_____
B-403	spices	_____
B-404	emotion	_____
B-405	speeding	_____

SEQUENCES

CAUSE-EFFECT WORDS—SUPPLY

Give one or more causes or reasons for the following effects or results.

	CAUSES/REASONS	EFFECTS/RESULTS
EXAMPLE:	nutrition, exercise	health
B-406	_____	fragrance
B-407	_____	waste
B-408	_____	casualties
B-409	_____	dizziness
B-410	_____	hesitation
B-411	_____	perspiration
B-412	_____	shyness
B-413	_____	light
B-414	_____	infection
B-415	_____	laughter
B-416	_____	fatigue

SIGNAL WORDS—SELECT

The following words and/or phrases are signal words that alert the reader to a relationship between statements.

Some signal words suggest **time order** (T-O):

_____T-O_____ He stopped at the library <u>before</u> he went home.

Some signal words suggest **contradiction** (CON):

_____CON_____ He wanted to stop at the library, <u>but</u> he needed to go directly home.

Some signal words of **cause-effect** (C-E) relationships call the reader's attention to the possibility that one statement <u>causes</u> or <u>results</u> in the second.

_____C-E_____ He stopped at the library <u>because</u> he needed information for his research paper.

In each of the following sentences the underlined signal word or phrase affects the meaning of the passage. Mark the sentence **T-O** if the signal word suggests time order, **CON** for contradiction, or **C-E** for cause-effect relationships.

B-417 _____ Margo didn't study for her chemistry course and <u>consequently</u> did not do well.

B-418 _____ Margo didn't study for her chemistry course and may <u>eventually</u> decide to drop the course.

B-419 _____ <u>Although</u> Margo didn't want to study for her chemistry course, she really didn't want to drop the course.

B-420 _____ <u>Since</u> Margo didn't study for her chemistry course, she did not do well.

B-421 _____ Margo's poor performance in chemistry was not due to lack of interest; <u>on the contrary</u>, she rather likes chemistry.

B-422 _____ Margo didn't take her chemistry examination <u>for</u> she was coming down with a cold.

B-423 _____ <u>While</u> Margo didn't study for her chemistry examination, she did like the course.

B-424 _____ <u>While</u> Margo was coming down with a cold she didn't feel like studying for her chemistry examination.

FLOWCHARTING

A flowchart is a diagram that represents a sequence of events. Flowcharting is useful for:

SEQUENCING
PICTURING STAGES
WRITING INSTRUCTIONS
SHOWING CYCLES
PLANNING
SOLVING PROBLEMS

Here is an example of a simple flowchart for writing a report.

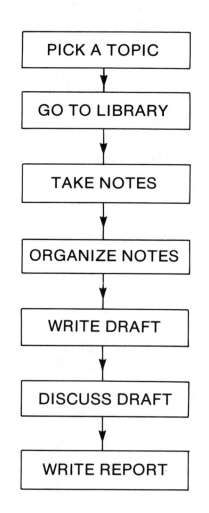

FLOWCHARTING

Flowcharts have become a useful tool of computer programmers. Programmers use a standard set of symbols so that the reader may quickly understand the **flow** of thought represented by the **chart**.

In the preceding flowchart only rectangles were used.

 RECTANGLES are used for actions or activities.

A standard flowchart begins with a "START" statement and ends with a "STOP" statement.

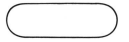 OVALS are used for "START" and "STOP."

A program in "standard form" looks like this.

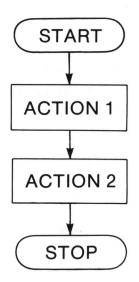

SEQUENCES

FLOWCHARTING FOR SOLVING PROBLEMS

Flowcharting can be used to reason through the solutions to practical and school-related problems.

EXAMPLE: Find the cost of eight gallons of gasoline if the price per gallon is $1.35. The flowchart below outlines the problem.

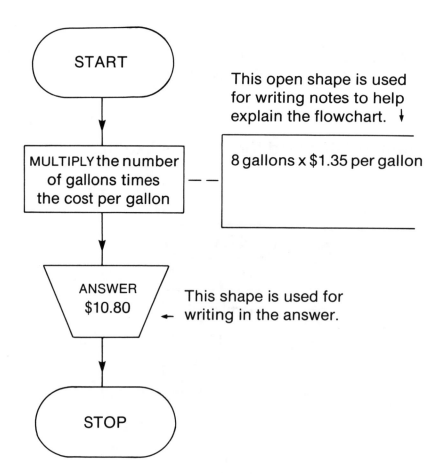

START

This open shape is used for writing notes to help explain the flowchart. ↓

MULTIPLY the number of gallons times the cost per gallon

8 gallons x $1.35 per gallon

ANSWER $10.80

This shape is used for writing in the answer.

STOP

FLOWCHARTING FOR SOLVING PROBLEMS

To calculate your baseball batting average you don't count the number of times you are "walked" or hit by a pitched ball as an official time at bat.

Your batting average is "hits" divided by "official times at bat."

B-425 Complete this flowchart and use it to calculate the batting average of a player who came up to bat 150 times. She was walked 23 times and hit twice by a pitched ball. She hit safely 45 times.

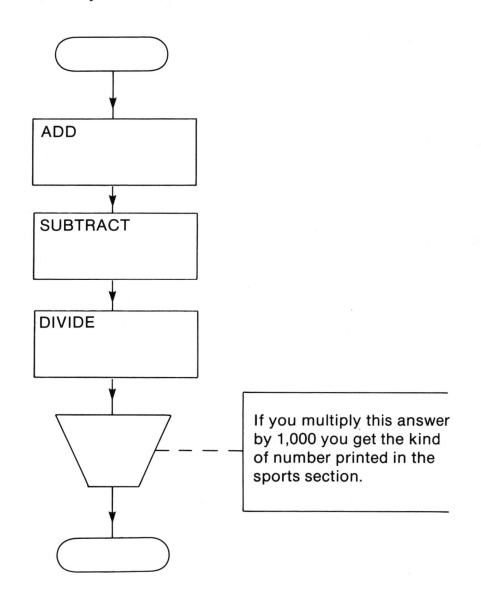

ADD

SUBTRACT

DIVIDE

If you multiply this answer by 1,000 you get the kind of number printed in the sports section.

FLOWCHARTING FOR SOLVING PROBLEMS

To find the average of a group of scores you add the scores and divide by the number of scores.

EXAMPLE: Find the average of 75, 87, 63, 59, and 92.

Step 1. Add the scores:
75 + 87 + 63 + 59 + 92 = 376

Step 2. Count the scores: 5

Step 3. Divide 376 by 5:   376 ÷ 5 = 75.2

Answer: 75.2 is the average of the five scores.

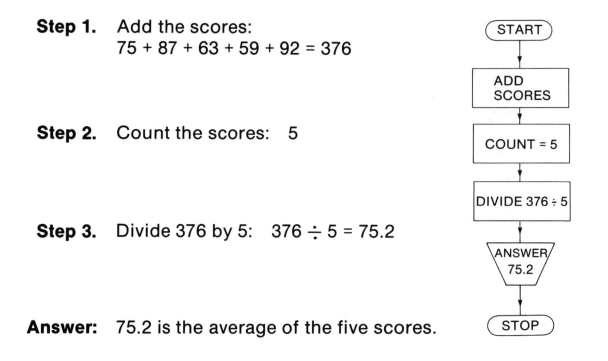

B-426 Construct a flowchart and use it to calculate the averages of these seven test scores:

63, 85, 96, 77, 89, 67, 93

FLOWCHARTING A SEQUENCE

In the preceding exercises you used ovals for "START" and "STOP" and rectangles for actions.

Two additional symbols are needed when flowcharting a sequence of events requiring that decisions be made.

 DIAMONDS are used for questions at decision points.

CIRCLES are used for answers at decision points.

Let's look at a flowchart that involves placing a long-distanc phone call at a pay phone. You do not wish to call collect and don't have a telephone credit card. The first time you dial you the wrong number.

The flowchart is shown on the next page.

FLOWCHARTING A SEQUENCE

Steps in making a phone call:

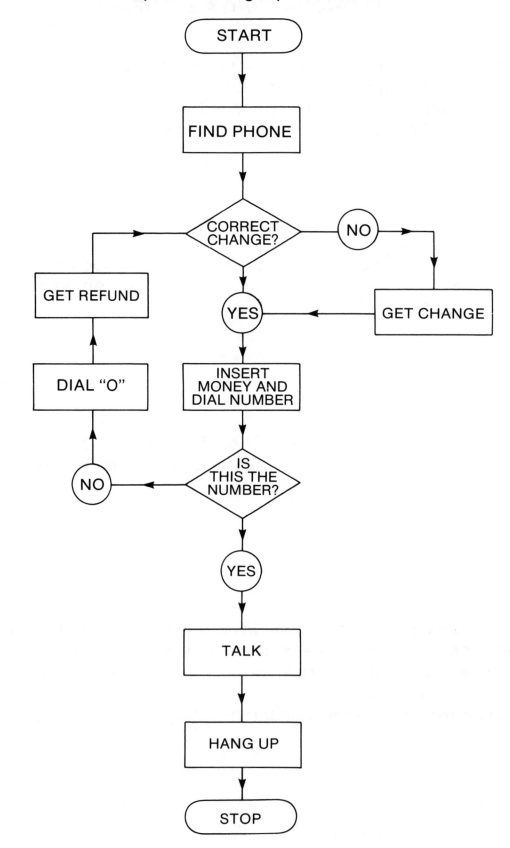

FLOWCHARTING A PLAN OF ACTION

B-427 In many hotels you find a flowchart that describes what to do in case of fire. Use the instructions below to fill in the flowchart that follows.

In the event of fire you should feel the door. If it is hot, remain in your room with the door closed. If the door is cool, open the door carefully and look for smoke in the hall. If there is smoke, remain in your room with the door closed. If there is no smoke, proceed to the exit.

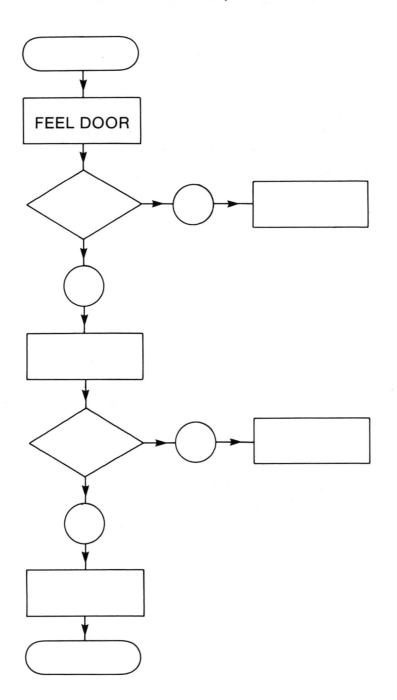

SEQUENCES

FLOWCHARTING—AVERAGE SPEED

B-428 Suppose your family travels 400 miles in 12 hours. Use this flowchart to find the average speed.

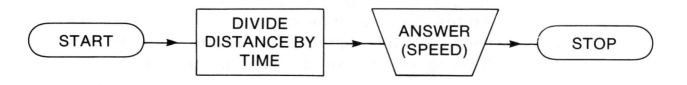

B-429 Now suppose you use only driving time in calculating average speed. Your family stopped twice for meals, took 45 minutes each time, and went sightseeing for 2½ hours. Use the flowchart below to calculate the average driving speed.

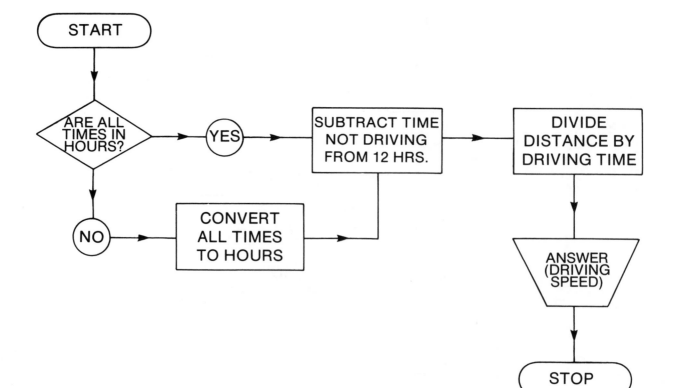

FLOWCHARTING AS AN AID TO PLANNING

B-430 Flowcharts can be used to show the steps someone must follow to get a job done. Fill in the flowchart below to show the steps Jane must take to order a birthday cake. Be sure to put direction arrows on the connecting lines.

Jane's mother needs help planning a birthday party for Jane's brother Bob. It is Jane's job to buy a birthday cake. She needs to find out if the nearest bakery can have the cake ready in time for the party. If the nearest bakery cannot have the cake done in time, then Jane will have to find a more distant bakery that will deliver the cake.

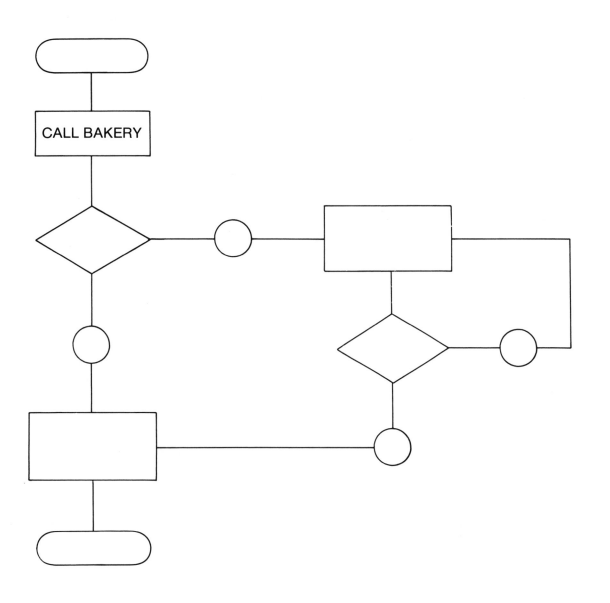

CALL BAKERY

FLOWCHARTING—COMPARISON SHOPPING

B-431 You are at the supermarket and are trying to decide which of the three sizes of Super Cleano laundry powder is the best buy. The 10-ounce regular size is priced at $1.20; the jumbo one-pound size costs $1.65; and the super-jumbo size weighs one pound, six ounces and sells for $2.30.

Draw a flowchart that details the steps that must be taken before deciding which size is the best buy. (Be sure to use the proper symbols as you construct this flowchart. Also, keep in mind that this is a long flowchart and may require two or more rows and/or columns.)

FLOWCHARTING A CYCLE

The water cycle below illustrates a process that repeats itself. Such events, having no beginning or end, can be represented by a cycle flowchart.

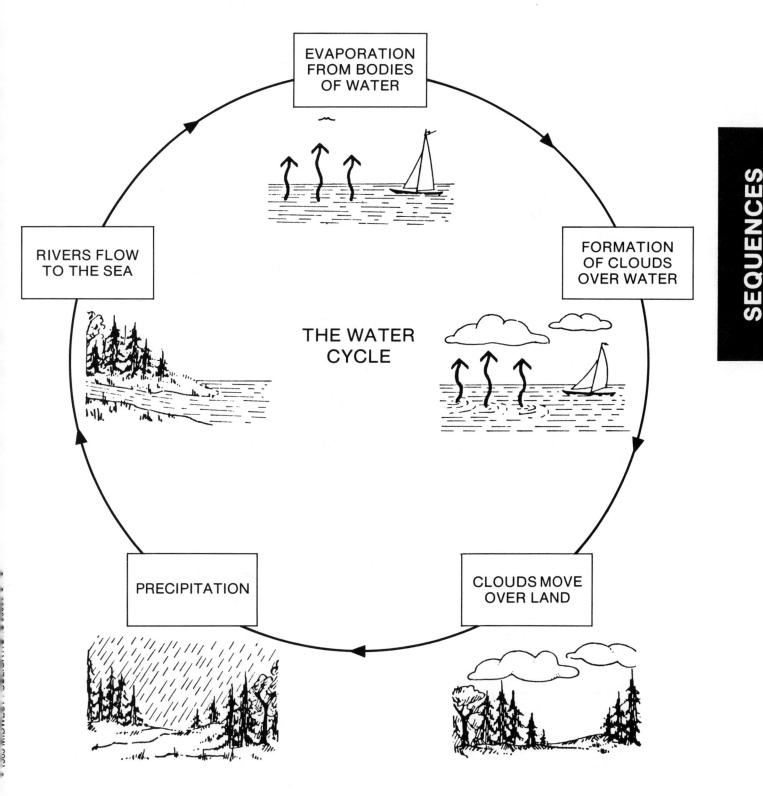

FLOWCHARTING A CYCLE

B-432 After reading these statements concerning the growth of plants and the food chain, assume that the first statement is the beginning of a cycle and rearrange the remaining statements in the order they would follow.

1. A corn plant is nourished by organic material in the soil.

2. A fox eats a sparrow.

3. The decomposing action of bacteria replenishes the soil with organic material.

4. Some corn is eaten by corn borer insects.

5. After the fox dies, the carcass is decomposed by bacteria.

6. Insects are eaten by a sparrow.

A corn plant is nourished by organic material in the soil.

_____

_____

_____

_____

_____

FLOWCHARTING A CYCLE

B-433 The order of events in the food chain is also a cycle. Use the information from the preceding exercise to fill in the flowchart of this food cycle. In each box, write the verb that results in the next step in the cycle. The line by each box should be filled in with the correct noun.

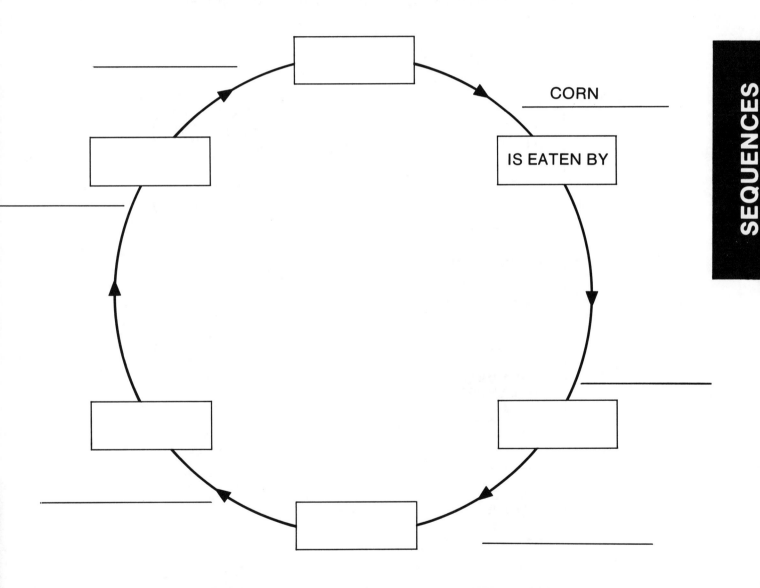

FLOWCHARTING A SEQUENCE

B-434　On a separate sheet of paper use these symbols and phrases to construct a flowchart outlining Danny's after-school trip to the mall. He must be home by 6 p.m. and is thinking about going to an afternoon movie. Use the symbol-phrases as many times as needed.

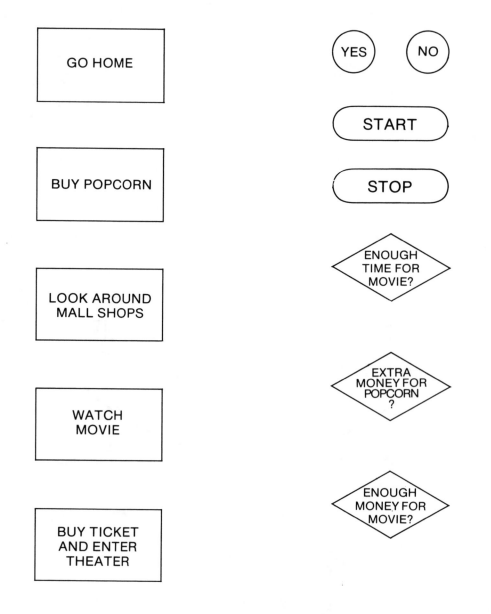

FLOWCHARTING A CYCLE

B-435 Your daily activities during the school year have a repetitive sequence. Use the symbols and phrases below to construct a cycle flowchart. Again, use a separate sheet of paper and use each symbol-phrase as many times as needed.

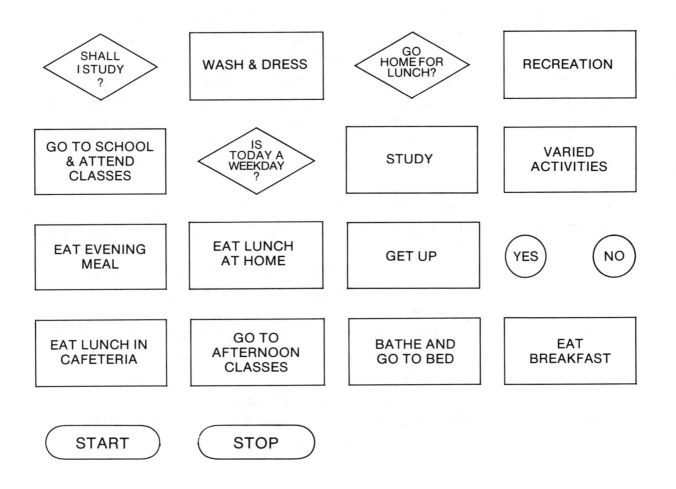

TIME INTERVALS OF A DAY—DEFINITIONS

While the concept of time is not so easy to explain or comprehend, understanding the definitions of the specific terms of time is important in our day-to-day lives. Understanding the definitions that follow* will help you answer the questions in this section and, hopefully, will also help you expand your concept of time.

afternoon	- the time period between noon and 6:00 p.m.
a.m.	- ante meridiem, the time between midnight and noon
dawn	- the first appearance of light in the morning; daybreak
daybreak	- the first appearance of light in the morning; dawn
daylight	- the light of day between dawn and dusk
dusk	- as it becomes dark; twilight; to make dark
evening	- the time period between 6:00 p.m. and midnight
forenoon	- the entire period of time between sunrise and noon
mid-afternoon	- the middle part of the afternoon, around 3 p.m.
midday	- the middle part of the day; noon
mid-morning	- the middle period from sunrise to noon, around 10 a.m.
midnight	- the middle part of the night; twelve o'clock at night
morning	- the period of time between midnight and noon, or dawn until noon
night	- the period of time between sunset and midnight
noon	- midday; twelve o'clock in the middle of the day
p.m.	- post meridiem, the time between noon and midnight
sundown	- the time the sun disappears for the night; sunset
sunrise	- the rising of the sun above the horizon; when it appears
sunset	- the time the sun disappears; sundown
twilight	- the time between sunset and darkness; dusk; a perceived light in darkness.

*These definitions are taken from *Thinking About Time/Book-2* © 1985 Midwest Publications, Pacific Grove, CA 93950. We are aware that some of the traditional definitions used may not apply to everyone's lifestyle. (Time has brought many changes.) These differences, however, offer many opportunities for class discussions.

INTERVALS OF A DAY—SELECT

B-436 Circle the times that occur between noon and midnight.

    a. 12:06 a.m.   **b.** 3:45 p.m.   **c.** 1:26 p.m.

    d. 9:18 a.m.   **e.** 8:53 a.m.   **f.** 11:25 p.m.

B-437 Circle the times that occur between midnight and noon.

    a. 11:32 a.m.   **b.** 2:32 a.m.   **c.** 4:53 p.m.

    d. 7:11 p.m.   **e.** 5:58 a.m.   **f.** 6:30 p.m.

B-438 Circle the times that occur within an hour of midday.

    a. 12:42 a.m.   **b.** 11:15 a.m.   **c.** 1:53 p.m.   **d.** 12:21 p.m.

B-439 Circle the times that occur within an hour of mid-afternoon.

    a. 1:35 p.m.   **b.** 2:43 p.m.   **c.** 3:41 p.m.   **d.** 2:24 a.m.

B-440 Circle the times that occur within an hour of mid-morning.

    a. 9:39 a.m.   **b.** 10:03 p.m.   **c.** 11:45 a.m.   **d.** 10:45 a.m.

B-441 Circle the times commonly considered to occur during the evening hours.

    a. 6:05 a.m.   **b.** 7:13 p.m.   **c.** 6:58 p.m.   **d.** 7:28 a.m.

B-442 Circle the time earliest in the morning.

    a. 3:40 a.m.   **b.** 12:08 a.m.   **c.** 7:10 a.m.

B-443 Circle the time latest in the morning.

    a. 11:46 p.m.   **b.** 10:57 a.m.   **c.** 12:21 p.m.   **d.** 11:07 a.m.

INTERVALS OF A DAY—SUPPLY

Examine these time intervals and supply the missing times to complete each sequence.

B-444 6:00 a.m., _____, 12:00 noon, 3:00 p.m., _____, 9:00 p.m.

B-445 _____, 9:40 p.m., 10:00 p.m., _____, 10:40 p.m.

B-446 12:00 noon, 9:00 p.m., _____, _____, 12:00 midnight

B-447 _____, _____, _____, 4:45 p.m., 5:30 p.m.

B-448 1:00 a.m., 7:00 p.m., _____, 7:00 a.m., _____

B-449 Examine the tide table below. What is the approximate interval between high tide and low tide? _____

B-450 What is the approximate interval between one high tide and the next? _____

B-451 What general trend do you see regarding when high tide will occur tomorrow, if you know what time it occurred today? _____

TIDE TABLE				
DAY	HIGH TIDE		LOW TIDE	
	A.M.	P.M.	A.M.	P.M.
1	2:50	3:11	9:32	9:24
2	3:59	4:18	10:35	10:28
3	5:00	5:19	11:29	11:19

204

INTERVALS OF A DAY—SUPPLY

B-452 Give the hour(s) of the day (or night) commonly associated with the terms listed below. Remember to use a.m. and p.m. correctly.

TERMS	TIME INTERVALS
EXAMPLE: afternoon	between noon and 6:00 p.m.
a. a.m.	_____
b. night	_____
c. dawn or daybreak	_____
d. midafternoon	_____
e. dusk or twilight	_____
f. p.m.	_____
g. forenoon	_____
h. daylight	_____
i. midmorning	_____
j. evening	_____
k. midday	_____

SEQUENCES

INTERVALS OF A DAY—SUPPLY

B-453 Give the terms most closely associated with the time periods listed below.

TIME INTERVALS   TERMS

EXAMPLE: 12 p.m.   _____noon or midday_____

  a. 2:45 p.m.   _____

  b. noon to midnight   _____

  c. sunrise to noon   _____

  d. 12 a.m.   _____

  e. 7 p.m.   _____

  f. 10:10 a.m.   _____

  g. midnight to noon   _____

  h. sunset to sunrise   _____

  i. daylight to dusk   _____

  j. sunset to darkness   _____

  k. dawn to noon   _____

LONG-TERM INTERVALS—DEFINITIONS

As you probably know, a "week," a "month," a "season," and a "year" are terms we apply to increasingly larger groups of days (7, 28 to 31, 3 months, and 365, respectively). However, you may not know that there are also terms we can apply to even longer time intervals.

decade — 10 years　　　　century — 100 years
score — 20 years　　　millennium — 1,000 years
era — an unspecified period of years having
　　　historical significance

It is also important to learn how prefixes affect the meaning of words. Listed below are the definitions of some time-related terms you are probably familiar with.

annually — happening once a year and/or every year
monthly — happening once a month and/or every month
weekly — happening once a week and/or every week

Now study the next list of definitions and note how the prefixes "bi-" and "semi-" affect the root words. It is also important to note that words that begin with bi- or semi- have different meanings.* The prefix **bi-** means: double; happening twice. The prefix **semi-** means: half.

biannually — happening twice a year, but not necessarily at
　　　　　　equal intervals
bimonthly — happening every two months
biweekly — happening every two weeks

semiannually — happening twice a year at equal intervals
　　　　　　　(every six months)
semimonthly — happening twice a month
semiweekly — happening twice a week

Look at the word biannual. Another word in our vocabulary closely resembles it — biennial. There are only two letters that are different, but they change the meaning of the words significantly. **Biennial** means happening every two years.

Other terms we should know:

perennial — happening every year for many years without
　　　　　　interruption
centennial — the celebration of a 100-year anniversary

*Some sources define these prefixes as meaning the same; but for the exercises in this book, follow the definitions given above.

INTERVALS OF A YEAR—SUPPLY

B-454 Define the following terms and use each in a sentence.

EXAMPLE: annual   occurring once a year
Thanksgiving is an **annual** celebration.

a. biannually   _____

_____

b. biennially   _____

_____

c. bimonthly   _____

_____

d. biweekly   _____

_____

e. centennial   _____

_____

f. century   _____

_____

g. decade   _____

_____

h. era   _____

_____

i. millennium   _____

_____

INTERVALS OF A YEAR—SUPPLY

B-455　Define the following terms and use each in a sentence.

a.　month　　　_____

_____

b.　monthly　　_____

_____

c.　perennial　_____

_____

d.　score　　　_____

_____

e.　season　　_____

_____

f.　semiannually　_____

_____

g.　semimonthly　_____

_____

h.　semiweekly　_____

_____

i.　week　　　_____

_____

SEQUENCES

TIME ORDER—RANK

B-456 Number these times from earliest to latest (remember that the day begins at midnight).

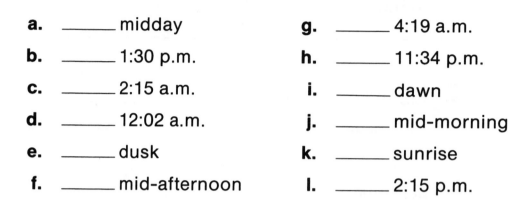

a.	_____ midday	**g.**	_____ 4:19 a.m.
b.	_____ 1:30 p.m.	**h.**	_____ 11:34 p.m.
c.	_____ 2:15 a.m.	**i.**	_____ dawn
d.	_____ 12:02 a.m.	**j.**	_____ mid-morning
e.	_____ dusk	**k.**	_____ sunrise
f.	_____ mid-afternoon	**l.**	_____ 2:15 p.m.

B-457 Number these time intervals from the shortest to the longest.

a.	_____ hour	**h.**	_____ day
b.	_____ year	**i.**	_____ season
c.	_____ week	**j.**	_____ minute
d.	_____ second	**k.**	_____ daylight
e.	_____ morning	**l.**	_____ month
f.	_____ decade	**m.**	_____ century
g.	_____ millennium	**n.**	_____ score

B-458 Number these measures of how often things occur from least often to most often.

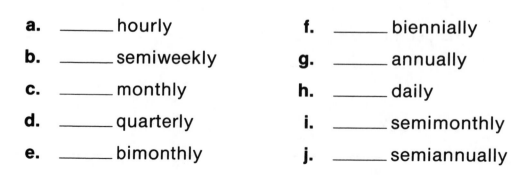

a.	_____ hourly	**f.**	_____ biennially
b.	_____ semiweekly	**g.**	_____ annually
c.	_____ monthly	**h.**	_____ daily
d.	_____ quarterly	**i.**	_____ semimonthly
e.	_____ bimonthly	**j.**	_____ semiannually

TIME INTERVALS—SELECT

Use these terms to complete the statements below. You may use an answer more than once.

annually	monthly
biweekly	semiweekly
daily	quarterly
hourly	weekly

SEQUENCES

B-459 Wedding anniversaries are celebrated _____.

B-460 Wages for employees of fast-food restaurants are usually figured at an _____ rate.

B-461 Payments on home mortgages are paid _____.

B-462 Employers must submit payments for income tax withheld from their employees' checks each April 15, July 15, October 15 and January 15. These payments to the Internal Revenue Service are made _____.

B-463 First-run, prime-time television series are usually broadcast _____.

B-464 Receiving a newspaper on Wednesdays and Sundays is _____ service.

B-465 Workers who are paid every other Friday are paid on a _____ basis.

B-466 Vitamins are usually taken on a _____ basis.

INTERVALS OF A YEAR—SUPPLY

The seasons of the year are determined by the number of hours of daylight compared to the number of hours of darkness.

The season of Spring begins when the number of daylight hours equals the number of dark hours. This day occurs when the sun is at a point in the sky known as the **vernal equinox**.

The next season, known as Summer, begins with the **Summer Solstice**. On this day the sun is at its highest point in the sky, and there are more daylight hours than at any other time of the year.

The following season, Fall, begins once again when the number of daylight hours equals the number of dark hours. This is the time of the **autumnal equinox**.

During the Winter the days are short and the nights are long. Winter begins with the **Winter Solstice**, when the sun is at its lowest point in the sky and there are fewer hours of daylight than any other day of the year.

In the United States the seasons begin on approximately the following dates:

Spring begins March 21
Summer begins June 21
Fall begins September 21
Winter begins December 21

B-467 Use the terms explained above to answer the following questions.

a. On what days of the year are there about the same number of hours of daylight and darkness in the United States?

Answer: _____

b. What season begins with the autumnal equinox?

Answer: _____

c. What season begins with the vernal equinox?

Answer: _____

d. What season begins with the day having the greatest number of hours of darkness?

Answer: _____

e. What season begins with the day having the fewest hours of darkness?

Answer: _____

© 1985 MIDWEST PUBLICATIONS 93950-0448

INTERVALS OF A YEAR—SUPPLY

This chart relating length of daylight to time of year will help you answer the questions below.

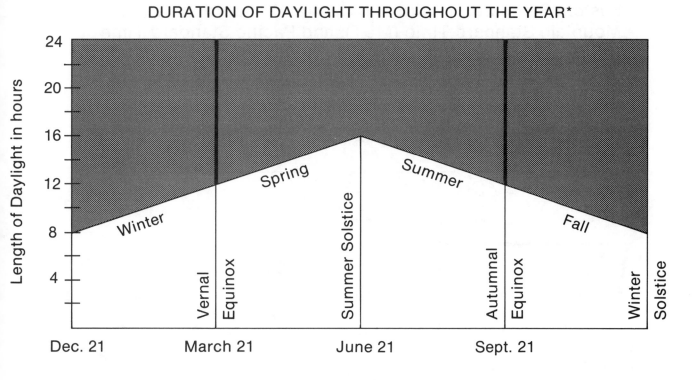

DURATION OF DAYLIGHT THROUGHOUT THE YEAR*

B-468 Give the times and a.m. or p.m. designations that people in your area** associate with the following.

   a. Sunset in December: _____

   b. Sunrise in July: _____

   c. Twilight in March: from _____ to _____

   d. Darkness in October: from _____ to _____

   e. Daylight in January: from _____ to _____

   f. Night in June: from _____ to _____

*An average for the continental United States.
**Your area may be different from the average — consult references.

TIME ZONES

In the continental United States there are four time zones — Eastern Standard Time (EST), Central Standard Time (CST), Mountain Standard Time (MST), and Pacific Standard Time (PST). Each time zone to the west is one hour earlier than its neighbor to the east. Use this time-zone map to answer the following questions.

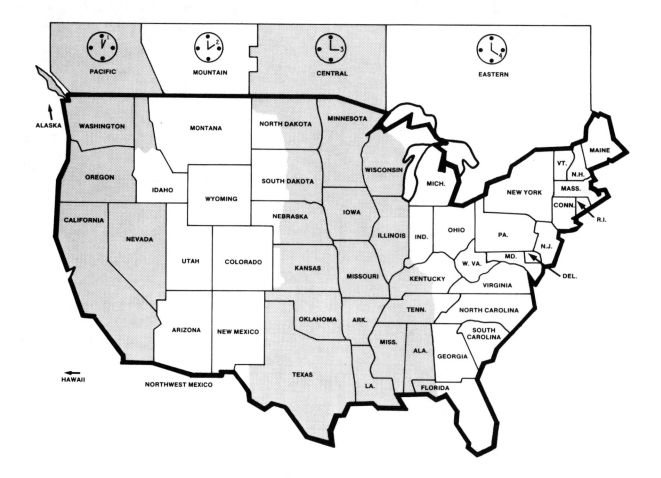

B-469   What time is it in Seattle, Wash., when it is 5:05 p.m. in Philadelphia, Pa.?   Answer: _____

B-470   What time is it in Philadelphia when it is 5:05 p.m. in Seattle? Answer: _____

TIME ZONES

Use the time-zone map on the preceding page to answer the following questions.

B-471 What time is it in Phoenix, Ariz., when it is 12:45 p.m. in Dallas, Tex.? Answer: _____

B-472 What time is it in Dallas when it is 12:45 p.m. in Phoenix? Answer: _____

B-473 What time is it in Detroit, Mich., when it is 9:20 a.m. in Chicago, Ill.? Answer: _____

B-474 What time is it in Chicago when it is 9:20 a.m. in Detroit? Answer: _____

B-475 What time is it in Los Angeles, Calif., when it is 12:15 a.m. in Phoenix? Answer: _____

B-476 What time is it in Phoenix when it is 1:25 p.m. in Miami, Fla.? Answer: _____

B-477 What time is it in Miami when it is 1:25 p.m. in Phoenix? Answer: _____

SEQUENCES

TIME ZONES

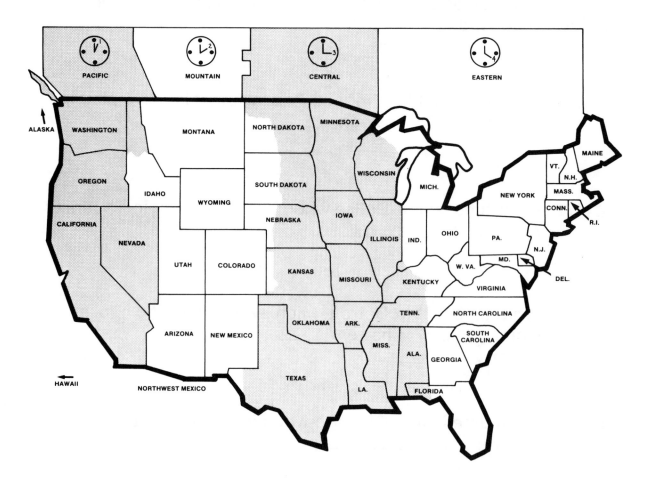

Use the time-zone map to answer the following questions.

B-478　Gina, who lives in Miami, Fla., wants to call her grandmother in Los Angeles, Ca., but she doesn't want to wake her. She knows that her grandmother gets up to 8:00 a.m. What is the earliest time that Gina can place her call?
Answer: _____

B-479　Mrs. Grantham took a non-stop flight from San Francisco, Calif., to Atlanta, Ga. She left San Francisco at 9:15 a.m. PST and arrived in Atlanta at 4:30 p.m. EST. How long did the flight actually take?　Answer: _____

TIME ZONES

Use the time-zone map on the preceding page to answer the following questions.

B-480 Kimberly's mother, an architect in Atlanta, has a contract to design a building in San Antonio, Tex. After her mother's flight left Atlanta, Kimberly discovered one of her mother's blueprints on the dining room table. Her mother has a layover in Houston from 12:43 p.m. to 1:50 p.m. Kimberly remembered that her mother usually waits for flights at the Ionosphere Club. During what time interval might Kimberly contact her mother in Houston about the missing plans?   Answer: _____

B-481 Mr. Horowitz took a non-stop flight from New York to Los Angeles. He left New York at 11:45 a.m. EST and arrived in Los Angeles at 2:35 p.m. PST. How long did the flight last?   Answer: _____

B-482 The time in Hawaii is three hours earlier than Pacific Standard Time. A former senator from Hawaii cited the strain of traveling and the difficulty of keeping in touch with his constituents as a factor in his not seeking reelection. During what hours in Washington, D.C., would he be able to reach business people in his state during their 9:00 a.m. to 5:00 p.m. workday?
Answer: _____

B-483 If a Hawaiian businessperson wanted to call during the Senator's 9-to-5 office hours, when could the call be placed?   Answer: _____

SEQUENCES

SCHEDULES

B-484　Before going to her 11:00 a.m. dance class with Helen last Saturday, Marta met Jenna and then Sandy. Each meeting lasted for one hour. Following a lunch date with Carol, she went to the mall with Shawn. After an hour with Shawn, she worked on her research paper at the library with Catherine. Catherine's brother Fred gave Marta a ride home. On the lines provided, write the person's name next to the time during which they met with Marta.

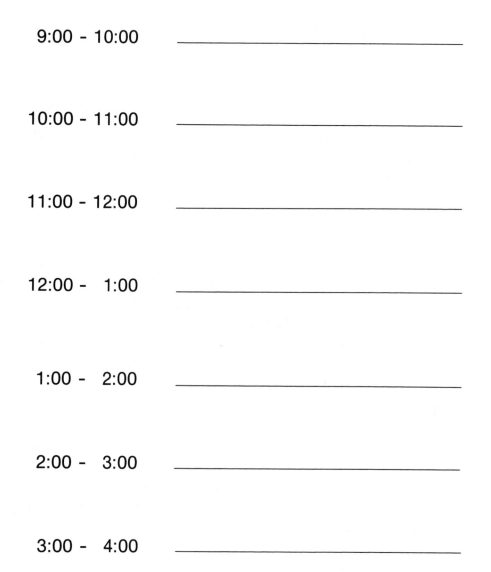

9:00 - 10:00 　　_____

10:00 - 11:00 　　_____

11:00 - 12:00 　　_____

12:00 - 1:00 　　_____

1:00 - 2:00 　　_____

2:00 - 3:00 　　_____

3:00 - 4:00 　　_____

SCHEDULES

B-485 Tina has chores to do after school lets out at 3:30. Tina's mom likes to eat supper from 6:00 to 6:30. Tina's young brother must be ready for bed by 7:30. Her jobs, and the time each requires, are listed below. On the schedule that follows, arrange these jobs in the order you would complete them.

30 minutes - to help her brother get ready for bed

30 minutes - to clean bedroom

30 minutes - to fold and put away clothes

30 minutes - to pick up her brother at the day-care center

30 minutes - to eat supper

  1 hour - to do homework

  1 hour - to prepare supper

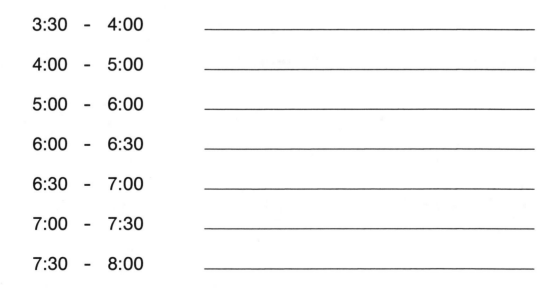

3:30 - 4:00 _____

4:00 - 5:00 _____

5:00 - 6:00 _____

6:00 - 6:30 _____

6:30 - 7:00 _____

7:00 - 7:30 _____

7:30 - 8:00 _____

SCHEDULES

B-486 Two movers, Gordon and Tad, want to unload their truck. Some of the jobs require that they work together; some do not. After reading the following requirements and list of things to be moved, write a schedule for unloading the truck.

REQUIREMENTS

1. Gordon and Tad have two hours to complete the unloading.
2. They can do one-person jobs at the same time.
3. The workbench is too heavy to move when it is full of tools.
4. The workbench must be filled with tools before they leave.
5. The lathe must be moved in before the workbench.
6. The garage must be swept before the heavy shop equipment is moved.

ONE-PERSON JOBS	TIME	TWO-PERSON JOBS	TIME
carry in paint cans	10 min.	move workbench	20 min.
carry in lumber	20 min.	move drill press	10 min.
carry in tools	20 min.	move lathe	20 min.
put paint cans on shelves	20 min.		
sweep garage	30 min.		
fill workbench with tools	40 min.		

Gordon's Jobs   **Two-Person Jobs**   **Tad's Jobs**

SCHEDULES

B-487   The Kim family is visiting Fun World. They are inside the grounds at 9:00 a.m. and leave the last amusement at 2:15 p.m. They want to hear a 45-minute rock concert at 10:00 a.m. and a jazz band play for half an hour at 1:45 p.m. The Kim children want to go on the roller coaster three times and the ferris wheel twice. There is a 20-minute wait for the roller coaster and a 15-minute wait for the ferris wheel. The children also want to spend two 45-minute sessions in the arcade. Lunch takes an hour.

Write a schedule that will permit these activities. Assume there is no waiting for the concerts and that the family is in line at an amusement at 9:00 a.m. The ride waiting time includes riding time.

Time	Activity
9:00 - 9:15	
9:15 - 9:30	
9:30 - 9:45	
9:45 - 10:00	
10:00 - 10:15	
10:15 - 10:30	
10:30 - 10:45	
10:45 - 11:00	
11:00 - 11:15	
11:15 - 11:30	
11:30 - 11:45	
11:45 - 12:00	
12:00 - 1:00	Lunch
1:00 - 1:15	
1:15 - 1:30	
1:30 - 1:45	
1:45 - 2:00	
2:00 - 2:15	
2:15	Leave for the parking lot

SEQUENCES

SCHEDULES

B-488 Phoebe must arrange her class schedule. She must take all the following courses each week but has a choice of the times of day she can take them. Write a weekly class schedule for Phoebe.

4 hours of science offered Tues. & Thurs. from 10-12 or 1-3

5 hours of math offered daily at 9 or 1

3 hours of computer offered Mon., Wed., & Fri. at 10 or 1

5 hours of language arts offered daily at 8 or 1

5 hours of lunch offered daily at 11 , 12, or 1

4 hours of social studies offered daily except Fridays at 11 or 2

3 hours of gym offered Mon., Wed., & Fri. at 8, 9, 10, 1, or 2

1 hour as audio visual assistant or library helper

2 hours of art offered Mon. & Wed. at 11 or 2

2 hours of music offered Tues. & Thurs. at 8, 9, 10, 1, or 2

1 hour of typing offered Fridays only at 11 or 2

	Monday	Tuesday	Wednesday	Thursday	Friday
8-9					
9-10					
10-11					
11-12					
12-1					
1-2					
2-3					

SCHEDULES

B-489   Mrs. Asher's mother has a severe cold and a respiratory infection. The doctor has prescribed several medicines and given other instructions to be followed. Mrs. Asher needs a treatment schedule to help her keep track of her nursing duties.

Use the doctor's instructions below to produce a treatment schedule.

Drink lots of fluids, at least 8 oz. every two hours.

Take the decongestant every eight hours.

Take an aspirin every four hours, but avoid taking aspirin on an empty stomach.

Take the antibiotic three times a day, just before meals.

Refill the vaporizer every four hours.

SEQUENCES

TIME	FLUIDS	DECONG.	ASPIRIN	ANTIBIOTIC	VAPORIZER
6:00 a.m.					
8:00 a.m.					
10:00 a.m.					
12:00 noon					
2:00 p.m.					
4:00 p.m.					
6:00 p.m.					
8:00 p.m.					
10:00 p.m.					
12:00 midnight					

SCHEDULES

B-490   Juan Santillo is manager of a fast-food restaurant. The restaurant is open seven days a week, and he must schedule his workers for a week in advance. Prepare a schedule for the workers from 8:00 a.m. to 4:00 p.m. following these guidelines:

1. Some workers are scheduled only in the morning and others only in the afternoon.

2. Work shifts are either four or eight hours long.

3. Two people are needed each hour on weekdays, and three people each hour on the weekends.

Beside each employee's name, list the day(s) he or she works and the total number of hours worked per week.

	Days	Total Hours
Anita (weekdays only)	_____	_____
Cheryl	_____	_____
Dino (weekends only)	_____	_____
Josh	_____	_____
Kim (afternoons only)	_____	_____
Leslie	_____	_____
Monroe	_____	_____
Pam (mornings only)	_____	_____

	Sunday	Monday	Tuesday	Wednesday	Thursday	Friday	Saturday
A.M.							
P.M.							

SCHEDULES—TOURNAMENTS

B-491　Eight schools are participating in a holiday basketball tournament. The pairings for the first round of games are shown. Use the following clues to determine the tournament results.

1. Washington H.S. and Roberto Clemente H.S. win no games.

2. Only South H.S. wins a total of two games.

3. Susan B. Anthony H.S. wins the championship.

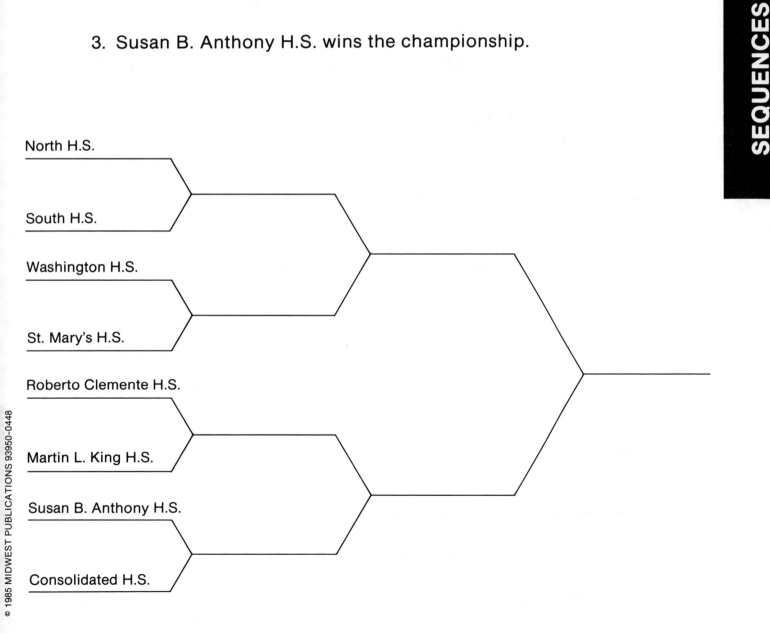

SCHEDULES—TOURNAMENTS

B-492   Use these clues to determine the winners in a girls' tennis tournament in which 16 girls compete. The tournament chart to be completed is on the next page.

1. Laura won three games.

2. No girl having a name containing four letters won any match.

3. The girl with the longest name won two matches.

4. Donna played Laura in the final game of the tournament.

5. Grace defeated Flora in the second round of matches.

B-493 a. List the girls that won the following number of matches:

Won No Matches		Won 1 Match	Won 2 Matches	Won 3 Matches
_____	_____	_____	_____	_____
_____	_____	_____	_____	
_____	_____	_____		
_____	_____	_____		

b. Which girl was not listed?   _____

c. Why? _____

SCHEDULES—CHART FOR EXERCISE B-492

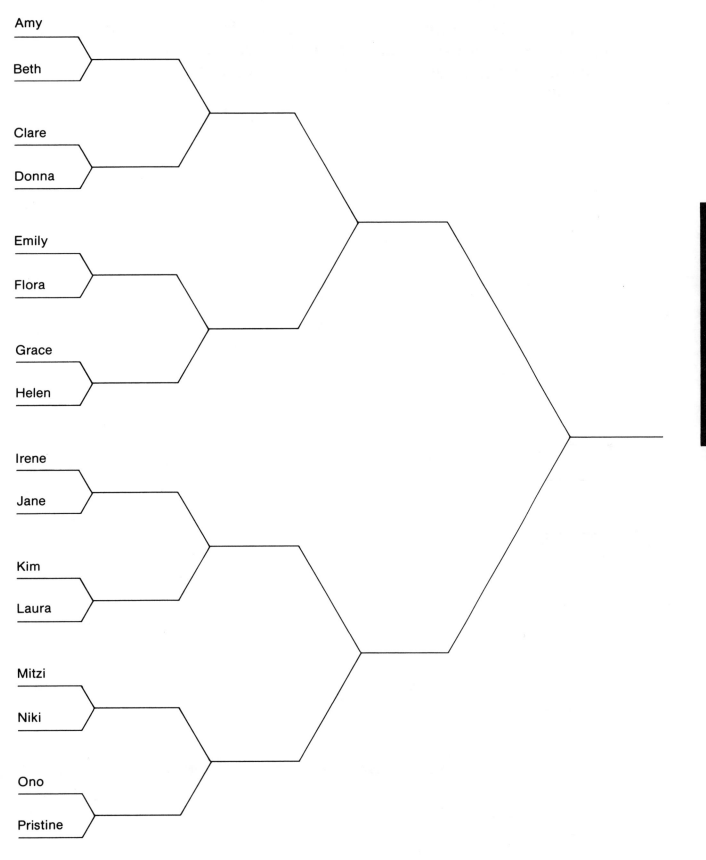

SEQUENCES

SCHEDULES—TOURNAMENTS

B-494   Here is another tournament pairing form. Construct a problem like Exercise B-492. Trade your problem with a classmate and then use this form to solve your classmate's challenge.

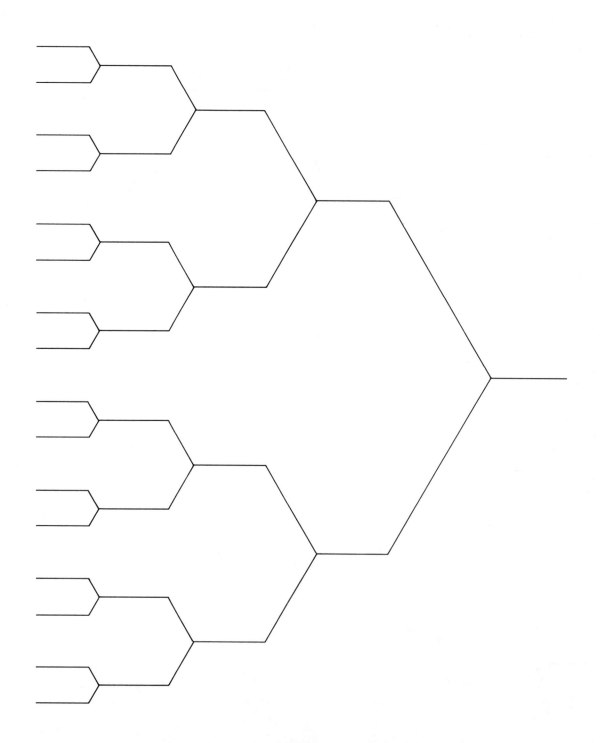

PARTS OF A WHOLE—SELECT

Read the four words listed for each exercise and decide which **one** represents a whole thing, as opposed to parts of the whole (represented by the other three words). Write the word that represents the whole on the line provided, then list the words that make up its parts.

EXAMPLE: closing, greeting, letter, signature

WHOLE __letter__ PARTS __greeting__, __closing__, __signature__

The words represent parts of a letter that you might write to a friend. So the WHOLE is the "letter"; and the PARTS are the "greeting," the "closing," and the "signature."

C-1   equator, globe, latitude, longitude

WHOLE _____ PARTS _____, _____, _____

C-2   brow, cheek, chin, face

WHOLE _____ PARTS _____, _____, _____

C-3   claw, hammer, handle, head

WHOLE _____ PARTS _____, _____, _____

C-4   expressway, median, ramp, shoulder

WHOLE _____ PARTS _____, _____, _____

CLASSIFICATIONS

PARTS OF A WHOLE—SELECT

Read the four words listed for each exercise and decide which **one** represents a whole thing, as opposed to parts of the whole (represented by the other three words). Write the word that represents the whole on the line provided, then list the words that make up its parts.

C-5   hem, jacket, lapel, seam

WHOLE _____ PARTS _____, _____, _____

C-6   cuff, inseam, pants, waist-band

WHOLE _____ PARTS _____, _____, _____

C-7   core, fruit, peel, pulp

WHOLE _____ PARTS _____, _____, _____

C-8   heel, shank, shoe, sole

WHOLE _____ PARTS _____, _____, _____

C-9   bicycle, chain, fork, frame

WHOLE _____ PARTS _____, _____, _____

C-10   clasp, coil, safety pin, shafts

WHOLE _____ PARTS _____, _____, _____

PARTS OF A WHOLE—SELECT

Read the four words listed for each exercise and decide which **one** represents a whole thing, as opposed to parts of the whole (represented by the other three words). Write the word that represents the whole on the line provided, then list the words that make up its parts.

C-11 barrel, cartridge, pen, point

WHOLE _____ PARTS _____, _____, _____

C-12 carriage, keyboard, ribbon, typewriter

WHOLE _____ PARTS _____, _____, _____

C-13 body, camera, film, lens

WHOLE _____ PARTS _____, _____, _____

C-14 book, margin, spine, text

WHOLE _____ PARTS _____, _____, _____

C-15 hammer, keys, piano, strings

WHOLE _____ PARTS _____, _____, _____

C-16 hub, rim, spoke, wheel

WHOLE _____ PARTS _____, _____, _____

CLASSIFICATIONS

PARTS OF A WHOLE—SELECT

Read the four words listed for each exercise and decide which **one** represents a whole thing, as opposed to parts of the whole (represented by the other three words). Write the word that represents the whole on the line provided, then list the words that make up its parts.

C-17   bowl, drain, sink, spigot

WHOLE _____ PARTS _____, _____, _____

C-18   burner, broiler, oven, stove

WHOLE _____ PARTS _____, _____, _____

C-19   bone, fat, steak, tissue

WHOLE _____ PARTS _____, _____, _____

C-20   celery, leaf, stalk, stem

WHOLE _____ PARTS _____, _____, _____

C-21   ice cream, sauce, sundae, topping

WHOLE _____ PARTS _____, _____, _____

C-22   bottle, lip, neck, shoulder

WHOLE _____ PARTS _____, _____, _____

C-23   bed, frame, mattress, spring

WHOLE _____ PARTS _____, _____, _____

© 1985 MIDWEST PUBLICATIONS 93950-0448

PARTS OF A WHOLE—SELECT

Read the four words listed for each exercise and decide which **one** represents a whole thing, as opposed to parts of the whole (represented by the other three words). Write the word that represents the whole on the line provided, then list the words that make up its parts.

C-24   band, case, face, watch

WHOLE _____ PARTS _____, _____, _____

C-25   tab, tape, zipper, teeth

WHOLE _____ PARTS _____, _____, _____

C-26   eyeglasses, frame, hinge, lens

WHOLE _____ PARTS _____, _____, _____

C-27   panel, rib, shaft, umbrella

WHOLE _____ PARTS _____, _____, _____

C-28   pulley, blind, slat, tape

WHOLE _____ PARTS _____, _____, _____

C-29   hem, pull, roller, shade

WHOLE _____ PARTS _____, _____, _____

C-30   base, cap, spring, stapler

WHOLE _____ PARTS _____, _____, _____

CLASSIFICATIONS

CLASS AND MEMBERS—SELECT

Read the four words listed for each exercise and decide which **one** represents the class to which the other words belong. Write the word that represents the class on the line provided, then list the words that are members of that class.

EXAMPLE: cupcake, dessert, pie, sundae

CLASS <u>dessert</u> MEMBERS <u>cupcake</u>, <u>pie</u>, <u>sundae</u>

C-31   gauges, indicators, meters, registers

CLASS _____ MEMBERS _____, _____, _____

C-32   folds, gathers, pleats, tucks

CLASS _____ MEMBERS _____, _____, _____

C-33   appliances, blenders, juicers, processors

CLASS _____ MEMBERS _____, _____, _____

C-34   bangs, braids, flips, styles

CLASS _____ MEMBERS _____, _____, _____

C-35   agreements, contracts, pacts, treaties

CLASS _____ MEMBERS _____, _____, _____

© 1985 MIDWEST PUBLICATIONS 93950-0448

CLASS AND MEMBERS—SELECT

Read the four words listed for each exercise and decide which **one** represents the class to which the other words belong. Write the word that represents the class on the line provided, then list the words that are members of that class.

C-36 collection, craft, game, hobby

CLASS _____ MEMBERS _____, _____, _____

C-37 culture, custom, language, religion

CLASS _____ MEMBERS _____, _____, _____

C-38 bacteria, decomposer, mold, yeast

CLASS _____ MEMBERS _____, _____, _____

C-39 debt, I.O.U., lien, mortgage

CLASS _____ MEMBERS _____, _____, _____

C-40 distance, inch, foot, mile

CLASS _____ MEMBERS _____, _____, _____

C-41 gallon, pint, quart, volume

CLASS _____ MEMBERS _____, _____, _____

C-42 tote bag, handbag, luggage, suitcase

CLASS _____ MEMBERS _____, _____, _____

CLASSIFICATIONS

CLASS AND MEMBERS—SELECT

Read the four words listed for each exercise and decide which **one** represents the class to which the other words belong. Write the word that represents the class on the line provided, then list the words that are members of that class.

C-43   monument, statue, tomb, tower

CLASS _____ MEMBERS _____, _____, _____

C-44   barge, ferry, freighter, vessel

CLASS _____ MEMBERS _____, _____, _____

C-45   abbreviation, flag, symbol, trademark

CLASS _____ MEMBERS _____, _____, _____

C-46   ounce, pound, ton, unit

CLASS _____ MEMBERS _____, _____, _____

C-47   business, manufacturing, sales, service

CLASS _____ MEMBERS _____, _____, _____

C-48   almanac, atlas, directory, reference book

CLASS _____ MEMBERS _____, _____, _____

C-49   agent, clerk, employee, secretary

CLASS _____ MEMBERS _____, _____, _____

SENTENCES CONTAINING CLASSES
AND SUBCLASSES—SELECT

In each sentence below there are three words that name members of a class. Underline these three words. On the lines beside each sentence write the words in order from the most general class to the most specific class. The general class (1) will contain the subclass (2) and the specific class (3). Write the most general class on line 1, the subclass on line 2, and the most specific class on line 3.

EXAMPLE: The orange is a popular citrus fruit.   1. <u>fruit</u>
"Fruit" is the most general class and   2. <u>citrus</u>
belongs on line 1. "Citrus" is a kind   3. <u>orange</u>
of fruit and belongs on line 2.
"Orange" is a kind of citrus fruit
and belongs on line 3.

C-50   We saw the flares across the road, a   1. _____
warning signal that the bridge was   2. _____
washed out.   3. _____

C-51   The weather report indicated that   1. _____
we could expect precipitation in   2. _____
the form of hail.   3. _____

C-52   The third chapter in the grammar   1. _____
book, the one on punctuation,   2. _____
includes lists of rules on the use   3. _____
of commas.

C-53   The Florida panther is a wildcat   1. _____
protected by endangered species   2. _____
laws.   3. _____

CLASSIFICATIONS

SENTENCES CONTAINING CLASSES
AND SUBCLASSES—SELECT

In each sentence below there are three words that name members of a class. Underline these three words. On the lines beside each sentence write the words in order from the most general class (on line 1) to the most specific class (on line 3).

C-54   Although Russell usually does well in mathematics, he has a hard time with quadratic equations in algebra.

1. _____
2. _____
3. _____

C-55   The marketing department, which plans advertising for the company, decided to use television commercials to sell the new products.

1. _____
2. _____
3. _____

C-56   As an investment, Ms. Hamilton bought ten shares of stock.

1. _____
2. _____
3. _____

C-57   Despite an ordinance prohibiting drink containers, including bottles, on the beach, someone left a broken flask partly buried in the sand.

1. _____
2. _____
3. _____

C-58   Quiche is a custard pie, which is often made with cheese and vegetables.

1. _____
2. _____
3. _____

C-59   Shawn went to the crafts section of the library to look for a book on tie-dying, a form of textile design using knots and string to make patterns.

1. _____
2. _____
3. _____

GENERAL TO SPECIFIC—RANK

Rank each group of words below from the most general class to the most specific class.

EXAMPLE:

dog, canine, terrier

<u>   canine   </u>   ⟶   <u>   dog   </u>   ⟶   <u>   terrier   </u>
(general class)   (subclass)   (specific class)

C-60   footwear, shoe, sneaker

————————— ⟶ ————————— ⟶ —————————

C-61   coin, currency, peso

————————— ⟶ ————————— ⟶ —————————

C-62   almond, nut, seed

————————— ⟶ ————————— ⟶ —————————

C-63   beverage, fluid, tea

————————— ⟶ ————————— ⟶ —————————

C-64   communication, media, television

————————— ⟶ ————————— ⟶ —————————

C-65   automobile, taxi, transportation

————————— ⟶ ————————— ⟶ —————————

C-66   groceries, produce, vegetables

————————— ⟶ ————————— ⟶ —————————

CLASSIFICATIONS

GENERAL TO SPECIFIC—RANK

Rank each group of words below from the most general class to the most specific class.

C-67   laws, ordinances, rules

_____ ⟶ _____ ⟶ _____

C-68   harmony, music, sound

_____ ⟶ _____ ⟶ _____

C-69   cabinet, furniture, storage

_____ ⟶ _____ ⟶ _____

C-70   cards, games, hobbies

_____ ⟶ _____ ⟶ _____

C-71   chemical, cleaner, detergent

_____ ⟶ _____ ⟶ _____

C-72   Asian, Korean, Oriental

_____ ⟶ _____ ⟶ _____

C-73   parallelogram, polygon, quadrilateral, rectangle, square

_____ ⟶ _____ ⟶ _____ ⟶

_____ ⟶ _____

DISTINGUISHING RELATIONSHIPS

Each word group below contains one of the following relationships:

P/W - parts of a whole
　EXAMPLE: animal,　　head,　　trunk,　　foot
　　　　　　　(whole)　　(part)　　(part)　　(part)

C/S - a general class and several subclasses
　EXAMPLE: animal,　　protist,　　invertebrate,　vertebrate
　　　　　　　(class)　(subclass)　(subclass)　(subclass)

G/Sp - a general class, a subclass, a more specific subclass of
　the previous subclass, and an even more specific subclass
　of that subclass

　EXAMPLE: animal, →vertebrate, → mammal, → dog
　　　　　　(class)　(subclass 1)　(more specific　(most specific
　　　　　　　　　　　　　　　　　　subclass)　　subclass)

The arrows help show that vertebrates are a subclass of
the class animals, mammals are a subclass of the class
vertebrates, and dogs are a subclass of the class
mammals.

Mark each group of words **P/W**, **C/S**, or **G/Sp** to describe the
relationship. Write and label each word as shown in the
examples. For general-to-specific classes, list from the most
general class to the most specific subclass and insert arrows.

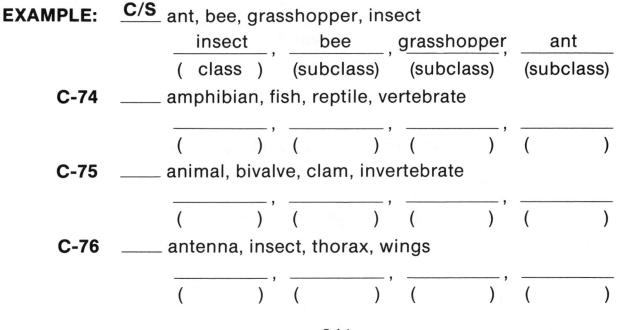

EXAMPLE:　__C/S__ ant, bee, grasshopper, insect

　__insect__ , __bee__ , __grasshopper__ , __ant__
　(class) (subclass) (subclass) (subclass)

C-74 ____ amphibian, fish, reptile, vertebrate

　_____ , _____ , _____ , _____
　(　　) (　　　) (　　　) (　　　)

C-75 ____ animal, bivalve, clam, invertebrate

　_____ , _____ , _____ , _____
　(　　　) (　　　) (　　　) (　　　)

C-76 ____ antenna, insect, thorax, wings

　_____ , _____ , _____ , _____
　(　　　) (　　　) (　　　) (　　　)

DISTINGUISHING RELATIONSHIPS

Mark each group of words **P/W**, **C/S**, or **G/Sp** to describe the relationship. Write and label each word as shown in the examples on page 241. For general-to-specific classes, list from the most general class to the most specific subclass and insert arrows.

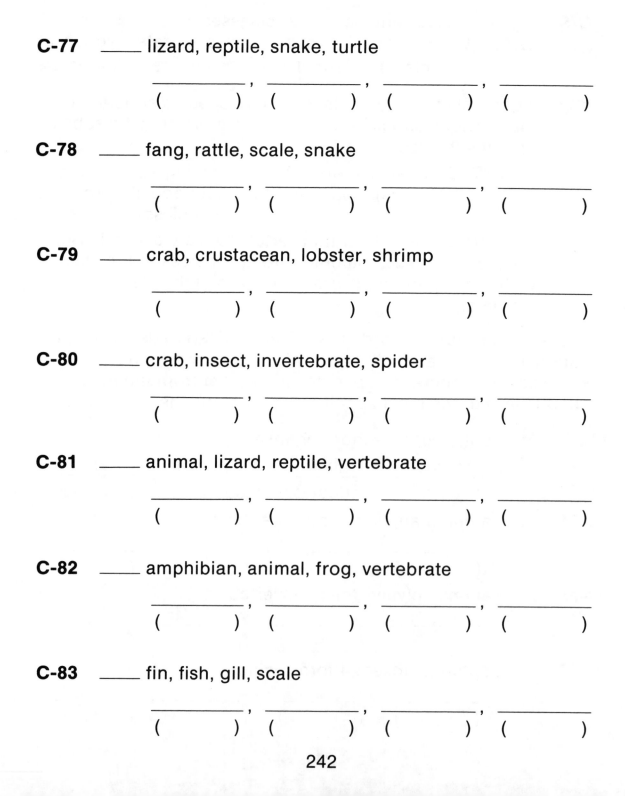

C-77 _____ lizard, reptile, snake, turtle

_____ , _____ , _____ , _____
(   )   (   )   (   )   (   )

C-78 _____ fang, rattle, scale, snake

_____ , _____ , _____ , _____
(   )   (   )   (   )   (   )

C-79 _____ crab, crustacean, lobster, shrimp

_____ , _____ , _____ , _____
(   )   (   )   (   )   (   )

C-80 _____ crab, insect, invertebrate, spider

_____ , _____ , _____ , _____
(   )   (   )   (   )   (   )

C-81 _____ animal, lizard, reptile, vertebrate

_____ , _____ , _____ , _____
(   )   (   )   (   )   (   )

C-82 _____ amphibian, animal, frog, vertebrate

_____ , _____ , _____ , _____
(   )   (   )   (   )   (   )

C-83 _____ fin, fish, gill, scale

_____ , _____ , _____ , _____
(   )   (   )   (   )   (   )

DISTINGUISHING RELATIONSHIPS

Mark each group of words **P/W**, **C/S**, or **G/Sp** to describe the relationship. Write and label each word as shown in the examples on page 241. For general-to-specific classes, list from the most general class to the most specific subclass and insert arrows.

C-84 _____ predicate, punctuation, sentence, subject

_____ , _____ , _____ , _____
(   )   (   )   (   )   (   )

C-85 _____ communication, discussion, media, writing

_____ , _____ , _____ , _____
(   )   (   )   (   )   (   )

C-86 _____ communication, debate, discussion, speaking

_____ , _____ , _____ , _____
(   )   (   )   (   )   (   )

C-87 _____ humor, irony, pun, satire

_____ , _____ , _____ , _____
(   )   (   )   (   )   (   )

C-88 _____ images, poetry, rhyme, rhythm

_____ , _____ , _____ , _____
(   )   (   )   (   )   (   )

C-89 _____ communication, dialect, language, speech

_____ , _____ , _____ , _____
(   )   (   )   (   )   (   )

CLASSIFICATIONS

DISTINGUISHING RELATIONSHIPS

Mark each group of words **P/W**, **C/S**, or **G/Sp** to describe the relationship. Write and label each word as shown in the examples on page 241. For general-to-specific classes, list from the most general class to the most specific subclass and insert arrows.

C-90 _____ exclamation, question, sentence, statement

_____ , _____ , _____ , _____
(   )   (   )   (   )   (   )

C-91 _____ fiction, mystery, narrative, novel

_____ , _____ , _____ , _____
(   )   (   )   (   )   (   )

C-92 _____ fable, lesson, parable, sermon

_____ , _____ , _____ , _____
(   )   (   )   (   )   (   )

C-93 _____ body, heading, letter, signature

_____ , _____ , _____ , _____
(   )   (   )   (   )   (   )

C-94 _____ fantasy, fiction, mystery, romance

_____ , _____ , _____ , _____
(   )   (   )   (   )   (   )

C-95 _____ autobiography, diary, letter, journal

_____ , _____ , _____ , _____
(   )   (   )   (   )   (   )

HOW ARE THESE WORDS ALIKE—SELECT

Circle the letter in front of the answer that **best** describes each class of words.

C-96   checked, plaid, striped

a. fabric
b. lined pattern
c. thread

C-97   whisk, beater, blender

a. appliance
b. mixing device
c. spoon

C-98   crane, hoist, pulley

a. lifting device
b. motor
c. weighing device

C-99   beard, mustache, whiskers

a. facial hair
b. strand
c. style

C-100   dial, selector, switch

a. channel
b. control device
c. frequency

C-101   client, customer, subscriber

a. advertiser
b. consumer of goods
   or services
c. merchant

CLASSIFICATIONS

HOW ARE THESE WORDS ALIKE?—SELECT

Circle the letter in front of the answer that **best** describes each class of words.

C-102　branch, fork, tributary

  a. bank of a river
  b. current of a river
  c. stream flowing into a river

C-103　cataract, rapid, waterfall

  a. direction of a river
  b. landform at the mouth of a river
  c. turbulence or fast-water motion in a river

C-104　bayou, marsh, swamp

  a. branch of a river
  b. channel in a river
  c. wetland of a river

C-105　bed, channel, levee

  a. bank of a river
  b. flow of a river
  c. part of a river

C-106　canyon, gorge, valley

  a. delta of a river
  b. flood plain of a river
  c. landform cut by a river

C-107　bay, inlet, lagoon

  a. gulf
  b. body of water partially surrounded by land
  c. spawning ground for fish

HOW ARE THESE WORDS ALIKE?—SELECT

Circle the letter in front of the answer that **best** describes each class of words.

C-108 coil, curl, spiral

    a. angle
    b. circle
    c. inward curve

C-109 arch, dome, vault

    a. curved line
    b. curved part of
       a building
    c. curved road

C-110 crescent, crook, hook

    a. curved object
    b. radius of a circle
    c. wave

C-111 arc, bend, bow

    a. angle
    b. curve
    c. sphere

C-112 crimp, dent, wrinkle

    a. irregular bend
    b. maze
    c. spiral

C-113 bulb, drop, oval

    a. coil
    b. rounded shape
    c. spire

CLASSIFICATIONS

HOW ARE THESE WORDS ALIKE?—SELECT

Each group of words below belongs to one of the classes given in the Choice Box. Select the class that **best** fits each group. The words in the Choice Box may be used more than once.

CHOICE BOX
first, follow, like, lift, soft

C-114 encourage, comfort, help _____

C-115 chase, go after, trail _____

C-116 admire, enjoy, prefer _____

C-117 foremost, initial, leading _____

C-118 low key, subdued, toned down _____

C-119 search, trace, track _____

C-120 champion, chief, head _____

C-121 gentle, mild, smooth _____

C-122 hoist, pick up, raise _____

C-123 original, pioneer, primary _____

C-124 cottony, silky, velvety _____

C-125 equal, same, similar _____

HOW ARE THESE WORDS ALIKE?—SELECT

Each group of words below belongs to one of the classes given in the Choice Box. Select the class that **best** fits each group. The words in the Choice Box may be used more than once.

CHOICE BOX
common, complete, rare

C-126   entire, total, whole _____

C-127   choice, elegant, superior _____

C-128   general, popular, universal _____

C-129   execute, fulfill, perform _____

C-130   normal, ordinary, regular _____

C-131   absolute, positive, utter _____

C-132   infrequent, occasional, seldom _____

C-133   attained, concluded, finished _____

C-134   customary, frequent, routine _____

C-135   joint, public, shared _____

C-136   exact, perfect, strict _____

C-137   exceptional, extraordinary, unique _____

C-138   cheap, inferior, second-rate _____

CLASSIFICATIONS

HOW ARE THESE WORDS ALIKE?—SELECT

Each group of words below belongs to one of the classes given in the Choice Box. Select the class that **best** fits each group. The words in the Choice Box may be used more than once.

```
┌─────────────────────────────┐
│         CHOICE BOX          │
├─────────────────────────────┤
│                             │
│      plan, result, start    │
│                             │
└─────────────────────────────┘
```

C-139 conclusion, decision, judgment _____

C-140 commence, generate, produce _____

C-141 intent, scheme, strategy _____

C-142 establish, found, launch _____

C-143 answer, outcome, solution _____

C-144 blueprint, design, project _____

C-145 assessment, calculation, computation _____

C-146 origin, root, source _____

C-147 method, purpose, way _____

C-148 draft, outline, sketch _____

C-149 consequence, effect, product _____

C-150 arrange, cast, devise _____

C-151 birth, creation, outset _____

C-152 chart, figure, outline _____

C-153 decision, determination, settlement _____

C-154 aim, intend, propose _____

C-155 introduction, preface, prologue _____

HOW ARE THESE WORDS ALIKE?—SELECT

Each group of words below belongs to one of the classes given in the Choice Box. Select the class that **best** fits each group. The words in the Choice Box may be used more than once.

CHOICE BOX

---

direct, heavy, open, track

C-156 bulky, hefty, weighty _____

C-157 imprint, mark, tread _____

C-158 aim, cast, point _____

C-159 ajar, clear, unlocked _____

C-160 trail, path, walkway _____

C-161 begin, launch, start _____

C-162 fat, overweight, stout _____

C-163 chase, follow, hunt _____

C-164 conduct, escort, guide _____

C-165 bare, exposed, uncovered _____

C-166 control, handle, manage _____

C-167 available, obtainable, public _____

C-168 grave, serious, severe _____

C-169 command, instruct, order _____

HOW ARE THESE WORDS ALIKE?—SELECT

Each group of words below belongs to one of the classes given in the Choice Box. Select the class that **best** fits each group. The words in the Choice Box may be used more than once.

CHOICE BOX
control, observe, strain, relieve

C-170 collect, contain, restrain _____

C-171 comfort, ease, soothe _____

C-172 extend, lengthen, stretch _____

C-173 conform, follow, obey _____

C-174 direct, handle, manage _____

C-175 replace, substitute, take over _____

C-176 injure, pull, overuse _____

C-177 behold, notice, perceive _____

C-178 labor, toil, work _____

C-179 excuse, exempt, spare _____

C-180 seep, sieve, sift _____

C-181 celebrate, commemorate, keep _____

C-182 pressure, stress, tension _____

C-183 comment, explain, remark _____

HOW ARE THESE WORDS ALIKE?—EXPLAIN

Each group of words below has something in common. On the line provided, explain how the words in each class are related.

EXAMPLE:

   newspaper, radio, television

   _____All bring the news._____

C-184 apparent, clear, obvious

_____

C-185 ramble, range, roam

_____

C-186 cast, critic, performance

_____

C-187 estate, manor, mansion

_____

C-188 modest, shy, timid

_____

C-189 fast, quick, swift

_____

C-190 force, might, vigor

_____

© 1985 MIDWEST PUBLICATIONS 93950-0448

CLASSIFICATIONS

HOW ARE THESE WORDS ALIKE?—EXPLAIN

Each group of words below has something in common. On the line provided, explain how the words in each class are related.

C-191 sled, sleigh, toboggan

_____

C-192 aquarium, wildlife park, zoo

_____

C-193 cable, lift, tram

_____

C-194 memory, program, terminal

_____

C-195 check, credit card, money order

_____

C-196 assume, expect, presume

_____

C-197 scorching, sweltering, tropical

_____

C-198 classical, jazz, rock

_____

HOW ARE THESE WORDS ALIKE?—EXPLAIN

Each group of words below has something in common. On the line provided, explain how the words in each class are related.

C-199 bright, keen, smart

_____

C-200 forecast, foretell, prophesy

_____

C-201 cash, funds, wealth

_____

C-202 apricot, peach, tangerine

_____

C-203 enormous, huge, vast

_____

C-204 billfold, purse, wallet

_____

C-205 likely, predictable, probable

_____

C-206 expand, extend, increase

_____

CLASSIFICATIONS

HOW ARE THESE WORDS ALIKE?—EXPLAIN

The following groups of words describe colors. Write the color or variation in color that each group has in common.

C-207 cherry, crimson, rose　　　　_____

C-208 brunette, chocolate, mahogany　　_____

C-209 charcoal, leaden, steel　　　　_____

C-210 amber, golden, lemon　　　　_____

C-211 ebony, pitch, jet　　　　　　_____

C-212 cardinal, crimson, scarlet　　_____

C-213 coral, peach, salmon　　　　_____

C-214 chalky, milky, snowy　　　　_____

C-215 ashen, pearly, smoky　　　　_____

C-216 auburn, cinnamon, rust　　　_____

C-217 indigo, royal, sapphire　　　_____

C-218 cream, eggshell, ivory　　　_____

C-219 burgundy, maroon, wine　　　_____

C-220 emerald, kelly, olive　　　　_____

C-221 aquamarine, teal, turquoise　_____

C-222 coal, ink, soot　　　　　　_____

© 1985 MIDWEST PUBLICATIONS 93950-0448

EXPLAIN THE EXCEPTION

The following groups of words contain one member that is an exception to the class. Explain how the similar words are alike and how the exception is different.

EXAMPLE:

area, measurement, perimeter, volume

Measurement is the exception. The other words

represent things that can be measured. Measurement is

the act of determining length, weight, volume, or time.

C-223 factors, multiplication, product, quotient

_____

_____

_____

C-224 climate, continent, temperature, weather

_____

_____

_____

C-225 character, force, might, strength

_____

_____

_____

C-226 order, sequence, ranking, value

_____

_____

_____

CLASSIFICATIONS

EXPLAIN THE EXCEPTION

The following groups of words contain one member that is an exception to the class. Explain how the similar words are alike and how the exception is different.

C-227 buzzard, eagle, hawk, turkey

_____

_____

_____

C-228 elevate, incline, slant, tilt

_____

_____

_____

C-229 canyon, ditch, gully, tunnel

_____

_____

_____

C-230 brow, lashes, lid, pupil

_____

_____

_____

C-231 continent, island, peninsula, ocean

_____

_____

_____

EXPLAIN THE EXCEPTION

The following groups of words contain one member that is an exception to the class. Explain how the similar words are alike and how the exception is different.

C-232 averaging, calculating, estimating, rounding

_____

_____

_____

C-233 alligator, frog, lizard, turtle

_____

_____

_____

C-234 depression, population, poverty, unemployment

_____

_____

_____

C-235 gallon, liter, pint, quart

_____

_____

_____

C-236 decide, inquire, question, research

_____

_____

_____

CLASSIFICATIONS

EXPLAIN THE EXCEPTION

The following groups of words contain one member that is an exception to the class. Explain how the similar words are alike and how the exception is different.

C-237 egg, pollen, seed, spore

_____

_____

_____

C-238 acute, parallel, obtuse, right

_____

_____

_____

C-239 intense, pastel, rich, vivid

_____

_____

_____

C-240 colon, comma, dash, period

_____

_____

_____

C-241 bus, monorail, subway, train

_____

_____

_____

SORTING INTO CLASSES

C-242   Sort the following words into the categories of PEOPLE, PLACES, and THINGS.

CHOICE BOX		
clinic, consultation, contract, contractor, curator, engineer, equipment, governor, instrument, investment, lecture, license, mechanic, mountains, museum, passenger, planet, reporter, secretary, software, telescope, teller, textbook, theater		
PEOPLE	**PLACES**	**THINGS**

CLASSIFICATIONS

SORTING INTO CLASSES

C-243 Sort the following food preparation terms into the categories of COOKING, CUTTING, FLAVORING, and MIXING.

CHOICE BOX			
beat, blend, boil, broil, chop, combine, dice, fold, grate, grill, grind, pickle, poach, roast, season, shred, simmer, slice, steam, sweeten, whip			
COOKING	**CUTTING**	**FLAVORING**	**MIXING**

SORTING INTO CLASSES

C-244   Sort the following animals according to what they eat. HERBIVORES eat only plants. CARNIVORES eat other animals. OMNIVORES eat plants or animals.

CHOICE BOX		
bears, butterflies, cattle, chickens, coyotes, deer, foxes, frogs, grasshoppers, humans, lions, mice, rabbits, seals, squirrels, wolves		
HERBIVORES	**CARNIVORES**	**OMNIVORES**

CLASSIFICATIONS

SORTING INTO CLASSES

C-245   Sort the following tools according to function or purpose: CUTTING, HOLDING, MAKING HOLES, MEASURING, SMOOTHING, TURNING.

CHOICE BOX				
axe, clamp, cleaver, drill, gauge, knife, lathe, needle, pliers, punch, saw, screwdriver, snips, tape, tweezer, vice, wrench, yardstick				
CUTTING	**HOLDING**	**MAKING HOLES**	**MEASURING**	**TURNING**

SORTING INTO CLASSES

Signal words tell you that a shift in meaning or a comparison is about to occur. Some signal words tell how long something lasts. Other signal words help you locate where something happened, while some help you understand when something happened.

C-246   Sort the following signal words into a group that describes PAST events, another that signals PRESENT events, and a group that suggests that an event will occur in the FUTURE.

CHOICE BOX		
afterward, bygone, contemporary, current, existing, following, former, hereafter, instant, later, modern, nowadays, obsolete, once, preceding, proceeding, succeeding		
PAST	**PRESENT**	**FUTURE**

CLASSIFICATIONS

SORTING INTO CLASSES

Signal words tell you that a shift in meaning or a comparison is about to occur. Some signal words tell when or how long something lasts; some warn that the next statement is the result of information that has just been given. Some signal words let you know that an addition or comparison is being made, while others alert you to prepare to shift meaning because an exception is coming.

C-247   Sort the following signal words into words that signal a COMPARISON, words that signal an EXCEPTION, and words that signal a RESULT. Using each word in a sentence will help you choose the right category.

CHOICE BOX		
although, because, better than, but, different from, due to, equally, for, hardly, however, if ... then, in spite of, instead of, in the same way, just as, larger than, like, not, only, same as, similar to, since, therefore, thus		
COMPARISON	**EXCEPTION**	**RESULT**

SORTING INTO CLASSES

Signal words tell you that a shift in meaning or a comparison is about to occur. Some signal words tell when or how long something lasts, others let you know that an addition or comparison is being made. Some signal words help you locate where something happened.

C-248   Sort the following signal words into words that signal when or how long — TIME words, words that signal that an ADDITION is being made, and words that signal the LOCATION or POSITION of an event.

CHOICE BOX		
above, across, after, again, also, among, and, another, around, as well as, at the same time, away, before, behind, below, beneath, beside, besides, between, during, extra, finally, higher, in front of, later, lower, meanwhile, next, now, off, on, once, out, over, second, soon, then, through, toward, under, until, upon, while		
TIME	**LOCATION/POSITION**	**ADDITION**

© 1985 MIDWEST PUBLICATIONS 93950-0448

CLASSIFICATIONS

SUPPLY THE CLASSES

C-249   In this exercise you must examine the words in the Choice Box and decide the characteristics by which they can be classified. Draw a diagram and sort these words into the classes you have selected.

CHOICE BOX
almonds, bananas, beans, beets, broccoli, cabbage, cantaloupe, carrots, cauliflower, corn, cucumbers, lemons, lettuce, oranges, peaches, pears, peas, pecans, pumpkins, radishes, rhubarb, spinach, strawberries, walnuts, yams

SUPPLY THE CLASSES

C-250 Examine the words in the Choice Box and decide the characteristics by which they can be classified. Draw a diagram and sort these words into the classes you have selected.

CHOICE BOX
acre, centimeter, cubic yard, cup, dozen, gram, kilogram, kilometer, liter, meter, mile, milligram, milliliter, millimeter, ounce, pint, pound, quart, score, square foot, square mile, square yard, ton, yard

CLASSIFICATIONS

SUPPLY THE CLASSES

C-251   Examine the words in the Choice Box and decide the characteristics by which they can be classified. Draw a diagram and sort these words into the classes you have selected.

CHOICE BOX
airplane propeller, bottle opener, chisel, clamp, crowbar, door knob, electric mixer, hammer, nail, nut, pencil sharpener, pliers, pulley

© 1985 MIDWEST PUBLICATIONS 93950-0448

OVERLAPPING CLASSES—MATRIX

C-252 Sort the following plants by type and growing location.

CHOICE BOX			
apricot, cabbage, cantaloupe, carnation, carrot, cauliflower, celery, cucumber, daffodil, grape, iris, lily, lime, magnolia, marigold, melon, morning glory, pineapple, plum, poppy, spinach, squash, tangerine, tulip, turnip, violet, zinnia			
	FLOWERS	**FRUITS**	**VEGETABLES**
ON TREES			
ON VINES			
ON STALKS OR IN THE GROUND			

CLASSIFICATIONS

OVERLAPPING CLASSES—MATRIX

C-253   On page 269 you selected the characteristics by which you sorted units of measure. You may have sorted the units according to a system of measurement (English, metric, or other), or you may have sorted according to the quantity being measured. In this exercise, use the matrix to classify the units of measure by both characteristics.

CHOICE BOX				
acre, centimeter, cubic yard, cup, dozen, gram, kilogram, kilometer, liter, meter, mile, milligram, milliliter, millimeter, ounce, pint, pound, quart, score, square foot, square mile, square yard, ton, yard				

	AREA	LENGTH	NUMBER	VOLUME	WEIGHT
ENGLISH SYSTEM					
METRIC SYSTEM					
OTHER					

© 1985 MIDWEST PUBLICATIONS 93950-0448

OVERLAPPING CLASSES—MATRIX

C-254   Sort the following words into groups that describe taste, touch, sound, or appearance. Use the matrix to show whether the connotation (implied meaning) of the word is generally favorable, generally unfavorable, or sometimes favorable and sometimes unfavorable. Words may be used in more than one matrix box.

CHOICE BOX			
babble, balmy, blinding, casual, cheerful, coarse, delicious, downy, fluffy, gaudy, harmonious, humming, irritating, nudging, rich, rotten, salty, scratchy, showy, shrieking, shrill, sour, spicy, stale, stinging, stylish, tart			

	TASTE	TOUCH	SOUND	APPEARANCE
GENERALLY FAVORABLE	rich			rich
GENERALLY UNFAVORABLE				
SOMETIMES FAVORABLE & SOMETIMES UNFAVORABLE				

EXAMPLE:

"Rich" can be used to describe a very sweet taste often associated with fancy desserts. "Rich" can also be used to describe the appearance of being dressed very elegantly. "Rich" fits into the matrix in the "generally favorable" row and in both the "taste" and "appearance" columns.

CLASSIFICATIONS

BRANCHING DIAGRAMS

C-255　　Basic groups of animals are called phyla. Arthropods, members of the largest phylum, have jointed legs and segmented bodies. The Arthropoda phylum contains many classes. The three best known are insects, crustaceans, and arachnids, which can be recognized by the number of body parts, legs, or antannae.

Look at the pictures of these arthropods and classify them on the branching diagram on page 275.

BEE

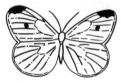

BUTTERFLY

COCKROACH

CRAB

FLY

MOSQUITO

MOTH

SCORPION

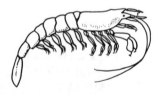

SHRIMP

SPIDER

TERMITE

WASP

DIAGRAM FOR EXERCISE C-255

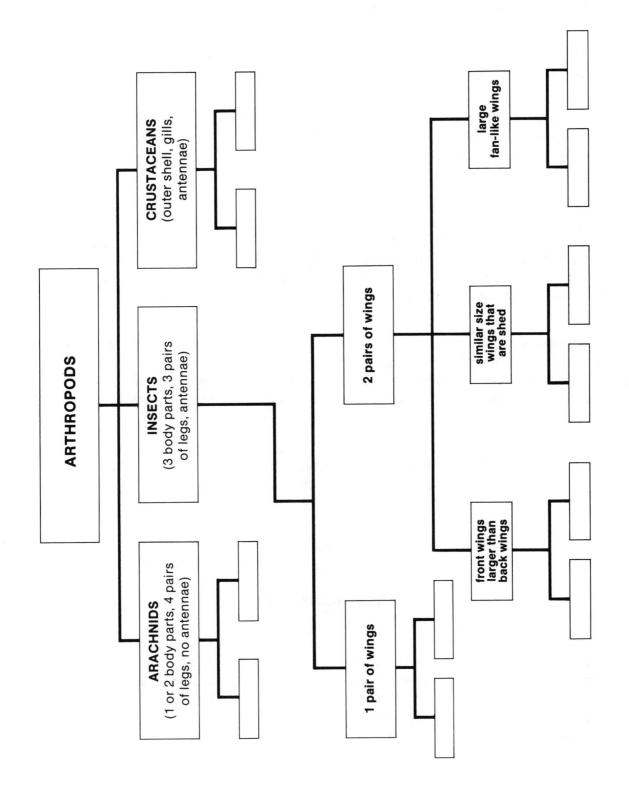

© 1985 MIDWEST PUBLICATIONS 93950-0448

CLASSIFICATIONS

BRANCHING DIAGRAMS

The sound of musical instruments is produced by vibrations. Instruments are named according to the manner in which the vibrations are produced. There are three basic ways to produce vibrations: vibrating air columns, vibrating strings, and vibrating surfaces or sheets.

Vibrating air columns are often produced by blowing. Instruments that are played by blowing include woodwinds and brasses.

Woodwinds are called "wood-winds" because the original instruments were carved from wood. Many modern "woodwinds," such as the flute and saxophone, are made of metal. Woodwinds are divided into two classes: edge-vibrated instruments and reed instruments.

To play an edge-vibrated instrument, the player forces air across the edge of an opening in a mouthpiece, rather than into a mouthpiece. A reed instrument is played by blowing through a mouthpiece, to which a thin, tapered slice of bamboo is attached. The bamboo slice, or "reed," is caused to vibrate by the flow of air.

Brasses are named for the metal from which they are made. Most modern brasses are still made from metal, although marching bands sometimes use lightweight plastic "sousaphones" in their brass sections. Brasses are played by blowing through a metal mouthpiece. Their vibrations are produced by lip action.

Stringed instruments are vibrated by hitting, plucking, or bowing. Percussion instruments are vibrated by striking a surface, sheet, or edge.

C-256 There are four large subclasses in a symphony orchestra. Use the diagram on page 277 to arrange the instruments listed below.

INSTRUMENTS

bass clarinet	flute	snare drum
bass drum	french horn	triangle
bassoon	harp	trombone
bass violin	oboe	trumpet
cello	piano	tuba
clarinet	piccolo	viola
cymbals		

DIAGRAM FOR EXERCISE C-256

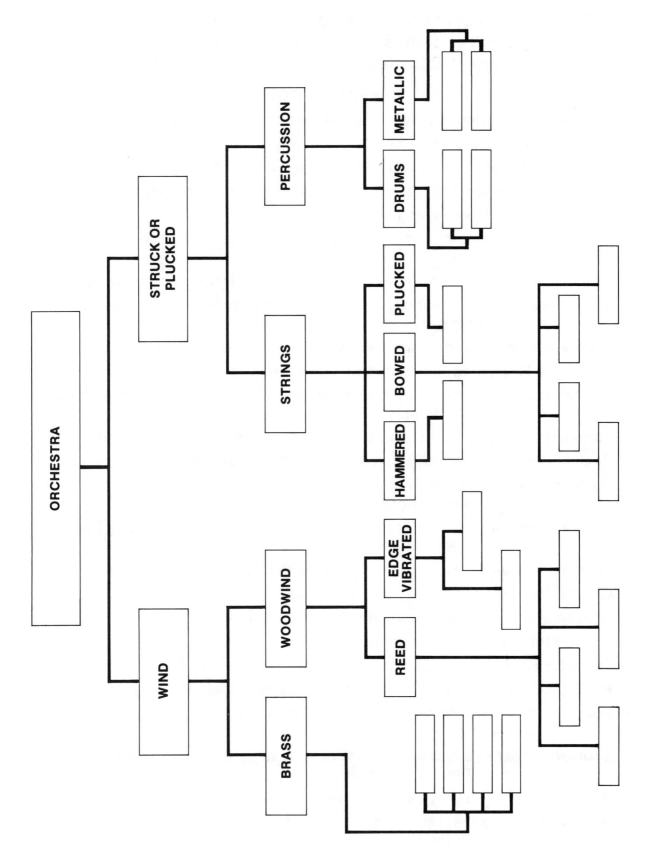

CLASSIFICATIONS

BRANCHING DIAGRAMS

C-257 While most people like dogs, few understand the variety and background of popular breeds of dogs. Use the branching diagram on page 279 to classify the following list of dogs.

BREEDS OF DOGS

Afghan Hound — large, longhaired hound that hunts by sight

Airdale — the largest terrier breed

Alaskan Malamute — sled dog with dramatic black and white face markings

Basset Hound — a scent-tracking hound with sad-looking eyes and long ears

Beagle — a small, brown and white scent-tracking hound

Boxer — a large, brown and white guard dog trained to work with police and the blind

Brittany Spaniel — a short-tailed, tall spaniel, usually orange and white

Chihuahua — the smallest dog, a member of the toy breed, has short hair and big ears

Cocker Spaniel — a short spaniel with long ears and a silky, wavy coat

Collie — a large, long-haired, herding dog originally from Scotland

Dachshund — a short-haired, brown hound with short legs, originally bred to track badgers

Dalmation — a large, black-spotted coach dog, a non-sporting breed

English Setter — a sporting bird dog with a silky coat and white markings

German Pointer — a short-haired, sporting dog with a brown head and white-spotted body

German Shepherd — bred as a herding dog, this popular guard dog has brown, thick fur

Golden Retriever — a sporting bird dog, with long, silky, golden hair

Great Dane — one of the largest guard dogs

Greyhound — a racing hound cued by the sight of its prey

Irish Setter — a sporting breed with long, dark red hair

Labrador Retriever — a black, short-haired sporting breed

Pekingese — a small, brown, long-haired toy breed with a dark pug nose

Poodle — a non-sporting breed that is often clipped into a stylized appearance

Scottish Terrier — a black terrier made popular by President Franklin Delano Roosevelt

Siberian Husky — a grey sled dog with a white face

Weimaraners — a grey, short-haired, German pointer; a sporting dog used for hunting

DIAGRAM FOR EXERCISE C-257

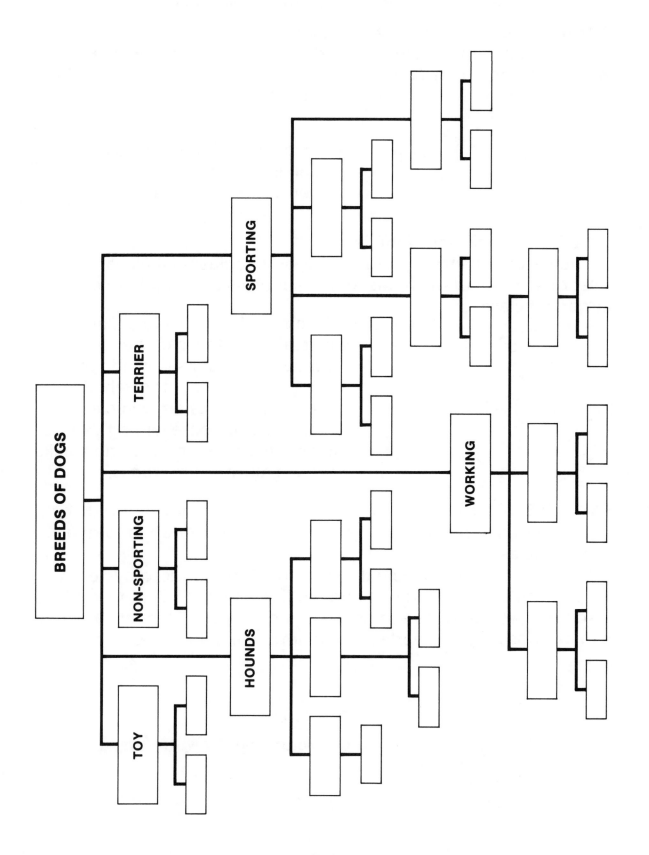

DIAGRAMING CLASSES

Diagrams can be used to show relationships.

EXAMPLE: bicycles, trucks, vehicles

The first diagram pictures two distinctly different subclasses within a common class. The large circle represents vehicles. The smaller circles represent bicycles and trucks.

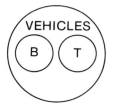

B = Bicycles

T = Trucks

A bicycle is a kind of vehicle, and a truck is a kind of vehicle. However, no truck is a bicycle.

EXAMPLE: truck, van, vehicle

The second diagram pictures a class-subclass-subclass relationship. All of the items in one subclass are members of a larger subclass.

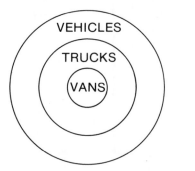

A truck is a kind of vehicle, and a van is a kind of truck. The circle representing trucks is inside the large circle representng vehicles because all trucks are vehicles. The smallest circle representing vans is inside the circle representing trucks because all vans are trucks.

EXAMPLE: bicycles, mopeds, motorcycles, vehicles

The third diagram pictures subclasses that overlap to form a third subclass.

Is there a form of bicycle that is also a form of motorcycle? A moped can be operated by peddling like a bicycle. A moped can also be powered by its engine like a motorcycle. This relationship can be shown by an overlapping diagram like this one.

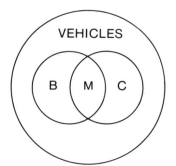

B = Bicycles

C = Motorcycles

M = Mopeds

280

DIAGRAMING CLASSES—SELECT

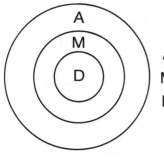

A = Animals
M = Mammals
D = Dogs

This diagram illustrates the relationship of the classes "Animals," "Mammals," and "Dogs." Decide how each word below is related to these three classes and darken the appropriate region of the corresponding diagram. If the word does not fit in any of these three classes, label it "O" for "Outside."

EXAMPLE:

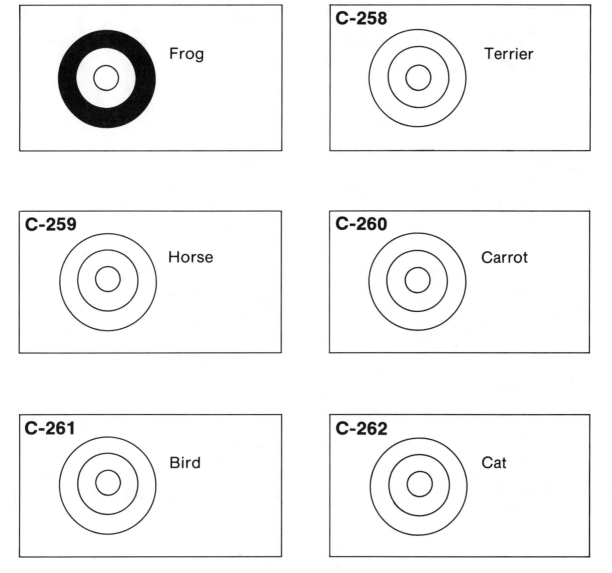

Frog	C-258 Terrier
C-259 Horse	C-260 Carrot
C-261 Bird	C-262 Cat

CLASSIFICATIONS

DIAGRAMING CLASSES—SELECT

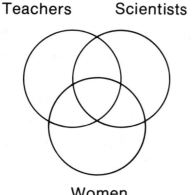

Teachers   Scientists

Women

This diagram illustrates the relationship of the classes "Teachers," "Scientists," and "Women." Decide how each person below is related to these three classes and darken the appropriate region of the corresponding diagram. If the person does not fit in any of these three classes, label the diagram "O" for "Outside."

EXAMPLE:

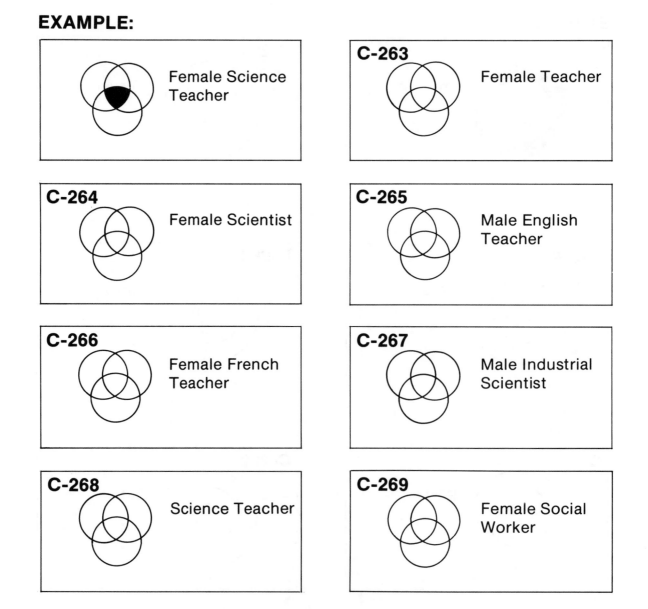

Female Science Teacher

C-263 Female Teacher

C-264 Female Scientist

C-265 Male English Teacher

C-266 Female French Teacher

C-267 Male Industrial Scientist

C-268 Science Teacher

C-269 Female Social Worker

DIAGRAMING CLASSES—SELECT

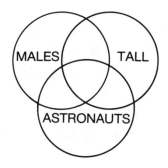

This diagram illustrates the relationship of the classes "Males," "Tall," and "Astronauts." Decide how each person below is related to these three classes and darken the appropriate region of the corresponding diagram. If the person does not fit in any of these three classes, label the diagram "O" for "Outside."

EXAMPLE:

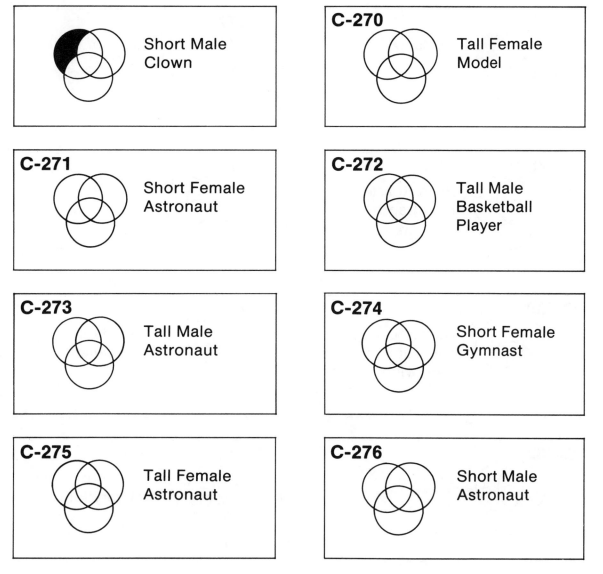

Short Male Clown

C-270 Tall Female Model

C-271 Short Female Astronaut

C-272 Tall Male Basketball Player

C-273 Tall Male Astronaut

C-274 Short Female Gymnast

C-275 Tall Female Astronaut

C-276 Short Male Astronaut

CLASSIFICATIONS

283

DIAGRAMING CLASSES—SELECT

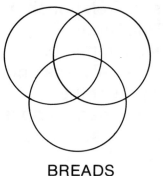

MEATS   VEGETABLES

BREADS

This diagram illustrates the relationship of the classes "Meats," "Vegetables," and "Breads." Decide how each of the foods below is related to these three classes and darken the appropriate region of the corresponding diagram. If the food does not fit in any of these three classes label it "O" for "Outside."

EXAMPLE:

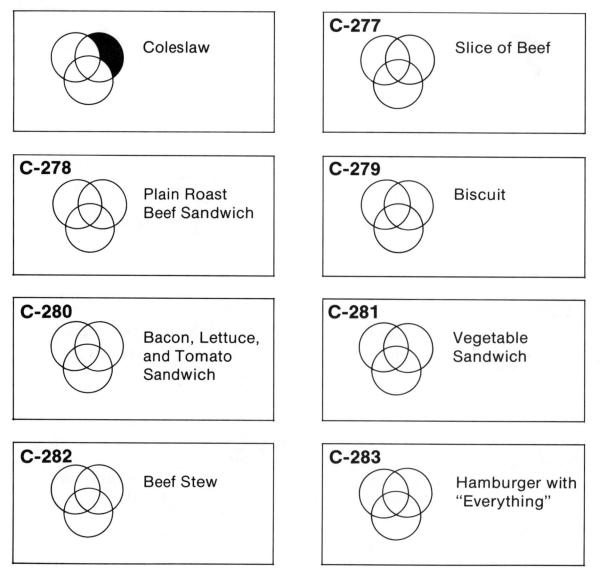

Coleslaw

C-277   Slice of Beef

C-278   Plain Roast Beef Sandwich

C-279   Biscuit

C-280   Bacon, Lettuce, and Tomato Sandwich

C-281   Vegetable Sandwich

C-282   Beef Stew

C-283   Hamburger with "Everything"

DIAGRAMING CLASSES—SELECT

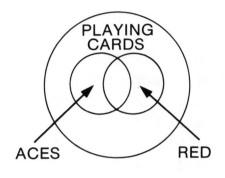

This diagram illustrates the relationship of the classes "Playing Cards," "Aces," and "Red." Decide how each item below is related to these three classes and darken the appropriate region of the corresponding diagram. If the item does not fit in any of these three classes, label it "O" for "Outside."

EXAMPLE:

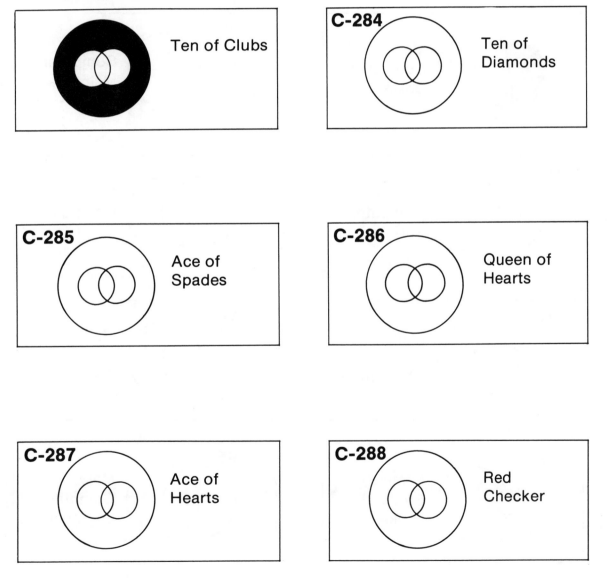

DIAGRAMING CLASSES—SELECT

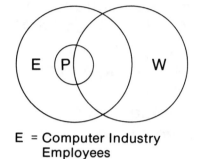

E = Computer Industry
    Employees
W = Women
P = Computer Programmers

This diagram illustrates the relationship of the classes "Computer Industry Employees," "Women," and "Computer Programmers." Decide how each person below is related to these three classes and darken the appropriate region of the corresponding diagram. If the person does not fit any of these three classes, label the diagram "O" for "Outside."

EXAMPLE:

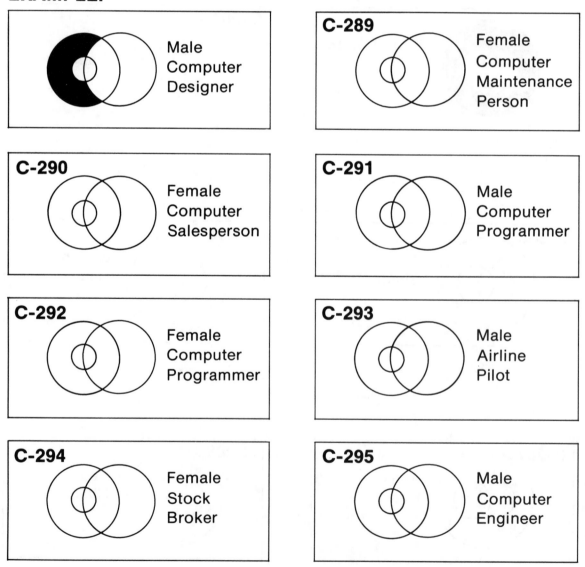

Male Computer Designer

C-289 Female Computer Maintenance Person

C-290 Female Computer Salesperson

C-291 Male Computer Programmer

C-292 Female Computer Programmer

C-293 Male Airline Pilot

C-294 Female Stock Broker

C-295 Male Computer Engineer

DIAGRAMING CLASSES—SELECT

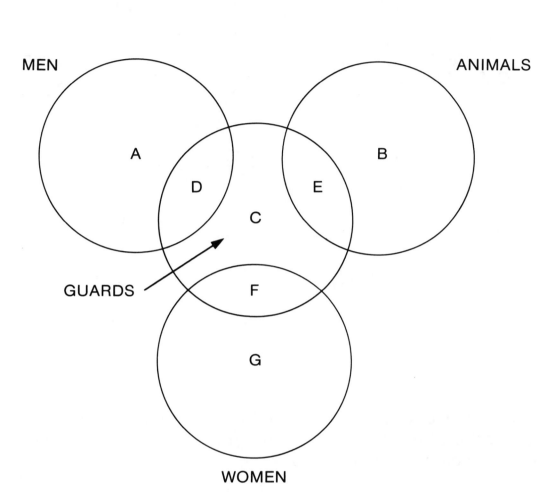

Study this diagram and decide in which region each of the descriptions below would fit. Write the letter representing the correct region on the line provided.

	DESCRIPTION	REGION
EXAMPLE:	male security officer	D
C-296	female police officer	_____
C-297	watchdog	_____
C-298	poodle	_____
C-299	burglar alarm	_____
C-300	lioness with cubs	_____

DIAGRAMING CLASSES—SELECT

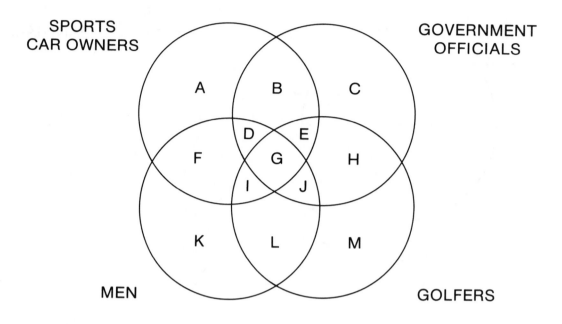

SPORTS
CAR OWNERS

GOVERNMENT
OFFICIALS

MEN

GOLFERS

Study this diagram and decide in which region each of the descriptions below would fit. Write the letter representing the correct region on the line provided.

	PERSON	**REGION**
EXAMPLE:	a woman judge who golfs and drives a station wagon	H
C-301	a congresswoman who plays only tennis and drives a Porsche	_____
C-302	a congressman who swims, jogs, and drives an Alfa Romeo	_____
C-303	a restaurant hostess who golfs and drives a compact car	_____
C-304	a male factory worker who golfs and owns a sports car	_____
C-305	President Eisenhower, who golfed but did not own a sports car	_____

DIAGRAMING CLASSES—DESCRIBE

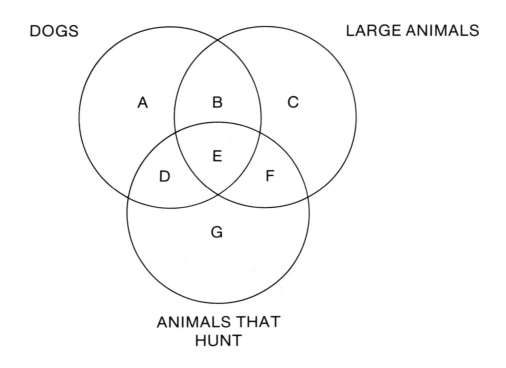

DOGS   LARGE ANIMALS

ANIMALS THAT
HUNT

Study the diagram above, then describe and name a member of the class that belongs in each region.

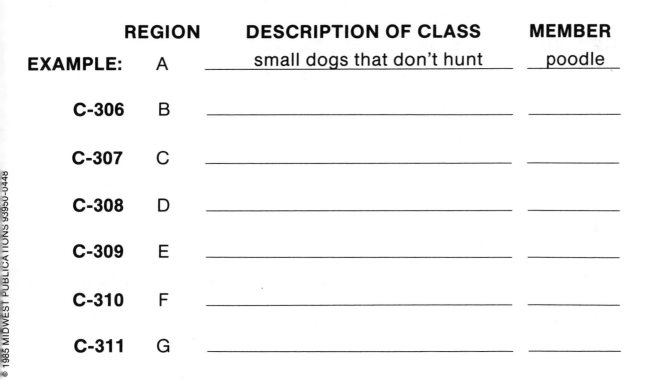

	REGION	DESCRIPTION OF CLASS	MEMBER
EXAMPLE:	A	small dogs that don't hunt	poodle
C-306	B		
C-307	C		
C-308	D		
C-309	E		
C-310	F		
C-311	G		

CLASSIFICATIONS

DIAGRAMING CLASSES—DESCRIBE

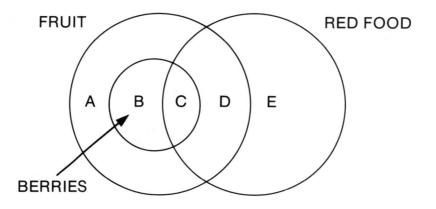

Study the diagram above, then describe and name a member of the class that belongs in each region.

	REGION	DESCRIPTION	MEMBER
EXAMPLE:	A	fruit that is not red and not a berry	banana
C-312	B		
C-313	C		
C-314	D		
C-315	E		

DIAGRAMING CLASSES—DESCRIBE

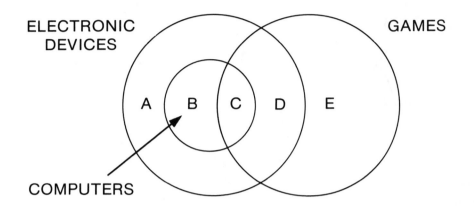

ELECTRONIC DEVICES   GAMES

A B C D E

COMPUTERS

Study the diagram above, then describe and name a member of the class that belongs in each region.

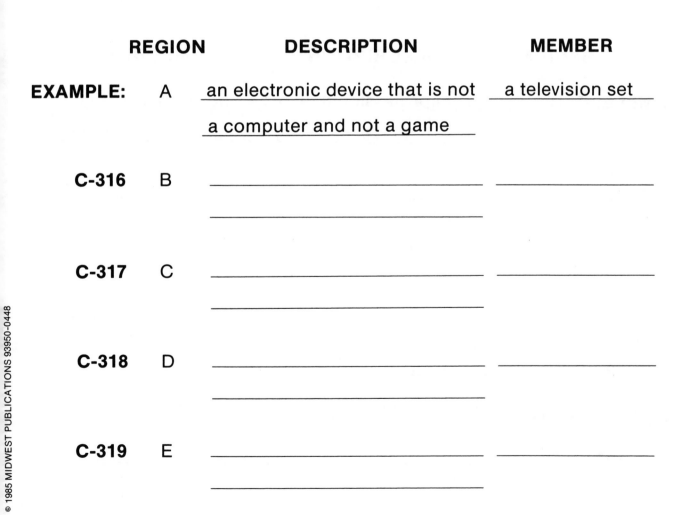

	REGION	DESCRIPTION	MEMBER
EXAMPLE:	A	an electronic device that is not a computer and not a game	a television set
C-316	B		
C-317	C		
C-318	D		
C-319	E		

CLASSIFICATIONS

DIAGRAMING CLASSES—DESCRIBE

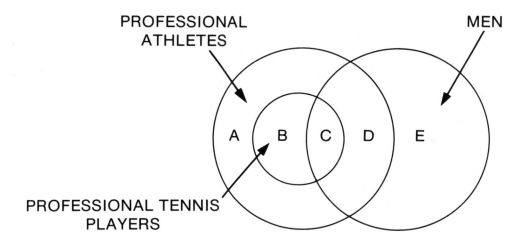

PROFESSIONAL
ATHLETES

MEN

PROFESSIONAL TENNIS
PLAYERS

Study the diagram above, then describe and name a member of
the class that belongs in each region.

	REGION	DESCRIPTION	MEMBER
EXAMPLE:	B	female professional tennis players	the Women's Tennis Assoc. champion
C-320	A		
C-321	C		
C-322	D		
C-323	E		

DIAGRAMING CLASSES—DESCRIBE

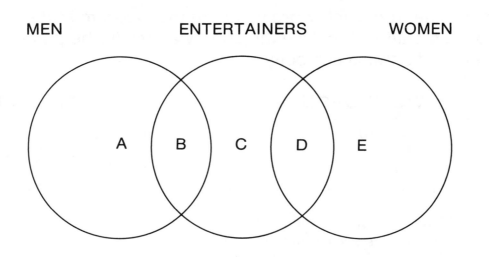

MEN   ENTERTAINERS   WOMEN

Study the diagram above, then describe and name a member of the class that belongs in each region.

	REGION	DESCRIPTION	MEMBER
EXAMPLE:	A	a man who is not an entertainer	a male doctor
C-324	B		
C-325	C		
C-326	D		
C-327	E		

CLASSIFICATIONS

DIAGRAMING CLASSES—SELECT THE DIAGRAM

Draw a line from each word group to the diagram that pictures the correct relationship. Use the abbreviations in the parentheses to label the diagrams correctly.

WORD GROUPS	DIAGRAMS

EXAMPLE:

Cheese (Ch)
Egg (E)
Ham (H)
Sandwiches (Sa)

The "sandwiches" diagram represents seven different sandwiches (cheese; egg; ham; ham & cheese; ham & egg; egg & cheese; and ham, egg & cheese).

C-328

Animal products (A)
Meat (M)
Pepperoni (P)
Sausage (Su)

C-329

Desserts (D)
Cookies (Co)
Pies (Pi)
Puddings (Pu)

C-330

Cakes (Ca)
Desserts (D)
Ice creams (I)
Pies (Pi)

C-331

Breads (B)
Grain Products (GP)
Muffins (Mu)
Whole Wheat (WW)

C-332

Cereals (Ce)
Oats (O)
Rice (R)
Wheat (W)

SANDWICHES (Sa)
Ch E
H

© 1985 MIDWEST PUBLICATIONS 93950-0448

DIAGRAMING CLASSES—SELECT THE DIAGRAM

Draw a line from each word group to the diagram that pictures the correct relationship. Use the abbreviations in the parentheses to label the diagrams correctly.

WORD GROUPS　　　　　　　　　**DIAGRAMS**

EXAMPLE:
Basketball (Bk)
Softball (So)
Sports (Sp)
Sports Girls Play (Sg)

C-333
Baseball (Ba)
Football (F)
Soccer (S)
Team Sports (T)

C-334
Individual Sports (I)
Outdoor Recreation (OR)
Recreation (R)
Swimming (S)
Team Sports (T)

C-335
Basketball (Bk)
Golf (G)
Outdoor Sports (OS)
Sports (Sp)
Sports Girls Play (Sg)
Team Sports (T)

C-336
Golf (G)
Outdoor Sports (OS)
Recreation (R)
Sports (Sp)

C-337
Camping (C)
Golf (G)
Outdoor Recreation (OR)
Outdoor Sports (OS)

C-338
Baseball (Ba)
Golf (G)
Outdoor Sports (OS)
Recreation (R)
Team Sports (T)

SPORTS (Sp)
Bk Sg So

CLASSIFICATIONS

DIAGRAMING CLASSES—SELECT AND EXPLAIN

The diagrams below illustrate the possible relationships between classes. In exercises C-339 through C-346 you will be asked to (1) decide how the two classes given are related; (2) write the phrase that describes the relationship (includes, is included in, overlaps, is separate from) in the blank provided; (3) label the diagram that best illustrates that relationship; and (4) write a sentence that expresses the relationship.

Class A **includes** class B.   all B are A

Class A **is included in** class B.   all A are B

Class A **overlaps** class B.   some A are B **and/or** some B are A

Class A **is separate from** class B.   no A are B **or** no B are A

EXAMPLE: The class TEACHERS (T) _____ the class MEN (M).

   Since not all teachers are men, you can say the class TEACHERS does not include the class men. This means the first diagram above does not fit.

   Since not all men are teachers, you can also say the class MEN does not include the class TEACHERS. This means that the second diagram above does not fit.

   Since some men are teachers, you cannot say the class TEACHERS is separate from the class MEN. This means the fourth diagram above does not fit.

   Since some men are teachers, and some teachers are men, you can say that the class TEACHERS overlaps the class MEN. This means the third diagram above fits. The overlapping part or intersection represents MEN TEACHERS, as illustrated below.

The class TEACHERS (T) __overlaps__ the class MEN (M).

Some men are teachers; some teachers are men.

SENTENCE

© 1985 MIDWEST PUBLICATIONS 93950-0448

DIAGRAMING CLASSES—SELECT AND EXPLAIN

In the exercises below: (1) decide how the two classes given are related; (2) write the phrase that describes the relationship (**includes, is included in, overlaps, is separate from**) in the blank provided; (3) label the diagram that best illustrates that relationship; and (4) write a sentence that expresses the relationship.

EXAMPLE:

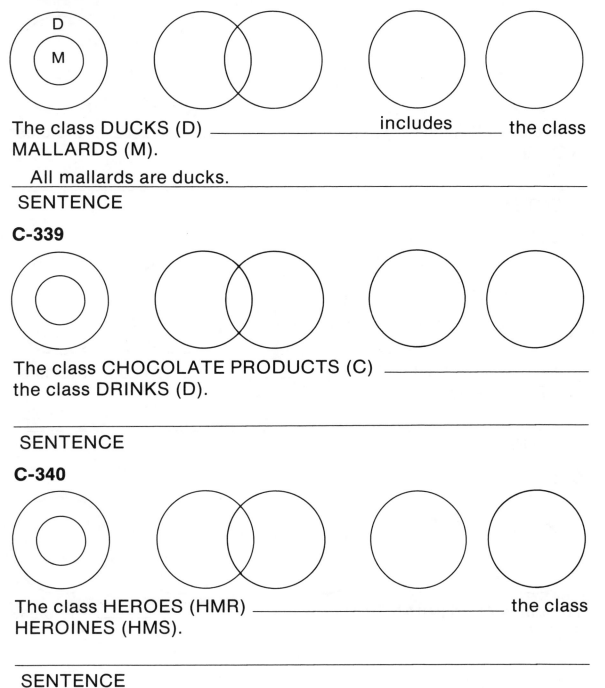

The class DUCKS (D) ———————— includes ———————— the class MALLARDS (M).

___All mallards are ducks._____
SENTENCE

C-339

The class CHOCOLATE PRODUCTS (C) _____ the class DRINKS (D).

_____
SENTENCE

C-340

The class HEROES (HMR) _____ the class HEROINES (HMS).

_____
SENTENCE

CLASSIFICATIONS

DIAGRAMING CLASSES—SELECT AND EXPLAIN

In the exercise below: (1) decide how the two classes given are related; (2) write the phrase that describes the relationship (**includes, is included in, overlaps, is separate from**) in the blank provided; (3) label the diagram that best illustrates that relationship; and (4) write a sentence that expresses the relationship.

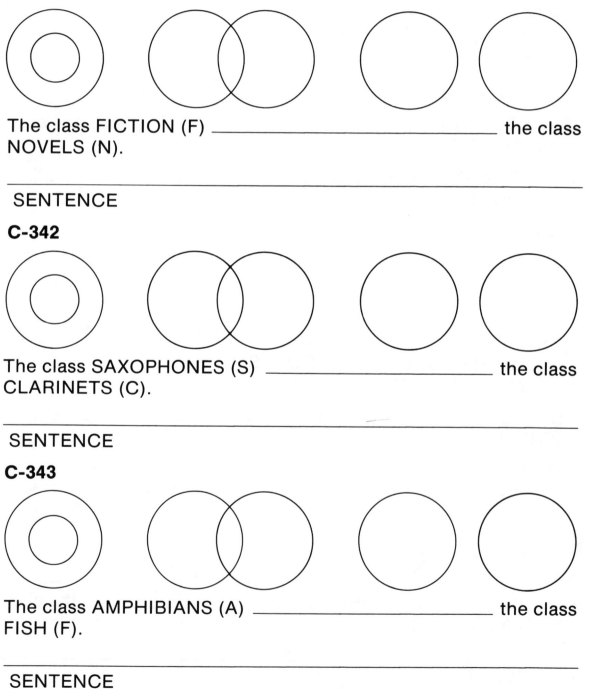

C-341

The class FICTION (F) _____ the class NOVELS (N).

SENTENCE

C-342

The class SAXOPHONES (S) _____ the class CLARINETS (C).

SENTENCE

C-343

The class AMPHIBIANS (A) _____ the class FISH (F).

SENTENCE

© 1985 MIDWEST PUBLICATIONS 93950-0448

DIAGRAMING CLASSES—SELECT AND EXPLAIN

   In the exercises below: (1) decide how the two classes given are related; (2) write the phrase that describes the relationship (**includes**, **is included in**, **overlaps**, **is separate from**) in the blank provided; (3) label the diagram that best illustrates that relationship; and (4) write a sentence that expresses the relationship.

C-344

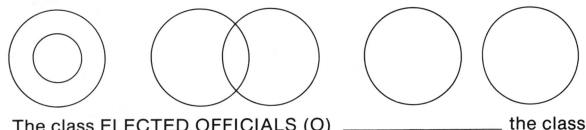

The class ELECTED OFFICIALS (O) _____ the class
STATE GOVERNORS (G).

_____

SENTENCE

C-345

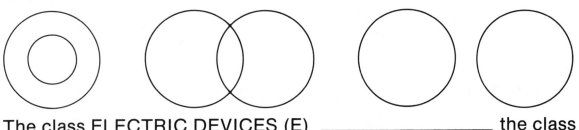

The class ELECTRIC DEVICES (E) _____ the class
SAWS (S).

_____

SENTENCE

C-346

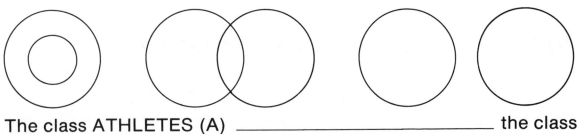

The class ATHLETES (A) _____ the class
GYMNASTS (G).

_____

SENTENCE

CLASSIFICATIONS

DIAGRAMING CLASS STATEMENTS

Read each statement, then select, label, and shade the diagram that best illustrates the statement. (NOTE: Some statements may not be true.)

EXAMPLE: Some cars (C) are fast (F).

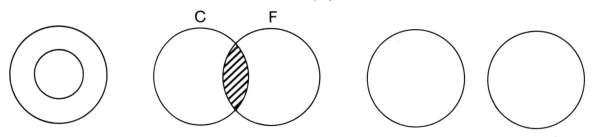

EXAMPLE: Some cars (C) are not fast (F).

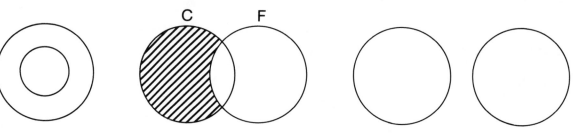

EXAMPLE: All cars (C) are vehicles (V).

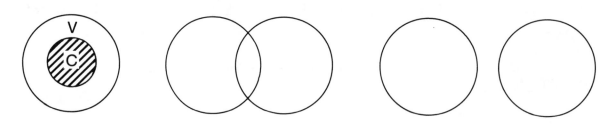

C-347 Some cars (C) are produced in America (A).

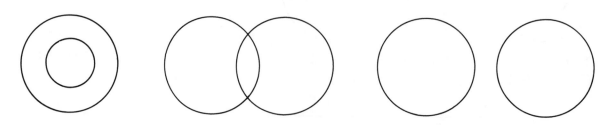

© 1985 MIDWEST PUBLICATIONS 93950-0448

DIAGRAMING CLASS STATEMENTS

Read each statement, then select, label, and shade the diagram that best illustrates the statement. (NOTE: Some statements may not be true.)

C-348   No Ford (F) is a Dodge (D).

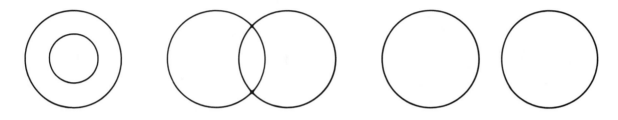

C-349   Some cars (C) are not produced in America (A).

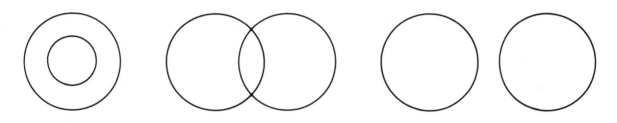

C-350   All Dodges (D) are vehicles (V).

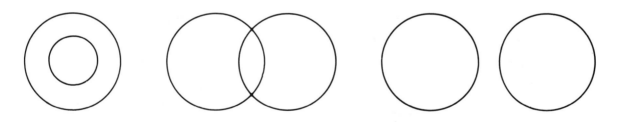

C-351   Some Dodges (D) are fast (F).

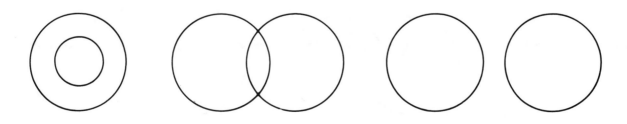

CLASSIFICATIONS

DIAGRAMING CLASS STATEMENTS

Read each statement, then select, label, and shade the diagram that best illustrates the statement. (NOTE: Some statements may not be true.)

C-352 All intelligent beings (I) are people (P).

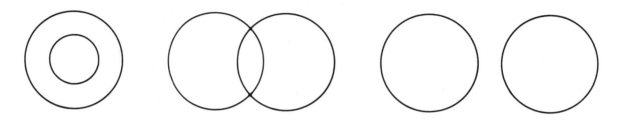

C-353 Some intelligent beings (I) are people (P).

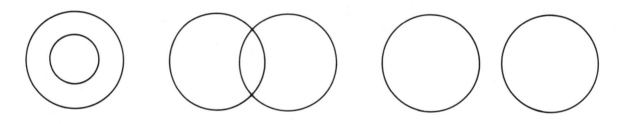

C-354 No intelligent beings (I) are people (P).

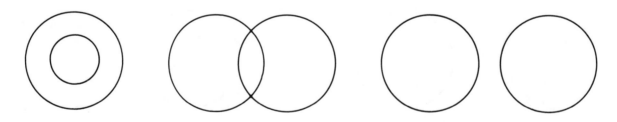

C-355 Some people (P) are not intelligent (I).

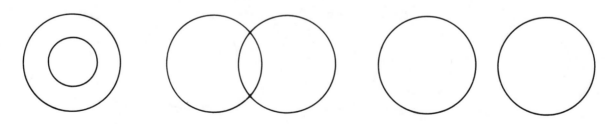

DIAGRAMING CLASS STATEMENTS

Read each statement, then select, label, and shade the diagram that best illustrates the statement. (NOTE: Some statements may not be true.)

C-356 Everyone (E) is intelligent (I).

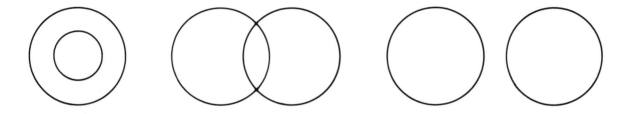

C-357 Some people (P) are intelligent (I).

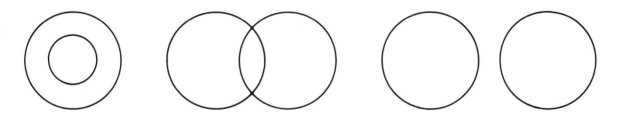

C-358 Not everyone (E) is intelligent (I).

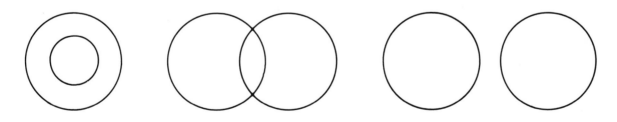

C-359 No one (N) is intelligent (I).

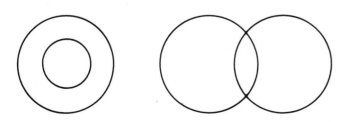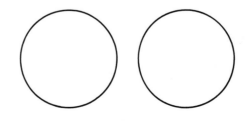

CLASSIFICATIONS

DIAGRAMING CLASS STATEMENTS—SUPPLY

Read each statement, then draw, label, and shade a diagram that best illustrates the statement. (NOTE: Some statements may not be true.)

EXAMPLE: Some plants (P) are green (G).

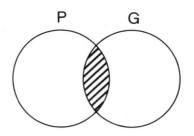

EXAMPLE: All flowers (F) are plants (P).

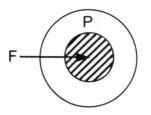

C-360   Some plants (P) are not green (G).

C-361   All marigolds (Ma) are flowers (F).

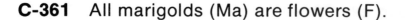

DIAGRAMING CLASS STATEMENTS—SUPPLY

Read each statement, then draw, label, and shade a diagram that best illustrates the statement. (NOTE: Some statements may not be true.)

C-362 Some flowers (F) grow on vines (V).

C-363 Both marigolds (Ma) and morning glories (Mg) are flowers (F).

C-364 Some flowers (F) do not grow on vines (V).

C-365 Marigolds (Ma) are flowers (F) that do not grow on vines (V), but morning glories (Mg) do.

CLASSIFICATIONS

DIAGRAMING CLASS ARGUMENTS

A simple argument consists of three statements: two premises and a conclusion.

EXAMPLE OF A SIMPLE ARGUMENT

Premise 1:   All actors (A) are performers (P).
Premise 2:   All comedians (C) are actors (A).
Conclusion: So all comedians (C) are performers (P).

The first step is to assume each premise to be true. Next, draw a diagram of premise 1 — just as you have done in exercises C-360 through C-365.

Diagram of Premise 1: "All actors (A) are performers (P)."

To describe this relationship, draw two circles so that all of circle A (actors) is inside circle P (performers).

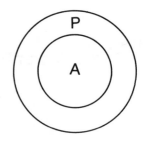

Next, diagram premise 2 (assume the statement is true).

Diagram of Premise 2: "All comedians (C) are actors (A)."

This premise requires that all of circle C (comedians) be inside circle A (actors).

DIAGRAMING CLASS ARGUMENTS

The final step is to combine the two diagrams to see if the conclusion can be shown.

Diagram of Conclusion: There is only one way these two diagrams can be combined.

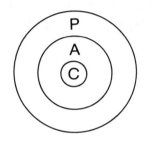

Since all of circle C (comedians) is inside circle P (performers), the diagram describes the statement "All comedians are performers," which agrees with the conclusion.

Since there is no way to draw C outside of P and still describe the meaning of the premise sentences, the conclusion **can** be shown.

EXAMPLE 2

Premise 1:   All actors (A) are performers (P).
Premise 2:   No editors (E) are performers (P).
Conclusion: No editors (E) are actors (A).

First, diagram premise 1.

"All actors (A) are performers (P)" requires that all of circle A be inside circle P.

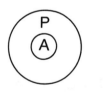

Next, diagram premise 2.

To describe the relationship "No editors (E) are performers (P)," draw two circles that do not overlap.

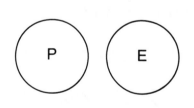

Finally, combine the two diagrams — there is only one possibility.

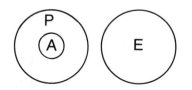

Since no part of circle E (editors) touches circle A (actors), the conclusion, "No editors are actors," **can** be shown.

CLASSIFICATIONS

DIAGRAMING CLASS ARGUMENTS
THIRD EXAMPLE

Premise 1:   All actors (A) are performers (P).
Premise 2:   All actors (A) are talented people (T).
Conclusion: So all talented people (T) are performers.

Premise 1 is the same as in the first and second examples. The smaller A (actors) circle can be anywhere within the larger P (performers) circle.

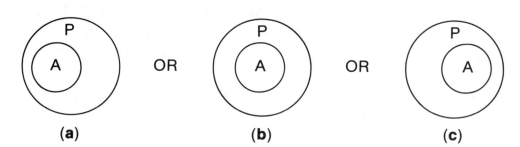

(a)   (b)   (c)

Premise 2, "All actors (A) are talented people (T)," is represented in a similar fashion.

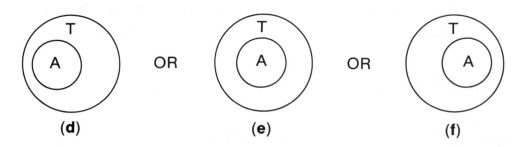

(d)   (e)   (f)

To test the **Conclusion,** "All talented people (T) are performers (P)," see if you can combine any of the above diagrams to find a diagram that does not fit the conclusion.

Combining (**c**) and (**d**) results in the following diagram:

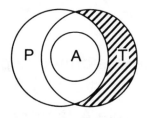

the shaded region represents "Talented people who are not performers."

   Since it is possible to draw T outside of P and still describe the meaning of the premise statements, the conclusion **cannot** be shown.

DIAGRAMING CLASS ARGUMENTS—SUPPLY

Draw a diagram for each argument and tell whether the conclusion **can** be shown or **cannot** be shown.

C-366

Premise 1:	All friends of Maria (FM) are friends of Sarah (FS).
Premise 2:	Ruth (R) is a friend of Maria.
Conclusion:	Ruth is a friend of Sarah.

C-367

Premise 1:	All friends of Maria (FM) are friends of Sarah (FS).
Premise 2:	Ruth (R) is a friend of Sarah.
Conclusion:	Ruth is a friend of Maria.

C-368

Premise 1:	Maria (M) is a friend of Sarah (FS).
Premise 2:	Ruth (R) is a friend of Sarah.
Conclusion:	Maria is a friend of Ruth (FR).

CLASSIFICATIONS

DIAGRAMING CLASS ARGUMENTS—SUPPLY

Draw a diagram for each argument and tell whether the conclusion **can** be shown or **cannot** be shown.

C-369

Premise 1:	Ruth (R) is not a friend of Sarah (FS).
Premise 2:	All friends of Maria (FM) are friends of Sarah.
Conclusion:	Ruth is not a friend of Maria.

C-370

Premise 1:	All cute creatures (C) are amusing (A).
Premise 2:	All babies (B) are cute creatures.
Conclusion:	All babies are amusing.

C-371

Premise 1:	All cute creatures (C) are amusing (A).
Premise 2:	Some babies (B) are cute creatures.
Conclusion:	All babies are amusing.

DIAGRAMING CLASS ARGUMENTS—SUPPLY

Draw a diagram for each argument and tell whether the conclusion **can** be shown or **cannot** be shown.

C-372

Premise 1:	All babies (B) are cute creatures (C).
Premise 2:	Some cute creatures are amusing (A).
Conclusion:	Some babies are amusing.

C-373

Premise 1:	All babies (B) are cute creatures (C).
Premise 2:	Some cute creatures are amusing (A).
Conclusion:	No babies are amusing.

C-374

Premise 1:	No babies (B) are amusing (A).
Premise 2:	Some babies are cute creatures (C).
Conclusion:	No cute creatures are amusing.

CLASSIFICATIONS

DIAGRAMING CLASS ARGUMENTS—SUPPLY

Draw a diagram for each argument and tell whether the conclusion **can** be shown or **cannot** be shown.

C-375

Premise 1:	All babies (B) are cute (C).
Premise 2:	All amusing things (A) are cute.
Conclusion:	All babies are amusing.

C-376

Premise 1:	All babies (B) are cute (C).
Premise 2:	All amusing things (A) are cute.
Conclusion:	No babies are amusing.

C-377

Premise 1:	Some babies (B) are cute creatures (C).
Premise 2:	Some babies are amusing (A).
Conclusion:	Some cute creatures are amusing.

DEFINITIONS THAT CONTAIN CLASSES—SELECT

A **definition** is a clear, exact statement of the meaning of a word. A good definition conveys enough information so that the reader knows precisely what the word means and what makes the word different from other similar terms.

A complete definition of a noun should contain the **class** to which the person, place, or thing belongs and the **characteristics** that make it different from others in its class.

Suppose you were asked to define a bicycle for someone who had never seen one.

EXAMPLE: A bicycle is something that kids ride to school.

The last part of the sentence, "something that kids ride to school," tells the reader that a bicycle is a vehicle, but the reader doesn't have enough information to distinguish a bicycle from a bus, subway, or tractor on which "kids ride to school."

EXAMPLE: A bicycle, which has two wheels and handlebars, is powered by pedaling with one's feet.

This definition gives the characteristics of a bicycle, but leaves the reader uncertain what the bicycle really is. It could be a game, an exercise device, or a generator of electricity.

To define the bicycle clearly, you must give
(1) the **class** to which it belongs and
(2) the **characteristics** that make it different from others in its class.

EXAMPLE: A bicycle is something people ride on (a vehicle), which has two wheels, handlebars for steering, and foot pedals by which it is propelled.

Read the following definitions for nouns and determine whether each is complete or incomplete. If the definition contains both the class to which the noun belongs and enough distinguishing characteristics, mark it **C** for **complete.** If the definition does not provide enough information, mark it **I** for **incomplete** and supply the missing information. Leave the class and characteristics lines blank if the definition is complete.

EXAMPLE:

____I____ A dime is worth ten cents or one tenth of a dollar.

_____a U.S. coin_____   _____
　　　　　　CLASS　　　　　　　　　　　　　　　CHARACTERISTICS

CLASSIFICATIONS

313

DEFINITIONS THAT CONTAIN CLASSES—SELECT

Read the following definitions for nouns and determine whether each is complete or incomplete. If the definition contains both the class to which the noun belongs and enough distinguishing characteristics, mark it **C** for **complete**. If the definition does not provide enough information, mark it **I** for **incomplete** and supply the missing information. Leave the class and characteristics lines blank if the definition is complete.

C-378 _____ A diamond is a playing field for baseball.

_____   _____
CLASS   CHARACTERISTICS

C-379 _____ A hurricane is a wind storm.

_____   _____
CLASS   CHARACTERISTICS

C-380 _____ A collie is a large long-haired, working dog sometimes used to herd animals.

_____   _____
CLASS   CHARACTERISTICS

C-381 _____ A tangerine is an orange-colored citrus fruit, commonly eaten in sections.

_____   _____
CLASS   CHARACTERISTICS

C-382 _____ A video game can be played by one or more people.

_____   _____
CLASS   CHARACTERISTICS

C-383 _____ Satisfaction means things are all right.

_____   _____
CLASS   CHARACTERISTICS

C-384 _____ A graph shows changes in conditions over a period of time.

_____   _____
CLASS   CHARACTERISTICS

DEFINITIONS THAT CONTAIN CLASSES—SELECT

Read the following definitions for nouns and determine whether each is complete or incomplete. If the definition contains both the class to which the noun belongs and enough distinguishing characteristics, mark it **C** for **complete**. If the definition does not provide enough information, mark it **I** for **incomplete** and supply the missing information. Leave the class and characteristics lines blank if the definition is complete.

C-385 _____ A pine is a cone-bearing evergreen tree.

_____   _____

CLASS   CHARACTERISTICS

C-386 _____ Intermission is when you get up in the middle of a game or concert and go to the rest room or concession stand.

_____   _____

CLASS   CHARACTERISTICS

C-387 _____ A set of pliers is a gripping tool with two handles that are operated by one hand.

_____   _____

CLASS   CHARACTERISTICS

C-388 _____ A desk is a piece of furniture.

_____   _____

CLASS   CHARACTERISTICS

C-389 _____ Love is tenderness, joy, and affection.

_____   _____

CLASS   CHARACTERISTICS

C-390 _____ Listening is intense concentration with interest.

_____   _____

CLASS   CHARACTERISTICS

C-391 _____ Fear is an emotion.

_____   _____

CLASS   CHARACTERISTICS

CLASSIFICATIONS

DEFINITIONS THAT CONTAIN CLASSES—SELECT

Read the following definitions for nouns and determine whether each is complete or incomplete. If the definition contains both the class to which the noun belongs and enough distinguishing characteristics, mark it **C** for **complete**. If the definition does not provide enough information, mark it **I** for **incomplete** and supply the missing information. Leave the class and characteristics lines blank if the definition is complete.

C-392 _____ A mallard is a type of wild duck.

_____ | _____
CLASS | CHARACTERISTICS

C-393 _____ A piano is a stringed instrument played by pressing keys that operate hammers.

_____ | _____
CLASS | CHARACTERISTICS

C-394 _____ Anger is when a person gets mad.

_____ | _____
CLASS | CHARACTERISTICS

C-395 _____ An expressway is a limited-access multilane highway.

_____ | _____
CLASS | CHARACTERISTICS

C-396 _____ Equality means people are treated fairly and justly.

_____ | _____
CLASS | CHARACTERISTICS

C-397 _____ A traffic jam is when too many cars and trucks are on the road.

_____ | _____
CLASS | CHARACTERISTICS

C-398 _____ A convertible is a kind of car.

_____ | _____
CLASS | CHARACTERISTICS

DEFINITIONS THAT CONTAIN CLASSES—SUPPLY

Write complete definitions of the following words. Put parentheses around the class and underline the characteristics in each definition.

EXAMPLE: blizzard

A blizzard is a <u>severe snow</u> (storm).

C-399   refrigerator

C-400   week

C-401   jeans

C-402   seat belts

C-403   rose

C-404   postage stamp

DEFINITIONS THAT CONTAIN CLASSES—SUPPLY

Write complete definitions of the following words. Put parentheses around the class and underline the characteristics in each definition.

C-405 automobile

C-406 resentment

C-407 dollar bill

C-408 education

C-409 lettuce

C-410 sister

C-411 calculator

ANALOGIES—INSTRUCTIONS

Here is an example to help you do analogy exercises.

EXAMPLE:

                                                                   CHOICE COLUMN

wrist : arm :: ankle : _____   foot
                                                           joint
                                                         leg

Step 1: Determine the relationship of the first two words of an analogy by writing them in a sentence. Use the words in the order that they appear. (The **wrist** is the joint at the lower end of the **arm**.)

Step 2: Write a second sentence, substituting the third word, "ankle," and a blank for the first two words. (The **ankle** is the joint at the lower end of the _____?)

Step 3: To determine which word in the Choice Column is related to ankle **in the same way as** arm is related to wrist, try each possibility (foot, joint, leg) in the blank to see which one fits best.

    a. "The **ankle** is the joint at the lower end of the **foot**." The ankle is at the upper, not lower, end of the foot, so "foot" is eliminated.

    b. "The **ankle** is the joint at the lower end of the **joint**." "Joint" describes the relationship, but it does not fit in the analogy sentence.

    c. "The **ankle** is the joint at the lower end of the **leg**." This is a true sentence, and the key words are related **in the same way as** the key words in the first sentence. **Leg** is the word that correctly completes the analogy.

ANALOGIES

ANTONYM OR SYNONYM ANALOGIES—SELECT

Study the first two words in each analogy and think about how they are related.(If the words are opposites, they are part of an ANTONYM analogy; if they are similar, they form a SYNONYM analogy.) To complete each analogy, decide which word in the Choice Column is related to the third word in the same way.

EXAMPLE:

CHOICE COLUMN

complex : simple :: extraordinary : ___average___

average
fancy
worthy

Complex and simple have opposite meanings and are known as antonyms. You must pick the word from the Choice Column that is an antonym to extraordinary. Both fancy and worthy are somewhat similar in meaning to extraordinary. **Average** is the opposite of extraordinary and should be written on the line.

CHOICE COLUMN

D-1 cautious : careful :: daring : _____

reckless
timid
watchful

D-2 import : export :: interior : _____

center
exterior
support

D-3 conceive : invent :: manufacture : _____

design
produce
plan

D-4 fore : front :: hind : _____

middle
rear
shoulder

D-5 excess : surplus :: lack : _____

fault
plenty
shortage

D-6 essential : required :: unnecessary : _____

extra
needless
vital

D-7 important : significant :: minor : _____

considerable
necessary
trivial

© 1985 MIDWEST PUBLICATIONS 93950-0448

ANTONYM OR SYNONYM ANALOGIES—SELECT

Study the first two words in each analogy and think about how they are related. (If the words are opposites, they are part of an ANTONYM analogy; if they are similar, they form a SYNONYM analogy.) To complete each analogy, decide which word in the Choice Column is related to the third word in the same way.

CHOICE COLUMN

D-8   safety : security :: danger : _____

cover
defense
peril

D-9   construct : build :: function : _____

operate
repair
replace

D-10   prospect : expectation :: reality : _____

anticipation
fact
hope

D-11   explore : search :: locate : _____

discover
miss
overlook

D-12   compose : create :: destroy : _____

establish
shape
wreck

D-13   enroll : enlist :: resign : _____

join
participate
quit

D-14   include : exclude :: superior : _____

inferior
interior
posterior

D-15   front : anterior :: rear : _____

center
interior
posterior

D-16   frontier : border :: interior : _____

coast
heartland
neighbor

D-17   frugal : thrifty :: extravagant : _____

careful
useful
wasteful

ANALOGIES

ANTONYM OR SYNONYM ANALOGIES—
SELECT MORE THAN ONCE

Study the first two words in each analogy and decide whether they are ANTONYMS or SYNONYMS. Complete each analogy by selecting the word from the Choice Box that is related to the third word in the same way.

+-------------------------+
| |
| **CHOICE BOX** |
| |
+-------------------------+
| |
| lead, leave, take |
| |
+-------------------------+

D-18 reach : arrive :: exit : _____

D-19 pursue : follow :: guide : _____

D-20 place : set :: remove : _____

D-21 permit : allow :: control : _____

D-22 join : unite :: detach : _____

D-23 enroll : join :: resign : _____

D-24 govern : manage :: direct : _____

D-25 trace : track :: guide : _____

D-26 present : confer :: acquire : _____

D-27 achieve : attain :: abandon : _____

ANTONYM OR SYNONYM ANALOGIES—
SELECT MORE THAN ONCE

Study the first two words in each analogy and decide whether they are ANTONYMS or SYNONYMS. Complete each analogy by selecting the word from the Choice Box that is related to the third word in the same way.

CHOICE BOX
after, back, far, past

D-28 here : near :: there : _____

D-29 there : here :: forth : _____

D-30 former : before :: latter : _____

D-31 forward : backward :: future : _____

D-32 present : here :: past : _____

D-33 former : latter :: before : _____

D-34 forward : present :: backward : _____

D-35 forward : backward :: forth : _____

D-36 here : there :: near : _____

D-37 forward : forth :: backward : _____

D-38 first : last :: front : _____

ANTONYM OR SYNONYM ANALOGIES—
SELECT MORE THAN ONCE

Study the first two words in each analogy and decide whether they are ANTONYMS or SYNONYMS. Complete each analogy by selecting the word from the Choice Box that is related to the third word in the same way.

CHOICE BOX
accept, pardon, reject, value

D-39 despise : detest :: cherish : _____

D-40 confess : admit :: forgive : _____

D-41 approve : decline :: agree : _____

D-42 question : approve :: doubt : _____

D-43 resist : oppose :: acknowledge : _____

D-44 scorn : appreciate :: degrade : _____

D-45 trust : suspect :: believe : _____

D-46 exclude : eliminate :: include : _____

D-47 authorization : permission :: assessment : _____

D-48 sentence : excuse :: condemn : _____

D-49 reserve : discard :: retain : _____

D-50 ideal : perfection :: esteem : _____

D-51 deny : admit :: refuse : _____

D-52 store : deposit :: rid : _____

D-53 appreciation : gratitude :: merit : _____

D-54 choose : select :: decline : _____

ANTONYM OR SYNONYM ANALOGIES—SELECT TWO

In these exercises, two members of an ANTONYM or SYNONYM analogy are supplied. From the Choice Box, select the two words that complete each analogy.

CHOICE BOX
completely, nearly, scarcely, usually

EXAMPLE:

altogether : <u>completely</u> :: approximately : <u>nearly</u>

D-55 definitely : _____ :: somewhat : _____

D-56 exactly : _____ :: almost : _____

D-57 exceedingly : _____ :: moderately : _____

D-58 perfectly : _____ :: partly : _____

D-59 extremely : _____ :: barely : _____

D-60 rarely : _____ :: frequently : _____

D-61 thoroughly : _____ :: hardly : _____

D-62 totally : _____ :: just : _____

D-63 infrequently : _____ :: often : _____

D-64 definitely : _____ :: commonly : _____

D-65 commonly : _____ :: seldom : _____

D-66 finally : _____ :: practically : _____

D-67 uniquely : _____ :: often : _____

ANALOGIES

ASSOCIATION ANALOGIES—SELECT

In the following ASSOCIATION analogies, the first two words of each are related in a certain way. Study the third word and decide which word in the Choice Column relates in a similar way.

EXAMPLE:

CHOICE COLUMN

flour : baking :: fabric : <u> sewing </u>

cloth
material
sewing

Flour is associated with baking just as fabric is associated with sewing. Since cloth and material are synonyms for fabric, the best answer is **sewing.**

CHOICE COLUMN

D-68   scale : weight :: compass : _____

direction
distance
mass

D-69   closet : clothes :: warehouse : _____

advertising
merchandise
sales

D-70   garment : alteration :: house : _____

construction
demolition
remodeling

D-71   can : bottle :: shell : _____

core
nut
pod

D-72   lake : reservoir :: river : _____

canal
rapids
waterfall

D-73   appetizer : dessert :: introduction : _____

contents
summary
title

D-74   speedometer : velocity :: thermometer : _____

degree
light
temperature

ASSOCIATION ANALOGIES—SELECT MORE THAN ONCE

In the following ASSOCIATION analogies, the first two words of each are related in a certain way. Study the third word and decide which word in the Choice Box relates in a similar way.

```
┌─────────────────────────────────────────────────┐
│                                                   │
│                   CHOICE BOX                      │
│                                                   │
├─────────────────────────────────────────────────┤
│                                                   │
│        add, divide, minus, multiply, sum          │
│                                                   │
└─────────────────────────────────────────────────┘
```

EXAMPLE:

add : plus :: subtract : _____minus_____

D-75   product : multiply :: quotient : _____

D-76   plus : add :: less : _____

D-77   quotient : product :: difference : _____

D-78   times : multiply :: plus : _____

D-79   dividend : divide :: factor : _____

D-80   factor : product :: addend : _____

D-81   factor : dividend :: multiply : _____

D-82   product : times :: difference : _____

D-83   factor : multiply :: addend : _____

© 1985 MIDWEST PUBLICATIONS 93950-0448

ANALOGIES

ASSOCIATION ANALOGIES—SELECT TWO

In these exercises, two members of an ASSOCIATION analogy are supplied. Complete each analogy by selecting the two words from the Choice Box that are associated in a similar way.

CHOICE BOX
colt, doe, ewe, fawn, ram, stallion

D-84 fawn : buck :: _____ : _____

D-85 buck : ram :: _____ : _____

D-86 ram : lamb :: _____ : _____

D-87 stallion : mare :: _____ : _____

D-88 mare : colt :: _____ : _____

D-89 fawn : lamb :: _____ : _____

D-90 doe : buck :: _____ : _____

D-91 mare : ewe :: _____ : _____

D-92 buck : stallion :: _____ : _____

© 1985 MIDWEST PUBLICATIONS 90059 2440

"KIND OF" ANALOGIES—SELECT

In the following KIND OF analogies, the first word of each is a "kind of" the second. Complete each analogy by selecting the word from the Choice Column that relates to the third word in the same way. (The third word will be a "kind of" the missing word.)

CHOICE COLUMN

EXAMPLE:

fluorescent : lamp :: diesel : ___engine___

bulb
engine
liquid

Flourescent is a "kind of" lamp. From the Choice Column, pick the word that diesel is a "kind of." The best answer is **engine**, because diesel is a kind of engine.

D-93 oxygen : gas :: water : _____

fuel
liquid
mixture

D-94 iron : metal :: granite : _____

atom
rock
soil

D-95 zucchini : squash :: cantaloupe : _____

fruit
melon
seed

D-96 tissue : paper :: silk : _____

dress
fabric
synthetic

D-97 ballpoint : pen :: watercolors : _____

clay
crayons
paint

D-98 dictionary : reference book : magazine : _____

issue
newspaper
periodical

D-99 movement : activity :: depression : _____

effort
mood
noise

ANALOGIES

"PART OF" ANALOGIES—SELECT

In the following PART OF analogies, the first word of each represents a "part of" the second. To complete each analogy, study the third word and decide which word in the Choice Column it is a "part of."

EXAMPLE:

scales : fish :: bark : _____tree_____

CHOICE COLUMN
dog
skin
tree

Scales are the outer part of a fish. Which word in the Choice Column answers the question, "Bark is the outer part of _____?" Dogs bark, but bark is not the outer part of a dog; so dog is not the answer. Skin is an outer part also, not something that bark is a part of; so it is not the answer either. But bark is the outer part of a tree, so **tree** is the answer.

D-100 tuner : television set :: valve : _____
dial
gauge
pipeline

D-101 brim : hat :: bill : _____
cap
coat
cuff

D-102 eyelid : eye :: shutter : _____
camera
film
nerve

D-103 officer : army :: manager : _____
company
employees
stockholder

D-104 ribs : chest :: rafters : _____
beams
joists
roof

D-105 lapel · jacket :: collar : _____
apron
shirt
tie

D-106 film : camera :: magnetic tape : _____
cassette recorder
projector
record player

"PART OF" ANALOGIES—SELECT THE RELATIONSHIP

Select the word from the Choice Box that explains the part/whole relationship in each of the following PART OF analogies.

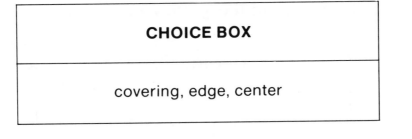

CHOICE BOX
covering, edge, center

EXAMPLE:

        margin : page :: border : picture ____edge____

     A margin is the edge of a page, and a border is the edge of a picture. So **edge** should be written in the blank space.

D-107   plaster : wall :: varnish : furniture _____

D-108   fringe : shawl :: hem : skirt _____

D-109   crust : pie :: shell : taco _____

D-110   perimeter : rectangle :: circumference : circle _____

D-111   axis : earth :: diameter : circle _____

D-112   shoulder : road :: rim : tire _____

D-113   peel : orange :: pod : pea _____

D-114   cob : corn :: core : apple _____

D-115   lip : bottle :: rim : cup _____

D-116   railing : stair :: fence : field _____

D-117   upholstery : furniture :: pillowcase : pillow _____

D-118   nucleus : atom :: sun : solar system _____

D-119   border : country :: coast : continent _____

D-120   median : road :: bisector : line _____

D-121   coat : person :: blanket : horse _____

D-122   eye : hurricane :: crater : volcano _____

ANALOGIES

"USED TO" ANALOGIES—SELECT

In the following USED TO analogies, the second word each describes what the first word is "used to" do. Complete each analogy by selecting the word from the Choice Box that relates to the third word in the same way.

CHOICE BOX
lift, turn, drive, stop

EXAMPLE:

bulldozer : push :: crane : _____lift_____

A bulldozer is used to push, just as a crane is used to lift. So **lift** should be written in the blank space.

D-123   rudder : steer :: brake : _____

D-124   gauge : measure :: gear : _____

D-125   clamp : hold :: crank : _____

D-126   strap : bind :: hoist : _____

D-127   seal : close :: valve : _____

D-128   wrench : twist :: jack : _____

D-129   needle : pierce :: plug : _____

D-130   bolt : fasten :: shaft : _____

D-131   pipe : connect :: engine : _____

© 1985 MIDWEST PUBLICATIONS 93950-0448

"USED TO" ANALOGIES—SELECT

In the following USED TO analogies, the second word of each describes what the first word is "used to" do. Complete each analogy by selecting the word from the Choice Column that is related to the third word in the same way.

EXAMPLE:

CHOICE COLUMN

glossary : define :: index : ___locate___

describe
explain
locate

A glossary is used to define, and an index is used as an aid to locating topics within a reference book. **Locate** is the best answer; an index is not used to describe or explain a topic.

D-132 vault : safeguard :: gallery : _____

collect
exhibit
store

D-133 exclamation : emphasize :: statement : _____

inform
question
warn

D-134 falsehood : deceive :: evidence : _____

exaggerate
prove
reply

D-135 imagination : create :: reason : _____

decide
depict
obscure

D-136 stilts : elevate :: foundation : _____

build
lower
support

D-137 valve : regulate :: gauge : _____

accelerate
indicate
restrict

D-138 radar : locate :: lens : _____

broadcast
observe
record

ANALOGIES

ACTION ANALOGIES—SELECT

An analogy that relates a person to what he or she does, or a thing to what it does, is called an ACTION analogy. Complete the following by selecting the word in the Choice Column that describes the action of the third word.

EXAMPLE:

surgeon : operates :: mechanic : ___repairs___

CHOICE COLUMN
cuts
removes
repairs

The main task that a mechanic performs is to **repair** a broken machine. As part of the repair task, the mechanic may need to cut or remove a part, but neither cutting nor removing is his main task.

CHOICE COLUMN

D-139   sheriff : arrests :: fugitive : _____

advances
flees
remains

D-140   pharmacist : dispenses :: librarian : _____

circulates
publishes
records

D-141   dilemma : confuses :: solution : _____

dissolves
disturbs
resolves

D-142   adjective : modifies :: conjunction : _____

acts
connects
names

D-143   dictator : rules :: conductor : _____

composes
directs
plays

D-144   guard : protects :: signal : _____

causes
performs
warns

D-145   flask : contains :: levee : _____

detects
rejects
protects

© 1985 MIDWEST PUBLICATIONS 93950-0448

"DEGREE OF" ANALOGIES—SELECT

In the following DEGREE OF analogies, the first word of each is related to the second according to the "degree of" the characteristic the words have in common. Complete each analogy by selecting the word in the Choice Column that is related to the third word to a similar degree.

EXAMPLE:

CHOICE COLUMN

definitely : maybe :: certain : __probable__

absolute
never
probable

Definitely is a stronger degree of likelihood than maybe, certain is a stronger degree of likelihood than **probable**. Absolute is a synonym for certain. Never suggests no likelihood of occurence.

CHOICE COLUMN

D-146 irritated : furious :: pleased : _____

disappointed
overjoyed
satisfied

D-147 loudness : sound :: brightness : _____

frequency
light
volume

D-148 dynamic : activity :: expert : _____

ability
value
witness

D-149 timid : confidence :: lazy : _____

capacity
motivation
skill

D-150 positive : certainty :: undeniable : _____

guess
hunch
proof

D-151 inaudible : blaring :: dim : _____

dull
glaring
shade

D-152 emergency : urgency :: continuously : _____

frequency
pitch
volume

ANALOGIES

MIXED ANALOGIES—SELECT TWO WORDS

Study the two words given in each of the following exercises and then pick two words from the Choice Box that will give you a complete analogy. These analogies are either ACTION analogies, ASSOCIATION analogies, or SYNONYM analogies.

EXAMPLE: speech : ___hear___ :: letter : ___read___

A speech is given for someone to hear, and a letter is written for someone to read. They are ASSOCIATED in a similar way. Although one talks when giving a speech, the active participant ("speaker") in a letter is the one who writes. Since "write" is not a choice, the analogy should be

"speech is to **hear** as letter is to **read**."

```
┌─────────────────────────────────────┐
│                                      │
│            CHOICE BOX                │
│                                      │
├─────────────────────────────────────┤
│                                      │
│         hear, read, see, talk        │
│                                      │
└─────────────────────────────────────┘
```

D-153   writing :_____ :: sound :_____

D-154   oral : _____ :: visual : _____

D-155   glimpse : _____ :: skim : _____

D-156   stare : _____ :: chatter : _____

D-157   correspondence : _____ :: conversation : _____

D-158   listeners :_____ :: speakers : _____

D-159   television : _____ :: stereo : _____

D-160   orator : _____ :: dancer : _____

D-161   debate : _____ :: movie : _____

D-162   lecture : _____ :: encyclopedia : _____

D-163   observers :_____ :: editors : _____

D-164   book : _____ :: recorded music : _____

MIXED ANALOGIES—SELECT TWO WORDS

Study the two words given in each of the following exercises and then pick two words from the Choice Box that will give you a complete analogy. These analogies are either ACTION analogies, ANTONYM analogies, ASSOCIATION analogies, or SYNONYM analogies.

CHOICE BOX
have, is, know, seems

D-165 apparent : _____ :: real : _____

D-166 get : _____ :: learn : _____

D-167 realize : _____ :: obtain : _____

D-168 fact : _____ :: hint : _____

D-169 learning : _____ :: possession : _____

D-170 object : _____ :: image : _____

D-171 heirloom : _____ :: memory : _____

D-172 forget : _____ :: lose : _____

D-173 keep : _____ :: remember : _____

D-174 proof : _____ :: theory : _____

D-175 wealthy : _____ :: wise : _____

D-176 existence : _____ :: appearance : _____

D-177 understand : _____ :: own : _____

D-178 person : _____ :: ghost : _____

D-179 collection : _____ :: education : _____

D-180 genuine : _____ :: counterfeit : _____

ANALOGIES

ANALOGIES—EXPLAIN

Study these analogies and decide how the words in each pair are related. On the lines provided, label each analogy and explain the relationship between the words in each pair. Select the best possible answer from the list below.

ACTION   KIND OF
ANTONYM   PART OF
ASSOCIATION   SYNONYM
DEGREE OF   USED TO

D-181 lace : tie :: button : fasten

_____

_____

D-182 barren : vegetation :: parched : moisture

_____

_____

D-183 crane : machinery :: bus : vehicle

_____

_____

D-184 heart : blood :: pump : water

_____

_____

D-185 silk : worm :: honey : bee

_____

_____

© 1985 MIDWEST PUBLICATIONS 93950-0448

ANALOGIES—EXPLAIN

Study these analogies and decide how the words in each pair are related. On the lines provided, label each analogy and explain the relationship between the words in each pair. Select the best possible answer from the list below.

ACTION	KIND OF
ANTONYM	PART OF
ASSOCIATION	SYNONYM
DEGREE OF	USED TO

D-186 always : occurrence :: doubtless : probability

_____

_____

D-187 mask : costume :: vest : suit

_____

_____

D-188 right : privilege :: duty : responsibility

_____

_____

D-189 know : understand :: ignore : overlook

_____

_____

D-190 bottle : contains :: sponge : absorbs

_____

_____

D-191 rind : watermelon :: shell : peanut

_____

_____

D-192 enamel : paint :: posterboard : paper

_____

_____

ANALOGIES

ANALOGIES—EXPLAIN

Study these analogies and decide how the words in each pair are related. On the lines provided, label each analogy and explain the relationship between the words in each pair. Select the best possible answer from the list below.

ACTION   KIND OF
ANTONYM   PART OF
ASSOCIATION   SYNONYM
DEGREE OF   USED TO

D-193 ready : preparation :: alert : awareness

_____

_____

D-194 aspirin : medication :: cider : beverage

_____

_____

D-195 moon : month :: sun : year

_____

_____

D-196 gate : entrance :: aisle : passageway

_____

_____

D-197 dictionary : spell :: calculator : compute

_____

_____

D-198 exhibit : museum :: painting : gallery

_____

_____

D-199 newspaper : periodical :: novel : book

_____

_____

© 1985 MIDWEST PUBLICATIONS 93950-0448

ANALOGIES—EXPLAIN

Study these analogies and decide how the words in each pair are related. On the lines provided, label each analogy and explain the relationship between the words in each pair. Select the best possible answer from the list below.

ACTION	KIND OF
ANTONYM	PART OF
ASSOCIATION	SYNONYM
DEGREE OF	USED TO

D-200 never : frequency :: none : amount

_____

_____

D-201 pat : butter :: bar : soap

_____

_____

D-202 span : bridge :: lane : highway

_____

_____

D-203 mirrors : reflect :: lenses : focus

_____

_____

D-204 pasture : ranch :: lawn : yard

_____

_____

D-205 drift : float :: glide : fly

_____

_____

D-206 composer : symphony :: sculptor : statue

_____

_____

© 1985 MIDWEST PUBLICATIONS 93950-0448

ANALOGIES

ANTONYM OR SYNONYM ANALOGIES—SUPPLY

Think about how the first two words of these ANTONYM or SYNONYM analogies are related. Complete each analogy by producing a word from your memory that relates to the third word in the same way that the second word relates to the first.

EXAMPLE:

former : latter :: before : _____after_____

Former means the first of two, and latter means the last of two. You need to supply a word that will complete the analogy and preserve the "first to last" relationship. (First and last are antonyms so you need to supply the antonym of before, which is **after**.)

D-207 beach : shore :: ocean : _____

D-208 interior : exterior :: entrance : _____

D-209 sheer : bulky :: thin : _____

D-210 carve : slice :: shear : _____

D-211 inhale : exhale :: inflate : _____

D-212 occasional : continual :: temporary : _____

D-213 humility : modesty :: vanity : _____

D-214 bureau : dresser :: cupboard : _____

D-215 casual : informal :: courteous : _____

D-216 waste : conserve :: squander : _____

© 1985 MIDWEST PUBLICATIONS 93060-0448

ANTONYM OR SYNONYM ANALOGIES—SUPPLY

Think about how the first two words of these ANTONYM or SYNONYM analogies are related. Complete each analogy by producing a word from your memory that relates to the third word in the same way that the second word relates to the first.

D-217 graph : diagram :: navigation chart : _____

D-218 advance : retreat :: promote : _____

D-219 choose : select :: reject : _____

D-220 preserve : maintain :: alter : _____

D-221 hamper : hinder :: aid : _____

D-222 recess : adjourn :: assemble : _____

D-223 assemble : construct :: demolish : _____

D-224 significant : petty :: major : _____

D-225 submit : yield :: resist : _____

D-226 repair : mend :: shatter : _____

D-227 disperse : distribute :: gather : _____

D-228 bow : stern :: front : _____

ANALOGIES

ASSOCIATION ANALOGIES—SUPPLY

In the following ASSOCIATION analogies, the first two words of each are related in a certain way. Complete each analogy by producing a word from your memory that relates to the third word in the same way that the second word relates to the first.

D-229   tree : row :: mountain : _____

D-230   oak : acorn :: pine : _____

D-231   scripture : minister :: script : _____

D-232   map : city :: blueprint : _____

D-233   model : airplane :: globe : _____

D-234   fever : degrees :: pulse : _____

D-235   doctor : infection :: dentist : _____

D-236   meter : yard :: liter : _____

D-237   shortcut : route :: discount : _____

D-238   charter : club :: constitution : _____

D-239   area code : telephone :: zip code : _____

"KIND OF" ANALOGIES—SUPPLY

In the following KIND OF analogies, the first word of each is a "kind of" the second. Complete each analogy by producing a word from your memory that relates to the third word in the same way that the second word relates to the first.

EXAMPLE:

granite : rock :: iron : _____metal_____

Granite is a kind of rock just as iron is a kind of **metal**.

D-240 cabin : house :: sedan : _____

D-241 novel : book :: pun : _____

D-242 bomber : plane :: destroyer : _____

D-243 prune : plum :: raisin : _____

D-244 cheddar : cheese :: wheat : _____

D-245 vinyl : plastic :: silk : _____

D-246 milk : liquid :: butter : _____

D-247 tumbler : glass :: carton : _____

D-248 basketball : sport :: chess : _____

D-249 dictionary : book :: auditorium : _____

D-250 expressway : road :: boulevard : _____

D-251 enamel : paint :: gasoline : _____

"PART OF" ANALOGIES—SUPPLY

In the following PART OF analogies, the first word of each represents a "part of" the second. Complete each analogy by producing a word from your memory that the third word would be a similar part of.

EXAMPLE:

tooth : tiger :: tusk : <u>elephant</u>

A tooth is the sharp mouth part of a tiger just as a tusk is the sharp mouth part of an **elephant**.

D-252   map : atlas :: word : _____

D-253   base : statue :: foundation : _____

D-254   singer : choir :: musician : _____

D-255   summit : mountain :: scalp : _____

D-256   shell : nut :: husk : _____

D-257   branch : trunk :: arm : _____

D-258   curtain : stage :: shade : _____

D-259   teeth : comb :: bristles : _____

D-260   net : tennis court :: goal posts : _____

D-261   telescope : observatory :: microscope : _____

"USED TO" ANALOGIES—SUPPLY

In the following USED TO analogies, the second word of each describes what the first word is "used to" do. Complete each analogy by producing a word from your memory that describes what the third word is "used to" do.

EXAMPLE:

thumb : grasp :: voice : _____speak_____

The thumb is used to grasp, and the voice is used to **speak**.

D-262   makeup : beautify :: mask : _____

D-263   styrofoam : insulate :: copper wire : _____

D-264   splint : support :: adhesive tape : _____

D-265   lecture : inform :: movie : _____

D-266   conveyor : move :: brake : _____

D-267   building : shelter :: vehicle : _____

D-268   needle : puncture :: blade : _____

D-269   notice : inform :: souvenir : _____

D-270   lamp : illuminate :: _____ : communicate

D-271   monument : commemorate :: _____ : indicate

D-272   graph : display :: _____ : locate

D-273   animal coloration : conceal :: shell : _____

ANALOGIES

ACTION ANALOGIES—SUPPLY

In the following ACTION analogies, the second word of each describes the action of the first. Complete each analogy by producing a word from your memory that describes the action of the third word.

EXAMPLE:

plants : decay :: iron : _____rust_____

Weather acts on plants to cause decay and acts on iron to cause **rust**.

D-274 jet engine : propels :: magnet : _____

D-275 archaeologist : digs :: chemist : _____

D-276 lawyer : defends :: jury : _____

D-277 doctor : prescribes :: counselor : _____

D-278 insult : offends :: compliment : _____

D-279 clerk : sells :: donor : _____

D-280 argument : divides :: treaty : _____

D-281 saver : deposits :: spender : _____

D-282 lotion : soothes :: treatment : _____

D-283 traitor : betrays :: patriot : _____

D-284 dictator : rules :: general : _____

D-285 blood : circulates :: water : _____

"DEGREE OF" ANALOGIES—SUPPLY

In the following DEGREE OF analogies, the first word of each is related to the second according to the "degree of" the characteristic that the words have in common. Complete each analogy by producing a word from your memory that is related to the third word to a similar degree.

EXAMPLE:

sprinkle : deluge :: flurry : ___blizzard___

Sprinkle and deluge are low and high degrees of rain. Flurry is a low degree of snow. Supply a word that means a high degree of snow, such as **blizzard**.

D-286   compact : sedan :: inn : _____

D-287   nibble : bite :: glimpse : _____

D-288   pat : slap :: poke : _____

D-289   heavy : weight :: far : _____

D-290   pitch : darkness :: glare : _____

D-291   inaudible : loudness :: dim : _____

D-292   bitter : taste :: stench : _____

D-293   tropical : heat :: polar : _____

D-294   perfume : fragrance :: harmony : _____

D-295   fury : anger :: delight : _____

D-296   trivial : important :: worthless : _____

D-297   remote : distance :: antique : _____

ANALOGIES

CREATE YOUR OWN ANALOGIES

D-298   Write two analogies to illustrate each of the following:

ANTONYM ANALOGIES

_____ : _____ :: _____ : _____

_____ : _____ :: _____ : _____

SYNONYM ANALOGIES

_____ : _____ :: _____ : _____

_____ : _____ :: _____ : _____

"PART OF" ANALOGIES

_____ : _____ :: _____ : _____

_____ : _____ :: _____ : _____

"USED TO" ANALOGIES

_____ : _____ :: _____ : _____

_____ : _____ :: _____ : _____

ACTION ANALOGIES

_____ : _____ :: _____ : _____

_____ : _____ :: _____ : _____

ASSOCIATION ANALOGIES

_____ : _____ :: _____ : _____

_____ : _____ :: _____ : _____

"DEGREE OF" ANALOGIES

_____ : _____ :: _____ : _____

_____ : _____ :: _____ : _____